Entangled Objects

Entangled Objects

Exchange, Material Culture, and Colonialism in the Pacific

Nicholas Thomas

Harvard University Press

Cambridge, Massachusetts

London, England

1991

Library of Congress Cataloging-in-Publication Data

Thomas, Nicholas.
Entangled objects: exchange, material culture, and colonialism in
the Pacific / Nicholas Thomas.
p. cm.
Includes bibliographical references and index.
ISBN 0-674-25730-8 (alk. paper).—ISBN 0-674-25731-6 (pbk. : alk. paper)
1. Material culture—Oceania. 2. Exchange. 3. Acculturation—Oceania. 4. Economic
anthropology—Oceania. 5. Oceania—Social life and customs. I. Title.
GN663.T46 1991
306.3'0995—dc20   91-9346   CIP

for
Pascal Boyer
and
Tony Tanner

Contents

Maps

Illustrations

Acknowledgments

An essay on the gift could hardly pass over its own debts, even if this one aims, among other things, to take Marcel Mauss's famous theory to pieces, in order to put together something different that owes rather more to work on colonial histories and material objects than writing upon that most canonized of anthropological topics, exchange. I could not have written the book in terms of the literature on prestations, the gift, reciprocity, debt, hierarchy, and so on, without recasting these issues in historical contexts and with respect to the cultural constitution of objects, not just because I do not want to bore readers in the way I was bored myself as a student by the anthropology of exchange, but also because most forms of the paradigm have been myopically liberal in their models of reciprocity and assumptions of consent among individual transactors (who are, it might be added, at once unsexed and male). Nearly all the societies which anthropologists made into case studies for exchange theory were or still are colonized, but this context of illiberal domination entered into these accounts, if it was mentioned at all, only as external contingency, never as a fact that needed to be central to analysis. In this book I make exchange into a prism for seeing what this discourse excluded—the uneven entanglement of local and global power relations on colonial peripheries, particularly as these have been manifested in capacities to define and appropriate the meanings of material things.

If this conceptual turn leads to irreconcilable analytical tensions, I know that I have only myself to blame; I doubt that any merits of this study could match the range and generosity of the advice, assistance, and encouragement I have received from people in the Pacific, librarians, institutions, colleagues, friends, and family. Although I wrote the book in Cambridge between March and October 1989, I drew upon earlier projects and interests going back to my undergraduate and graduate research, and any complete acknowledgment of people who helped, one way or another, would amount either to a long impersonal list or an autobiography. I have thus opted to thank those who helped in specific ways in notes at relevant points; nevertheless, there are many people I must mention here.

Caroline Humphrey and Stephen Hugh-Jones convened a seminar series in the Cambridge Social Anthropology department in early 1987 on barter and exchange; that prompted an initial exploration of the issues central here, but other people's papers and discussion, as well as conversations with Daniel Miller later that year, did much to provide me with questions for field research in Fiji in 1988. King's College, the Smuts Memorial Fund, and the Crowther-Beynon Fund of the Cambridge University Museum of Archaeology and Anthropology, supported that work; the Australian National University provided me with a travel grant in mid-1989 to spend some time with the Comparative Austronesian Project; in that period I was able to discuss drafts with Aletta Biersack, Don Gardner, and Maureen MacKenzie, as well as Chris Gregory, whom I had gotten to know in 1984 when I wrote a critique of *Gifts and Commodities* and with whom I have been agreeing and disagreeing in a productive way ever since. Others who read the typescripts in part or whole include James Carrier and Keith Hart; I received particularly valuable suggestions from Martha Macintyre (who also generously provided some unpublished field material) and Ranajit Guha, who helped me reduce the book's entanglement in the colonialist discourses that it tries to criticize. My approach to colonial culture has been stimulated particularly by Chris Pinney and Roger Keesing; with respect to what I try to do in Chapter 4, Harriet Guest's suggestions and encouragement were more important than I imagine she realizes. Anonymous readers' reports obtained by Harvard University Press, and Lindsay Waters's guidance, have helped me forestall misreadings and elaborate upon certain arguments. A Queen Elizabeth II Research Fellowship granted by the Australian Research Council enabled me to revise the book while affiliated with the Department of Prehistory and Anthropology at the Australian National University, which generously provided various facilities; the first two maps in the book were prepared by Mrs. Joan Goodrum in that department. An earlier version of parts of Chapter 5 appeared as "Material Culture and Colonial Power: Ethnological Collecting and the Establishment of Colonial Rule in Fiji," *Man* 24 (1989), 41–56. I thank the publisher for permission to make use of the material here.

Although books are usually cited in annotations or a bibliography, I must signal the importance for this project of Marilyn Strathern's *The Gender of the Gift* and Chris Gregory's *Gifts and Commodities*, already mentioned; although I have disagreed categorically with certain arguments in these works, both have been crucial in enabling me to locate my own position and have furnished a number of more specific analytical problems. Bernard Smith's *European Vision and the South Pacific* was never far from my desk; though first published thirty years ago, the contemporary salience of Smith's concerns is acute, particularly in the context of questions about representation and imperialism raised by Edward Said—a writer whom I have not cited at all here; I hope, however, that the influence of his interests and politics will be apparent.

In various sections below I argue that gifts in the southwestern Pacific often do not extinguish debt generated by other gifts; instead they can be seen to display enduring conditions of indebtedness that arise from relationships, from the substance of sociality. In this sense, this book is meant to be a partible return gift displaying my dependence on the people whose conversation, writing, and companionship made it possible—to Margaret Jolly, especially, whose support and work have been crucial. For not taking any of my academic work too seriously, I thank Anna Jolly, who drew my attention to more useful things like parks and bike rides. I also have a sense of profound debt to the people of Korolevu, Navosa, Fiji, and particularly the Suguvanua family, who adopted me; but I imagine that the gifts I made in the village expressed that better than this sort of product, which is rather less fetishized in their place.

The lack of interest in disciplinary boundaries in the humanities and social sciences at King's College helped me arrive at an idea of what I wanted to write; of many friends there I must mention Pascal Boyer and Tony Tanner, whose concern and support were unfailing.

Entangled Objects

Introduction

In an account of India which was published in 1800, the Carmelite missionary Paolino, whose ethnographic authority rested upon a residence of no less than thirteen years, remarked upon the failure of the local people to adopt imported commodities:

> Though the Indians see daily before them the furniture and cooking utensils of the Europeans, they have never yet thought proper to make use of them. The customs prevalent among them above three thousand years ago still remain unchanged.[1]

This was, of course, a classic Orientalist statement. The nonuse of introduced articles was taken as a negative condition which had to be explained, and explanation turned upon the image of a custom-bound race resistant to innovation. In his annotations to Paolino's text, the distinguished natural scientist, geographer, and ethnologist Johann Reinhold Forster subverted this appeal to otherness.

> There are various reasons which prevent the Indians from imitating the household furniture and cooking utensils of the Europeans. The poorer sort of people cannot do it, on account of their circumstances; and the rich will not, because they hate and detest the whites, by whom they are oppressed. Besides, many of the European customs, articles of furniture, &c. are not suited to the climate of India. The attachment of the Indians to every thing handed down to them by their ancestors, arises from that pride prevalent among all little cultivated nations, who, like the Chinese for example, consider what they themselves possess to be the best in the world.[2]

This book amounts to an elaboration upon Forster's critique. Like any other writer, he of course had his own interests in imagining other nations or cultures, which I need not consider here. The point is

1

rather that he sought to displace an essentialist claim about patterns in the use of material culture with historical and political specificity. The failure to adopt Western articles stemmed not from some cultural principle or innate inability but from factors such as poverty, political hostility, local unsuitability, and what he saw as a rather immature kind of national pride.

A great deal has been written since about exchange relations among non-Western peoples, and about the nature and consequences of those between them and Europeans. The introduction of European material artifacts into tribal societies has generally been seen not just in negative terms but as emblematic of the disintegration of indigenous cultures in the face of imperial expansion. Although related questions concerning cultural contact and change have been extensively discussed within anthropology, the debate which has been more prominent in the discipline has revolved around the economic forms and transaction types which are distinctive to non-Western and especially tribal societies. "The gift," "reciprocity," "gift exchange," and related topics have figured prominently in the work of Mauss, Malinowski, Firth, Sahlins, and Lévi-Strauss; the critique of some of this literature was central to the opening polemic of Bourdieu's *Outline of a Theory of Practice*, perhaps the most important work of anthropology theory of the seventies; and more recently, writers such as Annette Weiner, Chris Gregory, and Marilyn Strathern have extended earlier perspectives in widely discussed studies. Faced with the proliferation of theoretical texts and ethnographic and historical studies, the reader might well ask if there is anything more to be said, but the direct or indirect stimulus of feminism in recent reappraisals in itself signals the politicized and unstable character of the discourse. Although all forms of scholarly practice and writing are, in some respects, gender-marked and politically inflected, history and especially anthropology differ from subjects such as entomology in the sense that there are very direct ways that conceptions of one's own social relations and cultural identity are connected to available public discourses about power and sex and to the topics of routine academic investigation. Disputes about the custody of children in Europe, America, and Australia might, for instance, lead one to raise different questions about notions of parenthood in India and Amazonia—even if the influence of culture at home upon the questions asked of ideology abroad is not acknowledged.

The political turn that underpins this book relates not so much to gender as to a symbolic structure which is, however, profoundly gendered—the discourse of colonialism. Although anthropologists have generally been critical of missionaries, capitalist expansion, and administrative intrusions, they have resisted the implications of colonial history and transcultural exchange for the sorts of people typically studied. Most of the writing alluded to above conceives of tribal societies and even places such as Indonesia and India as authentic, meaningfully stable domains which differ fundamentally from Western social regimes and which resist interpretation on the basis of Western categories. Modern anthropology has been, in a fundamental sense, about "other cultures." The fact of difference is thus anterior to any contingent similarities between ourselves and other peoples, as it is to our mutual entanglement. There is thus scope for slippage between the idea that others' names for beliefs and practices may be different and the discursive strategy which specifies that they must be different. The exercise of endlessly elaborating on the metaphors, key symbols, concepts of the person and agency, and indigenous views of time and history must be taken at one level as a reasonable reaction to the imposition of European categories upon beliefs and social relations which, obviously, often are different. But insofar as this has become the diagnostic attribute of the discipline, it must be recognized that anthropology is a discourse of alterity, a way of writing in which us/them distinctions are central, and which necessarily distances the people studied from ourselves.[3] Actual variation among European people and among those abroad can only be understated; actual variation between ourselves and them can only be magnified. Such a perspective seems also to depend upon a radical denial of history. The manifold and problematic engagements of various classes of Europeans, North Americans, or Australians with various colonized peoples, and the equally asymmetrical contacts and combats between Third World nation-states and tribal peoples within their borders, are part of a shared history which has continuing ramifications in the process of "development" and numerous regional political instabilities.

Here I am mostly concerned not with these immediacies but with their prehistories in processes of mutual appropriation and unequal exchange on colonial peripheries. In dealing with indigenous exchange regimes, transactions, and the uses of material culture, this work resists the notion that indigenous responses or practices are to be explained through some clarification of an alternate cultural order. I am not denying that cultural categories salient to objects and exchange are locally distinctive; rather, I stress that their elaboration must take account of the full range of transaction forms, instead of only those which accord with Maussian stereotypes of the gift economy. The theoretical background to these critiques is elaborated upon in Chapter 1; this provides the terms for contrasts between different forms of Oceanic exchange relations, drawing particularly upon Fiji, the Marquesas, and the western Solomon Islands in Chapter 2. The argument sustains the importance of the distinction between commodities and gifts but demands that it be disconnected from the opposition between European and indigenous societies. The critique is, however, intended to be internally unstable, since the notions of gift and commodity which are to be resituated are themselves recast and distorted through a succession of case materials. Accounts of early Fijian systems evince relations between gift and debt quite different to those postulated in Mauss's famous theory, and a wider range of evidence from indigenous Oceanic societies suggests that there is a broad continuum between systems in which it is possible to substitute only people for people, or food for food, and those in which a wide range of expansive conversions are permitted. The second point draws upon earlier writing, especially from New Guinea, but my extension of these discussions proposes that in some systems of the second type, forms of alienation and what are virtually commodity transactions occur. The general view that Melanesian, Polynesian, or any other tribal societies can be regarded as communal or "gift" economies is thus rejected.

The problem of such unitary conceptions of indigenous economies is that they suppress the entanglement with other systems such as capitalist trade. In some areas, entanglement with colonizing agents of various kinds has gone on for hundreds of years and has prompted a distinctive indigenous historical consciousness in which local customs and solidarity are explicitly contrasted with the inequality characteristic of relations with outsiders. But such contacts are not only historically crucial—they also energize a new way of thinking about material culture.[4]

One of the central ideas of the later sections of this work is that objects are not what they were made to be but what they have become. This is to contradict a pervasive identification in museum research and material culture studies which stabilizes the identity of a thing in its fixed and founded material form. In a preface to a volume on Cook voyage artifacts, Adrienne Kaeppler noted that "the importance of collections from Cook's voyages often lies in the fact that his expeditions were the first to make extensive contact with the local inhabitants. The objects traded to the ships are, therefore, relatively free from European influence."[5] This is perhaps a more specific form of a view enunciated by other theoreticians of material culture: artifacts are thought to have "advantages over written records of behaviours and belief in being concrete, objective, difficult to distort, and little subject to personal or ethnocentric bias."[6] I do not want to invalidate the analysis of non-Western art or the historical reconstruction of transformations of material culture which such an observation enables, but the only useful departure point would, I think, amount to the reverse of these assumptions. Just as iron hatchets are inevitably useful and meaningful in a new way when they are appropriated by a head-hunting culture, the things which the producers of culture in Europe and America have put into museum cases or set up as sources for styles in paintings and fabric patterns have become and are becoming different.[7] Creative recontextualization and indeed reauthorship may thus follow from taking, from purchase or theft; and since museums and exhibitions of history and culture are no less prominent now than in the epoch of world's fairs, that is a sort of entanglement that most of us cannot step outside. As a way of breaking up us/them oppositions, I pretend that there is a kind of symmetry between indigenous appropriations of European artifacts and the colonial collecting of indigenous goods; these cultural histories and varieties of interested recontextualization are explored in Chapters 3 and 4 respectively. The final chapter returns to island societies and argues that contemporary forms of gift giving and ceremonial exchange do not evince alternate social logics as much as their historical constitution and the effect of the reifications of indigenous cultures and their singular patterns of exchange, which have emerged through the histories explored in the preceding discussions. I thus place chapters about the nature of objects and consumption between the opening and concluding sections, which deal with forms of circulation; I begin with questions about exchange that are initially abstract, situate these in precolonial and early colonial social contexts, and then return to these issues, after having discussed colonial histories and consumption, in the "post-colonial" present. The way exchange is viewed in the final chapter, with respect to the objectification of identity and the politics of ethnicity, depends on the discussion in the middle chapters. I hope it is clear that material artifacts and appropriation do not amount merely to new topics for scholarly industries but constitute a set of issues that have many ramifications for how we interpret both past and present societies.

Although I draw extensively and disproportionately upon materials I know best—from Fiji and eastern Polynesia—this is a comparative study which extracts items from the ethnography of New Guinea and the Solomon Islands, from the histories of New Zealand and Micronesia. Regional specialists will probably not forgive me, but it should be obvious that this exercise has been engaged in highly selectively and with the purposes of wider argument (and not proper contextualization) in mind. I have written this way partly in order to disfigure the anthropological project toward an accurate account of one stable culture by presenting a multiplicity of narratives and parts, but I am also motivated by a sense that an intermediate level of theory and analysis seems sadly lacking in much anthropology. On one side, there are treatises and hypotheses about ritual, myth, cognition, ethnicity, class, and gender; and on the other a mass of ethnographies. The discipline is almost devoid of works which are synthetic either for geographical regions or in thematic terms. This derives clearly from an intensification of disciplinary professionalism, but the associated specialization and introversion inevitably damage the prospects for wider conversations. This book does not aim to be synthetic in a Lévi-Straussian sense, or to establish general models, or any kind of definitive account; it focuses on the transposition of concepts rather than their formulation; it puts forward a succession of events, narratives, and relations and argues at a regional level about patterns of cultural history and social variation.

1

Objects, Exchange, Anthropology

I remembered my anger and shock when I perceived that the treasures I had rescued were being treated carelessly, ill used, not given
their pride of place; and then I smiled to myself at my concern as
I realized that even in my journeys to Mirror City I had abducted
treasures from their homeland, placed them in strange settings,
changed their purpose, and in some cases destroyed them to make
my own treasures even as my niece was doing in her playhouse.
And here I was being trapped also within one of the great themes
of fiction—the gift, the giver, the receiver and the thing received,
a theme so basic it is embedded in the grammar and syntax of the
language where it lies like a trap or a shaft of light.

Janet Frame, *The Envoy from Mirror City,* 1985

Exchange relations seem to be the substance of social life. Inequality
is often expressed through unfairness in distribution or contempt in
giving, just as egalitarianism is manifested in careful reciprocity and
parity. Words such as "contempt" refer to emotive states, but exchange
is always, in the first instance, a political process, one in which wider
relationships are expressed and negotiated in a personal encounter.
Hence the particular characteristics of transactions at once reflect and
constitute social relationships between both groups and individuals:
affines, strangers, enemies, lovers. Evaluations of entities, people,
groups, and relationships emerge at the moment of a transaction;
subversion can proceed through the assertion of reciprocity in the face
of dominance. These possibilities are general, but the forms of prestations differ between social contexts and societies. The overt calculation of value and the matching of quantities are routine in some
contexts and hideously inappropriate in others. Expectations about
action and ambience are very diverse: sometimes one should settle up

7

at once—but to return a gift directly is frequently to wound. Some transactions appear simply to concern things—one does not go into a shop to establish or consolidate a social relationship. Others appear to have purely "social" objectives which lack any "economic" rationale. These observations not only are familiar to anthropologists but also spell out a kind of commonsense practical knowledge which everyone who can manage social dealings has. People have a grasp, not so much of a code of behavior as a set of possibilities, of what amounts to generosity or offensive behavior under certain circumstances, of the morality or immorality of acts of giving and taking.

Our common sense does not, however, extend to the principles and values which are implicit in other economic systems—not even, necessarily, to other people's forms of capitalism, let alone to tribal economies which seem more intransigently unlike and more removed from our own culture and economy. The distinctive forms of prestations and value in such systems deserve to be recognized—since much of the action of indigenous peoples in dealings with intrusive Westerners has been rendered childlike or irrational because of ignorance of the contexts of particular transactions.

Cultural differences must thus be acknowledged and interpreted, but should not occasion a kind of writing in which tribal people inhabit a domain completely separate from our own.[1] Ahistorical representation, and the broader narrative of evolutionary pseudo-history, place them at a distance, which obscures our mutual engagement in economic, political, and cultural relationships. Everyone is now tied up in a historical network of global relations; this assumption does not determine everything at a local level and does not specify cultural categories or responses, but it does play a part in explaining the distinctiveness of modern life in the West as well as the peculiar combinations of transformation and intransigence on the colonial periphery. Just as in a local situation, the centrality of exchange in everyday practice should not lead to a view of social life or experience as wholly or primarily "transactional"; transactions may manifest, but do not encompass, the larger field of power relations that constitutes the circumstances of colonized populations. The properties of exchange relations derive from broader cultural structures and premises, from inequalities and asymmetries in rights over people, social groups, and their products—and also from the histories which engender cultural and political transformations of notions and relations. Exchange thus mediates conditions and relations that are not, or not wholly, constituted within the immediate frame of exchange. If actions and events are to be understood politically, they need to be situated historically: many of the factors which make a particular exchange relation distinctive are not visible in its enactment but must be traced through the longer-term dynamics of the social situation.

Ethnographic inquiry into economic practice should thus reflect a combination of local and global historical perspectives. Interpretation, and particularly reflection upon what has been witnessed ethnographically, leads to the constitution of an image of difference: a world which in many subtle ways resists and deflects our own expectations about economics and society. The presentation of a dish of food can be an expression of one's humility before a superior or a pushy reminder of a discrepancy in wealth. But this world of nuances is not a system of arcane meanings, a philosophical playground; rather it is practically muddled like everything else—symbolic miracles take place "while someone is eating or opening a window or just walking dully along."[2] Moreover, this world is not only in the same time and dimension as our own, but has been partly constituted through transactions between societies, through our mutual entanglements. As individuals we Europeans or Americans may or may not have face to face contacts with the indigenous peoples of the Pacific or the Amazon, but we are all caught up in international relations of production and appropriation which stretch across the spaces separating us. The transpositions of objects are conspicuous features and effects of these relations. Television documentaries suggest that these tribal people seem to be less themselves as they use our material culture—cloth and radios and metal tools—while we flock to see their tools and art hung up in our museums.[3] A book like this must thus attend not only to culturally specific forms of value and objectification, but also to the wider histories of appropriation and recontextualization.

Prestations and Ideology

Talking about aspects of the culture and economy of other peoples is difficult partly because of the general role which representations of "others" play in the constitutive myths of Western society. A broad contrast can be made between two uses of simple societies in this ideological process. Those who take a positive view of modern history, and regard contemporary industrial civilization essentially as a rational achievement which is disjunct from a tradition-bound past, have usually been committed to some sort of evolutionism. In this conception, primitive customs are opposed to modern institutions as magic is to science, but some kind of continuity is often also postulated. There is an evolutionary interest in identifying the origins of constitutive features of civilization (such as writing and the state), and aspects of contemporary "primitive" society can be interpreted as embryonic or intermediate forms.

In many social movements, and in certain currents of academic discourse, a view quite opposed to this has developed. Industrial society, capitalism in particular, has been seen as a source of impoverishment and misery unprecedented in human history and as the cause of mass alienation in human life. The notion of alienation has, of course, some specific philosophical meanings, but in sections of the contemporary environmental movement, as well as in much other modern thought, there is a strong sense that individuals are divorced from a whole range of activities which properly constitute human nature. They engage in highly mechanized or specialized work, are drawn into a larger, impersonal, industrial world, and out of a "community" or network of authentic, kin-structured relationships that characterized societies closer to nature.[4] This ideology of primitivism thus celebrates simple societies because they display what has been lost and provide a model for a more wholesome and fulfilling way of living. This is clearly the direct antithesis of the modernist celebration of progress, rather than a way of thinking which transcends the narrative of social evolution. There is, of course, a great gulf between the crude misconstructions of other peoples' lives as examples of a utopian connection to nature and professional anthropological writing, but celebration of the degree of solidarity, equality, and coherence in small-scale societies is nevertheless manifestly imbued with romanticism.

Exchange relations have long been significant as a marker in these evolutionary narratives which situate—irrespective of particular adjudications—elements of "their life" as origins for particular institutions of "our life." I have in my mind an unusually clear, but socially decontextualized, image of barter. I suppose I acquired this through elementary social studies, perhaps even at primary school. The scene takes place at an oasis, on a river bank, or near some sort of border. I see the people who have traveled to this spot giving some object in exchange for some very different object: pottery jugs for fabric, for instance. Because the local people do not have money, they equate quantities; several pairs of sandals are worth one jug. Money is thus implicit in its absence. The image is a kind of origin myth; as in Marx's similar "mystery" of the equivalence of a quarter of corn and some hundredweight of iron[5]—the absent term of course being human labor power—a solution is posed in terms of its problem. But what is most *telling* about the image of barter is that it does *not* speak: it is a spectacle or silent film in which we see things change hands. We have no sense of what is said or thought, and the image fades before we discover what becomes of the things, what people make of them subsequently. The objects' properties and uses thus appear to be self-evident, while participants' motives are either transparent or irrelevant.[6]

Economic topics were not of great interest to nineteenth-century anthropologists, but it is significant that insofar as the area of inquiry was recognized at all, this silent film of barter dictated the narrative. This is apparent from the questionnaire which Sir James Frazer circulated to his informants—the very numerous missionaries, colonial officials, and other travelers with whom he corresponded about primitive customs and beliefs. His brief section under the heading "Trade and commerce" ran as follows:

219. Do the people trade among themselves or with neighbouring tribes? What products are especially exchanged? Is there a special class of traders or merchants? 220. Are there regular markets? If so, how are they established? How often are they held? What customs are observed in connexion with them? 221. Have they the custom of "the silent trade"? That is, do they barter goods with other tribes or with Europeans without personal contact, each side depositing its wares in certain spots and carrying away the wares of the other side without speaking or meeting? 222. Have the natives any kind of money or anything that passes for money, such as cattle, shells, salt, axes, &c.? Do they employ weights and measures? What are their standards of weight and measure?[7]

"Savage commerce" is thus the exchange of utilitarian values. The observer perceives the primitive condition in negative terms, in terms of what is missing (in this instance true money)[8] and then notes the gradual emergence, in what are taken to be slightly more advanced savage societies, of "early forms" of money or primitive government. This particular area was not explored by Frazer himself, but an exponent of Frazerian anthropology wrote a whole book on "the silent trade."[9]

A figure long regarded as one of the founders of modern anthropology shifted economics from the margins to the center of ethnological inquiry. Bronislaw Malinowski had a strong polemical interest in turning his back upon the kind of speculative and detached anthropology epitomized by Frazer's questionnaire. As is well known, he placed great emphasis on localized and intensive ethnographic study which adopted the native point of view. The aim was to see institutions and behavior in native terms, rather than in the context of some grand hypothetical scheme. The famous kula[10] trading system of southeastern Papua—still a dynamic and developing network—was a signifier in this polemic because it differed dramatically from expectations about "primitive commerce." In Malinowski's first summary report of the kula, he noted that Melanesian trade was well known through the publications of C. G. Seligman and others, but that the examples described involved utilities and food which were often transported into areas short of such resources.[11] These systems accorded roughly with what he called "the usual a priori notion of savage trade": "an exchange of indispensable, or, at least, useful things, done under pressure of need by direct barter, or casual give and take of presents, without much ceremony and regulation. Such a conception would almost reverse all the essential features of the *Kula*."[12]

Malinowski thus had a strategic interest in asserting that the kula did in fact invert a utilitarian, nonceremonial stereotype of primitive exchange. This led him to exaggerate the contrast: he insisted, for instance, that the necklaces and armshells which comprised the key valuables were exchanged only against each other and played no part in other transactions; they were in no sense a kind of money which could be substituted for other goods or services. It is now apparent that on this point he actually misled his readers. Like shell valuables elsewhere in Melanesia, kula items could be used in a great variety of ways—in payment for food, canoes, assassinations, and so on.[13] Although Malinowski acknowledged that something more like barter also took place, he claimed that this constituted a separate sphere of transactions which were never muddled or connected with kula gifts.[14] This distinction has also been rejected in recent historical and ethnographic research.[15]

Modern kula exchange: Vakutan people leaving the island of Kitava at the end of a kula trip, 1977.

I will return to these revisions of Massim exchange. What is significant here is that Malinowski's intellectual project led him to represent Trobriand practices as strictly ceremonial, and as having no particular link with the history of our society. The movement from Frazer's questions to Malinowski's ethnography is from the direct subordination of their world to ours, to a romantic counter-modernism in which selected features of their world serve to relativize and destabilize cherished features or cultural tenets of our own. In modern anthropology this has been the most pervasive and enduring rhetorical structure. From Margaret Mead to Clifford Geertz, and in many more recent studies, the ethnographic case serves as an argument for difference and the contingency of our own cultural models. The kula, Samoan sex roles, and the Balinese polities known as *negara* confounded Western assumptions about economics, gender, and the state respectively, but the rhetorical game has too often led to an extension of real differences. Dilemmas about relativism and the imposition of Eurocentric values can be set aside if it is recognized that the play of assertion and negation is a condition of anthropological talk. Moreover, it is also a feature of indigenous peoples' own coding of practices and ethnic differences. Forms of prestations are also signifiers within similar debates about cultural contrasts and social alternatives among tribal peoples. This is another way of recognizing that they have their "anthropology"—if anthropology is essentially discourse upon social and cultural values based on material about others—and thus leads us to a more realistic and immediate sense of indigenous peoples as co-subjects in a wider system.

The Inalienability of the Gift

The terrain of the gift, of "archaic" exchange as a form in its own right, was opened up by Malinowski and Marcel Mauss; the elaborations and critiques of their writings are numerous and will not be analyzed in detail here. However, my theoretical reference points include two discussions drawing extensively from Mauss—C. A. Gregory's distillation of ideas of gift and commodity, and Annette Weiner's exploration of inalienable wealth—and an innovative theoretical essay by Arjun Appadurai on commodities, which draws on more diverse and nonstandard sources. In the acknowledgments I alluded to the fact that a book about exchange could hardly overlook its own debts, so I will briefly review and situate these studies.

In Gregory's view objects take the form of gifts and commodities in clan-based and class societies respectively. In the former, the processes of consumption and personification, or the self-replacement of people, predominates; in the latter, production and objectification (the making of commodities) are the dominant processes. The exchange relation of a commodity is a relationship between things, a relation of price or equivalence: x quantity of article A $=$ y quantity of article B. Once a transaction has been effected there is no excess which must in some sense be accounted for socially. The transactors are strangers in a state of reciprocal independence which persists after the transaction. The exchange relation of gifts, by contrast, is one between people. Gregory, following Mauss and others, proposes that the fundamental principle is that the giver acquires some sort of superiority over the receiver: a relationship of indebtedness is therefore established. Gifts are inalienable things which move between people who are mutually entangled in an array of rights and obligations, people who are "reciprocally dependent."[16] As far as the status of things themselves is concerned, Gregory suggests that while commodities have prices, gifts have rank. Kula armshells and necklaces are, for instance, ranked on the basis of size and, as a category, rank higher than articles such as polished axe blades and foodstuffs.[17] This theory can be crystallized into a series of oppositions:

commodities	gifts
alienable	inalienable
independence	dependence
quantity (price)	quality (rank)
objects	subjects[18]

The set of dichotomies provides a useful departure point by showing that gifts are radically different from commodities. Indebtedness may not necessarily take a universal form, and the precise character of the singularity of the gift will require further clarification, but the differences can provisionally be seen to emerge sharply from the fact that giving always has a distinctly *social* effect: mistakes made in giving have consequences that commodity transactions almost never have. In many societies, the presentation of an extravagant gift implying a relationship of intimacy or commitment which the receiver or others present feel is entirely lacking, could only lead to embarrassment or mistrust. The durability of the effects of such a gift (or its refusal) have no parallel in the domain of a commodity transaction. I mention something like a Western birthday party in order to disambiguate this opposition from that between capitalist or industrial societies and tribal systems.

These distinct forms could be elaborated upon much further, as Gregory did for the case of Papua New Guinea. Precisely because the theoretical contrast is developed with such clarity, the question arises of whether the postulated gift is anything other than the inversion of the commodity. At the same time, some of its specific features, such as the notion that the donor acquires superiority through giving,[19] are derived from ethnographic cases and have no theoretical necessity or generality. I therefore treat "the gift" not as an ideal type to which prestations in clan societies may accord with to a greater or lesser degree, but as a foil for a range of differences and mutations.[20] For instance, while "inalienability" does seem to be a crucial attribute of things in some contexts, the nature of the indissoluble bond certainly varies in consequential ways.

In other words, there should be a movement of perspective from economic abstractions to historical forms. But at the analytic level it seems useful to add three major qualifications to Gregory's account. These concern the nature of alienability and inalienability, the differentiation of things, and the associations between transactors.

Confusion might arise from the Marxist slant of *Gifts and Commodities*, since the conception of alienation developed there depends less upon Marxian or Hegelian antecedents than upon Mauss's general proposition that in "archaic" societies there is confusion or conflation of persons and things. (The tenet arose partly from Mauss's interest in archaic jurisprudence and "early" forms of contracts and pledges.) Hence "objects are never completely separated from the men who exchange them."[21] This is quite a different proposition from the materialist idea that objects are or should be inalienable *from their producers*, a point which is of considerable importance for the interpretation of exploitation and appropriation within gift economies. At the level of philosophical anthropology, the making of a product involves the objectification of one's work, and an object may thus be said to permanently embody an aspect of one's practical activity. But there is clearly a disjunction between this ontological fact and the way associations between producers, objects, and subsequent users are culturally represented. It is not inevitable that it will be acknowledged that a thing would not exist without someone's labor. In many cases, in fact, the authorship of producers may be unrecognized or only partially acknowledged. Where more than one person, or more than one class of persons (both men and women, both specialists and others) makes a contribution, the work of one may be marginalized and rendered inessential if not elided altogether.[22] Moreover, the strong association taken to be constitutive of inalienability may be with a person for whom a thing was produced or with someone who has acquired it under particular circumstances. This occurs, for instance, in the eastern Polynesian systems where the *tapu* of a high-ranking man or woman could draw almost any object which passed above his or her body or any mediating object into a close association with the person. Once a thing had passed over a *tapu* person's head, its subsequent use by another would endanger both parties. It may be desirable at certain points to recover these implications of what might be loosely described as a Marxist or production-oriented perspective, but for conceptual clarity it is important to recognize that the issue does not arise in a strictly Maussian theory.

Another general set of problems concerning inalienability arises from the fact that the connection between the general proposition and the specific theory which postulates gifts that generate debt and compel a return is by no means clear. Jonathan Parry has suggested that the crucial sources of Mauss's argument were not the Maori and Polynesian cases generally discussed but examples from Hindu India, which are drawn into an evolutionary argument about the origins of modern contracts. According to Parry, this dimension of Mauss's argument has been overlooked in dominant Malinowskian readings.[23]

Whatever the precise sources of Mauss's thesis, it is clear that the dictum that persons and things are confounded is merely a general premise. Although the notion that a gift carries something of the donor or former user with it may be sustained, the principle of the superiority of the donor, and the compulsion to provide a return gift, cannot be derived from this broader postulate. These propositions, though constantly repeated in Maussian economic anthropology, are obviously ethnographic generalizations which ought to be subject to contest and reformulation. Other kinds of gifts—both of objects and relations in the domain of kinship—have been extensively witnessed and interpreted ethnographically but have not been incorporated into theoretical abstraction.

The second qualification concerns the differentiation of objects. The discussion has tended to confound—as in a sense it should—types of prestations and material objects. A gift is indeed both a thing and a kind of act, but the emphasis upon the social relation has been almost to the exclusion of the nature of the object. With respect to Gregory's point that commodities have price while gifts have rank, it is certainly the case that virtually everything in capitalist society can have a monetary value placed upon it. Even things like personal relationships, reputations, and parts of the body which are usually thought of in nonmonetary terms are occasionally priced for insurance, litigation, or blackmail. Sexual activity is more ambiguous in that although there are obviously notions specifying that it should be a mutual gift, everyone is aware of its commoditization in prostitution and the more or less subtle ways in which one party can demand or offer sex in return for something else. What makes these moments of commoditization disturbing or immoral are the ways in which things and services are culturally constructed: sex has a proper meaning which is taken to be distorted through objectification. Similarly, we are (or at least I am) shocked and angered by the practice of purchasing organs from impoverished Brazilians to repair the bodies of the rich; such a judgment is enabled by a concept of the integrity of the person and the inalienability of body parts—a concept that is a moral and political necessity. The debate is about the exchangeability of things and depends upon their culturally specific features; theorization of the circulation and the politics of value can be partial only insofar as it is restricted to principles of exchange, such as the application of the fundamental standard of money. My argument is thus that an understanding of forms of prestations can generate a sense of actual movements and values only if it is synthesized with another cultural domain—in which things are differentiated and in which appropriate kinds of transactions and restrictions are specified.[24] That is, a particular article can be understood as something which can be given, but only at certain times; or as one which may be sold anywhere, to anyone; or as something which it would always be improper to give away or sell. The introduction of this set of questions disables the simple connection between the gift/commodity opposition and any distinction between traditional and modern societies, or clan and class, by establishing a greater degree of diversity and contingency than this evolutionary dichotomy can contain. The point, though, is not merely to identify complexity but to connect it with political and historical contexts. Through discussion of commoditization in colonized Solomon Islands societies, I develop this line of argument in a later section. Here I sketch out a counterpoint—the sentiment-burdened gift in the modern industrial situation.

A ring may be initially a commodity produced in a factory or by a craftsman for sale. In the shop, it is likely to be an alienated thing divorced from its producer, but some high-class or "craft" jewelry is regarded, like art, as the output of a creative master. In this case the association may be mentioned or paraded when the article is shown off; a signature or mark may express the thing's origin and the fact that it is an objectification of the creator's work and intellect. (The same applies to a greater degree to antique pieces which have histories: associations not only with the producer but also with illustrious former owners may be celebrated.) If the ring becomes a wedding ring, it acquires the character of a highly specific kind of gift which cannot move beyond one context without becoming something else. This gift is performative in the sense that its transmission, when accompanied by the right words in the right context, is constitutive of the conjugal relationship which it subsequently stands for. It is important that it is something which can be worn on the person virtually continuously, since this manifests the (notionally) essential, noncontingent character of the married state.[25] In the case of engagement rings, the signifier and the signified are so closely connected that the breaking of the engagement can be effected—and in a strict sense can *only* be effected—by the handing back of the ring. More intricate aspects of relations and their distortions can also be signified by the situations of rings or remarks upon them. As Tony Tanner has noted with respect to *Madame Bovary*, the ring is "an exemplary sign" such that confusions between Charles and Emma over a "false engagement ring" as opposed to a token of love in the opera at Rouen connote a larger deprivation of meaning produced by the disorder and transgression of adultery.

> Emma tries to explain, but when he still cannot understand the function of these deceptive props in the story she says impatiently, "Qu'importe?" . . . If you cannot distinguish—either for the purposes of narrative interpretation or those of social identification—a false engagement ring from a real one, or a deceitful sign from a gift of love, then you are bound to encounter very serious problems of meaning and value . . . At one stage she could explain (to herself) the difference between marriage and adultery, between what she saw as a meaningless contract and what she felt to be the extreme significance of passionate love, but she is entering the stage when these distinctions are confounding and equivalizing themselves, and her final response is, in effect—"Qu'importe?"[26]

Hence the artifact is not simply a valuable object of exchange or even a gift that creates relations of one sort or another but also a crucial index of the extent to which those relations are sustained or disfigured. The failure to recognize the distinctions that artifacts stand for suggests a succession of other failures: "To the extent that a recognition of meaning is withheld from the sign [the ring], so too it is withheld from the relationships and bonds that it is supposed to signify."[27]

Neither particular signification nor types of relations signified are stable in the lives of particular rings. It is frequently the case that both engagement and wedding rings are bequeathed or otherwise transmitted from grandmothers or mothers to daughters. It might be argued that this is often an empty ritual, but in many cases, and especially where transmission across alternate generations is involved, it probably genuinely reflects the sustaining of an intergenerational female link in a context where patriliny is dominant, and, more significantly, the formation of immediate nuclear families tends to diminish other kinship ties. The fact that the thing has become inalienable has a significant impact upon the contexts in which it is exchangeable. In this case, these are reduced virtually to one: the handing down of the thing to a female descendent. It would be unusual for a ring to be given away to a friend or a woman related affinally, and it would be strange to lend such an article in any context—not because it is valuable and unique, since it may not be valuable—but because of its particular character and association with one's personal history. But an owner may be forced by poverty to dispose of her jewelry: under these circumstances the absent article may retain associations for the former holder, who experiences some loss precisely because it was an inalienable thing entangled with her life history. For other people, however, it is a detached commodity, stripped of associations and just like any other in the shop.

Perhaps wrong in the details, this conjectural ethnography nevertheless indicates that the intrinsic and attributed properties of objects have an impact upon their exchangeability. The fact of some articles being highly restricted arises not merely from the existence of "spheres of exchange" of the kind identified by anthropologists in various societies, but from more specific cultural constructions. The conjugal relation, intergenerational female link, or a domestic group could be seen as a "sphere of exchange" within which certain sorts of transactions take place, but this would not explain the particular features of certain sorts of gifts: the elucidation of these acts depends, of course, upon what items such as rings, garments, foods, and so on, are seen to convey. It may be objected that rings are singular and atypical, and that considerations of this kind are thus incidental to the development of indigenous exchange and the pattern of trade on colonial peripheries; but the analysis below attempts to establish that it is precisely such factors which prompt people to barter some things and not others.

My story of the ring also reveals the discrepancy which often separates personal estimation from systemic value. An object can acquire singular meaning for a person because it was given by a particular relative or friend, or because of a connection with an event (a tree planted on the day of someone's death). The particular relation with such a thing is not necessarily an individual or idiosyncratic matter—a meaning may be restricted to a neighborhood community or a subcultural group but may nevertheless entail something tantamount to inalienability and in that respect differ from the configuration of value in broader social terms. These perspectival differences are not peculiar to "complex" Western societies: a Tubetube (Massim) man used the example of the value of the ethnographer's lost ring to explain that the meaning of an owned kula shell, a *kitom* or *kitomwa*,[28] for him or for someone else would not be the same as its meaning for future holders:

MARTHA MACINTYRE: How does it work?

PANETAN: *Kitomwa*, its work is like a sign, just the same as some sign on a tree. It is the same as you were telling me the story of your Grandmother's ring, that one. When it was her ring it was to show that she was engaged, but you hold that ring to remember your Grandmother. You can look at it every day and keep her in your mind. It is the same with *mwagolu*, the hair necklaces our ancestors wore during mourning. You wear your ring and it shows people [something]. Our widows wore a *mwagolu* and it shows—it reminds—herself and others who look at it. We all know something about that person, but not what she has in her own mind. It is the same with a *kitomwa* . . . If I use it to call my wife, it shows my love for my wife. It shows my respect for my family, for her place. Because it has made a path there it reminds people of all the work that will go up and down during marriage . . . But when that marriage is finished or people put it on another path then it is their *kitomwa*. Its sign is different then, perhaps they pay compensation or *kune* [do kula] with it. It's up to them.[29]

If it is allowed that value can be reinterpreted in specific social contexts, as well as at an abstract level of economic logic, then it must be appreciated that the estimations people make draw upon a range of historical and sentimental considerations, which may qualify, specify, or even negate wider systemic criteria such as scarcity, utility, and cultural categorization.

The third aspect of Gregory's model which requires comment concerns the status of parties to both gift and commodity exchange. The relationship of "reciprocal independence" between transactors does not mean that there is no social relationship. Strangers are named as such because one does have associations with them, which may be managed in various ways through expectations and precautions. The strangers with whom individuals in Western societies deal in buying and selling are usually not threatening, but strangers in other contexts are often potentially dominating or dangerous. An asymmetrical relationship, rather than a condition of equality, is presumably a more typical background to transactions, and it would seem unfortunate if this was only to be appreciated indirectly through notions of supply and demand. It is also a notable feature of gift exchange that the parties are frequently *not* "reciprocally dependent," if these words imply that they are in an essentially equivalent position. In many contexts, the particular character of the agency of one member of a clan makes him or her dependent with respect to another—because of some ritual status, because of gender, or, in the context of ceremonial exchange, because there is some categorical difference such as that entailed in hypergamy, where wife-takers rank higher than wife-givers. A capacity to generate debt is not inherent in every prestation; it is not necessarily the case that the donor acquires some superiority, even of a merely temporary kind.

The nature of specific prestations is thus dependent, not just on the form of prestation or on the conjuncture of such forms and cultural constructions of objects, as has already been asserted, but also on the political and cultural construction of agency, which differentiates people's capacities through relations of mutual, but distinctly uneven, dependence.[30]

Immobile Value

The question of inalienability has also been explored recently by Weiner, who draws more directly from Maussian usage and the cases which Mauss originally discussed. Her concern is to establish that there is a category of "inalienable wealth":

> Whatever happens to these objects, they are perceived to belong in an inherent way to their original owners. Inalienable possessions are imbued with affective qualities that are expressions of the value an object has when it is kept by its owners and inherited within the same family or descent group. Age adds value, as does the ability to keep the object against all the exigencies that might force a person or a group to release it to others. The primary value of inalienability, however, is expressed through the

power these objects have to define who one is in a historical sense. The object acts as a vehicle for bringing past time into the present, so that the histories of ancestors, titles, or mythological events become an intimate part of a person's present identity.[31]

Weiner proceeds to consider various valuables, some of which are completely inalienable and are kept out of all circulation, whereas others, such as Samoan fine mats, are "partially inalienable." In addressing the question of why such goods should be bound to their owners, she makes connections, in the Maori case, between cloth in various forms and birth, death, and the transmission of power from deities to persons; in an analogous manner, greenstone adz heads and ornaments were also used in life-crisis rituals and represented descent lines. Both kinds of *taonga* (valuables) thus embodied a collective life-force and a fusion of ancestors and living owners: they were "the proof of a group's immortality."[32] This leads to a general thesis concerning a "solution" to the problems of the fragmented character of social life and the inescapability of loss, death, and decay. An inalienable thing permits one to transcend this condition through its permanence, but the social necessity of engaging in exchange makes the achievement of inalienable association with a badge of immortality difficult and inevitably partial. The need to give can be dealt with in part through replacement, which is seen as somewhat compromised since the most singular valuables cannot be equated with return gifts. The "dynamics of social exchange" are thus located in keeping, giving, and replacement, but the first term is accorded primacy: keeping "concentrates identity into a symbol of immortality."[33]

The value of this perspective is that it shifts attention from the forms of prestation to the characteristics of particular kinds of objects.[34] The limitations of Weiner's analysis arise from the fact that, like the works of Mauss and Gregory, it is oriented toward a general type rather than historic actualities. The emphasis is thus always upon broader similarities rather than the differences between particular kinds of valuables and the distinctive purposes which some may have. The "badge of identity and immortality" is no doubt an important type, but this must be understood either as a restricted class or as a category which does not have the same properties as other kinds of valuables. In this case, there is no necessary nexus between the need to exchange and subtraction or loss, since the valuables which may be given away in certain contexts such as marriage are not always the same as those which become historical narrative-bearing artifacts of social life. In fact it is arguably *the purpose* of certain kinds of valuables to be alienated, to move against aspects of kinship or other forms of debt, and their disposal represents an accomplishment rather than a loss.

Difficulty arises partly from the fact that the pregnant term "inalienability" may be being used to refer to relations between things and persons which are not all quite the same. It is odd, in the light of subsequent discussion, that the word was not actually used by Mauss himself: the term translated as "inalienability" is generally *immeuble*, which actually has rather distinct meanings concerning the fixity of property in medieval law, although *aliénabilité, inaliénabilité*, and related terms are obviously French words, and the origins of the English words are all Old French and Latin.[35] Of course, the focus here is not what Mauss might or might not have intended but what concepts are appropriate now; this discrepancy, however, does compound the uncertainty concerning what exactly is taken to be characteristic of the gift.

Is it really the case, for instance, that a thing can never be definitively transmitted, such that it belongs in an unqualified sense to someone else? Can the interest of a producer, "owner," or donor never be categorically erased? This, if true, would be a strong proposition. It is no doubt the case, as Weiner notes, that some objects or interests such as shell body decorations or rights in land may be exchanged without ever losing "their identity and attachment to the lineage that originally owned them."[36] But do such cases, concerning articles which might be compared with heirlooms and regalia, really characterize gifts or even inalienable gifts as a class? A woman who presents a mat to a woman in another village, thereby creating a debt, cannot go and take it back without asking. Probably she could not even reasonably request it back. Are there thus other kinds of inalienability—where for instance a thing can have social effect, in that it creates debt, or where the object will always be associated, in memory, with another person or group? Of course, in neither of these cases do the former owners or users have residual interest in what can be done with the article. There is thus a distinction to be made between control and persisting rights on one side, and memories and cultural associations on the other. The gift of an object may frequently relate to rights or debts in a distinct register (of nurture or kinship) and thus cannot itself be the matter of persisting claims. And all these types would seem distinct from the "keeping" variety of inalienability discussed in Weiner's work.

Parallel comments might be made about Daniel Miller's important and wide-ranging analysis of cultural objectification, which likewise claims our attention on behalf of the neglected material object. This synthesis of concepts abstracted from Hegel, Marx, and Simmel, among others, and diverse case materials, cannot be fully discussed here, but it is relevant that the departure point in a dialectical construction of culture as objectification leads to particular emphases in the interpretation of objects. Hegel is said to have "illustrated a continual process of societal self-creation through objectification and sublation";[37] the second term refers to the reabsorption of something which is external or has been externalized and is equated by Miller with consumption.[38] Miller's aim in part is to criticize various forms of modernist and postmodernist elitism in which consumption is regarded negatively as an expression of mass capitulation to industrial overproduction; in contrast to such attributions of passive receptivity to the consumer, Miller emphasizes that the process may entail active appropriation, which turns a particular product to purposes unforeseen by the manufacturers:

> The motor scooter was developed in Italy as the feminine equivalent of the more macho motorbike . . . These images are, however, transformed in a manner not intended by the producers (though later picked up and encouraged by them), but which is established rather through articulation with emergent polarities in British youth cultures. The motorbike takes on an association with the rockers which is then contrasted with the motor scooter's place in the mods' sense of style; the latter representing a more continental "soft" image as against the rocker's American "hard" image.[39]

The example and the overall line of Miller's argument centralize the objectification *of identity*, that is, the ways in which artifacts express individual or collective subjects. There is, as it were, a one-to-one relationship between a material thing (or a particular array, such as a style of home decoration) and the expression of belonging or difference. Idiosyncrasy, for instance, can be expressed through unusual choices, or by avoiding clothes or kinds of furniture which would convey affiliation with a subculture.

There is certainly great scope for analysis of the appropriation of things as objectifications of local or national identity-projects in the south Pacific. Janet Keller has recently discussed the potential and emerging importance of baskets and various other plaited artifacts for the diverse cultures of Vanuatu: "Plaited products may continue to be fully elaborated in local detail as important emblems distinguishing the peoples of Vanuatu, and yet, as shared productions of a technology with common features, can simultaneously represent ni-Vanuatu identity."[40] Similarly, in Papua New Guinea string bags (*bilums*) are already vehicles both for local style and new Melanesian identity: the overall form expresses the latter while specific patterns and looping or knotting techniques convey the former.[41]

Though a useful departure point, the focus on the projection of identity, is, I suggest, ultimately restrictive. Artifacts can be significant as markers of other people with whom one does not identify; they can signify difference, contest, and relatedness; they can also be created in order to represent histories or events rather than subjects or can be subsequently seen in those terms. The potential uses of artifacts do not constitute a plethora that is too extensive to be analyzed, but they cannot be reduced to a unitary model or process such as the chain of objectification and sublation. My curiosity avoids any constrictive typology of object-meanings in an abstracted domain of man, subject, and object, and is instead aroused by the variety of liaisons men and women can have with things in the conflicted, transcultural history of colonialism.

The problems that have been enunciated derive from a more general distinction between the projects of the theorists I have discussed and what is attempted here. Mauss's interest was principally in identifying a generality rather than the differentiation or classification of practices. He diverges from postulated Western principles in order to discover the distinct logic of the gift—what counts theoretically is always "the" gift. I suggest that this is also true of Gregory's extension of the Maussian framework, Weiner's useful exploration of types of "inalienable wealth," and Miller's theory of consumption. Although all feature ethnographic distinctions, such as Mauss's between the potlatch and the total prestation, the rhetorical emphasis of writing is always upon similarities. What animates these texts is the scope for reducing various cases to the overall form that is focused upon. This is no doubt a necessary movement in any intellectual effort, but once the distinctiveness of a particular entity or process has been established, the general concept needs to be fractured; not split up, as a partitioned essence in a formalistic typology, but instead scattered through the nuances of practice and history.

The Promiscuity of Objects

Much theory and analysis in economic anthropology has turned upon divisions between "traditional" and "modern" forms, that is, upon evolutionary distinctions of one sort or another. It is no doubt useful to represent the social differences between larger categories of political and economic types. Without entirely denying the worth of such generalized discriminatory exercises, it must be said that in most instances these have merely reformulated constructions of primitivism or alterity through ethnographic specificity and have often, in any case, taken by-products of colonialism to be the core structures or hallmarks of tribal or Asiatic authenticity (as in Dumont's sociology of caste). The point is not to shift the pursuit of an ethnographic essence back into precolonial history, but rather to displace such exercises through an analysis of processes and grounded regional distinctions which actually relate to peoples rather than rhetorical types. When scrutinized in this manner, the grand polarities almost always turn out to be implausible. I have already drawn attention to the enduring significance of the gift in the ordinary social life of the West—there is more to the economy than supermarkets and the Dow Jones index— and will also insist that commoditization occurs on a relatively wide scale in some "tribal" exchange systems.

Appadurai's recent reconstruction of the category of the commodity has some direct bearing on this effort and also represents the healthy deconstruction of us/them polarities now under way. Appadurai starts with Simmel's claim that exchange consists essentially in mutual sacrifice, in the matching of demands and desires. Contrary to the Marxist view, value thus has no prior or absolute basis but originates in actual or imagined exchange. Rather than pursuing Simmel into the theory of money, Appadurai proceeds to discuss the politics of value, that is, the process through which cultural assumptions and relations entailing power create regimes of exchange. The focus, however, is on things themselves, rather than on forms of exchange such as gift giving, barter, or sale and purchase. Instead, the "commodity situation" of things becomes a way of examining circulation, restriction, and the creation of privilege through strategies such as diverting and "enclaving" commodities. The "commodity situation" of a thing is a phase in its longer history or "social life" in which "its exchangeability (past, present, or future) for some other thing is its socially relevant feature."[42] This "can be disaggregated into: (1) the commodity phase in the social life of any thing; (2) the commodity candidacy of any thing; and (3) the commodity context in which any thing may be placed."[43]

These terms refer, first, to *phases*. A thing is not immutable, but may move in and out of a commodity state: a shirt purchased and given to a family member ceases to be a commodity and becomes merely an article for personal use, which in many cases would never be given or sold to anyone else (unless "handed down" or recommoditized through donation to a charity shop). As this is a temporal feature, the commodity *candidacy* of a thing is a categorical or conceptual aspect: objects and services are culturally represented in various ways such that they may or may not be considered exchangeable. Certain things, such as shell valuables, money, Fijian mats, and second-hand cars are obviously eminently disposable and in some cases exist primarily for exchange. By contrast, certain foods, land, and one's religious adherence may frequently be regarded as nonexchangeable, and may never be candidates for commoditization. *Phase* and *candidacy* are mediated by the thing's commodity *context*, which refers to the social arenas in which things may be more intensely or appropriately exchanged. It is obvious that placing something in a market rather than a house usually emphasizes its exchangeability and prompts commodity flows, but it is also the case that things such as shell valuables can often be exchanged only in ritualized formal contexts. "Thus, commoditization lies at the complex intersection of temporal, cultural, and social factors."[44]

For me, this set of insights is liberating: in conjunction with established understandings of spheres of circulation and classifications of things, insistence upon the fact that objects pass through social transformations effects a deconstruction of the essentialist notion that the identity of material things is fixed in their structure and form. Hence, although certain influential theorists of material culture have stressed the objectivity of the artifact, I can only recognize the reverse: the mutability of things in recontextualization. Axes, old cars, striped condoms—they are never things embodying pure or original templates or intentions. The use of a truck in the New Guinea highlands as the "big-man's" prestige valuable is no distortion of a straightforward machine commodity; any thing shifts through phases, within which it can be used at certain times as a claim about design, a new product, a potential way of getting cash, a marker not just of status but of a certain kind of taste (stylish *old* Jaguars versus the more common new kind), an aggressive way of expressing taste against its absence, a means of violence or seduction, and later a marker of a period, a relic, a souvenir; all this as well as a way of cutting a tree, traveling somewhere, or having safe sex. The symbolic and political claims and risks are always engaged with what some visions would split off as fundamental or straightforward uses—but what could be more fundamental than making a political claim or representing difference? What we are confronted with is thus never more or less than a succession of uses and recontextualizations.

Appadurai proceeds to develop further general ideas about exchange paths, diversions of valuables, and the political effect of restricting or enclaving things in certain ways, and he argues for a general category of "tournaments of value," including such things as kula and art auctions—which can be seen as "complex periodic events that are removed in some culturally well-defined way from the routines of economic life" in which participation is a privilege and a basis for status competition. Although I will not discuss these propositions in detail here, I must express disagreement with one of Appadurai's theoretical moves.[45]

The very positive emphasis upon the existence of commodities in a wide range of societies leads, I think quite unnecessarily, to a suppression of the distinction between the commodity and the gift. It is true, as Appadurai notes, that this has often been not just exaggerated but polarized, and his perspective on the social lives of things permits us to examine transformations of gifts into commodities and vice versa (an area Gregory had discussed in the case of Papua New Guinea). But to abandon the distinction altogether seems to obscure precisely the factors which mark the biographies of objects and sometimes break them apart through recontextualization and transgression. The cultural violence in seizing a headdress or ornament and listing it in a curiosity catalogue or squabbling over its price can be appreciated only if its initial, singular, inalienability is specified. The overall form of the prestation dictates the ramifications of transactions and the significance of any enduring association with a producer or former owner. Moreover, ignoring the distinction between gifts and commodities precludes an analysis of economic systems as totalities, as conjunctures of prestation forms with arrays of material culture and social relations, rather than as any one of these separate fields. Of course, it is obvious why Appadurai does this, because there have been numerous studies of economic systems; his interest, like that of Weiner and Miller, is in opening up the neglected area of the cultural constitution of objects. But a more satisfactory historical and political perspective would put together the sets of concepts developed by Gregory and Weiner on one side and Appadurai and Miller on the other (among various other writers): the absences in each case are the strengths of the other. This retention of the theory of forms of prestations is especially important in any work dealing with cross-cultural exchange, which frequently entails differing assumptions or claims about whether a thing is a commodity or a gift, as well as divergent views of the commodity candidacy of things and the context of exchange itself.

Value: A Surplus of Theories

Much of what I have written above avoids an issue central to the concerns of many of the writers referred to, an issue that has proved contentious and intractable for several traditions of economic and anthropological thought, namely, the nature of value and the way in which it is appropriately conceptualized. Although I do not attempt any new integration of approaches and do not rely consistently upon one formulation of what value is, my usage is not intended to be totally erratic, and I suggest briefly that, out of many, there are three perspectives on value which are analytically productive in particular inquiries of the kind pursued here. The question of whether these ought to be drawn into one comprehensive theory is of less interest to me than their localized, strategic effect.

What is private and idiosyncratic is normally outside the vision of the social sciences, but it seems important to recognize that artifacts can have peculiarly personal value arising from some association with an individual's biography, that—as was noted above—passes largely unrecognized in both collective scales of value and in the systemic dynamics of transactions. This kind of value, like the heirloom status of the treasures discussed by Weiner, is not a principle of exchange but a principle that is excluded by, or is incompatible with, exchange; and in this sense it can hardly be accommodated by any theory that takes value to emerge at the moment of circulation. The identification of this form of value could lead to a kind of micro-ethnography, like the history of a ring, that would specify why certain garments or books mean so much. But it is not my intention to dissolve the economic into the personal. While I would insist that the systemic cannot entirely encompass the idiosyncratic, the more important point is that evaluations of particular artifacts will often conflict: a situation of exchange, or one in which one party attempts to impose exchange upon another, is thus inevitably a politicized field entailing compromise, subordination, acquiescence, refusals, and so on. In cross-cultural exchange on colonial peripheries, in particular, the discrepancies between estimations of value are one of the crucial sources of conflict.

Of course, this form of value, which is probably recognized more in common sense than in either anthropological or economic theories, is salient to material culture and exchange only in a distinctly particular and partial way. With respect to processes of circulation, especially in the complex forms typical of marriage and mortuary presentations in Oceania, a more systemic approach is clearly required. Here a distinction may be identified between attempts to understand the values of things exchanged through reference to some underlying or prior equivalence,[46] and studies that emphasize their difference; the second perspective, which has emerged in work derived from one strand or another of symbolic anthropology, effectively repudiates any interest in establishing some imperfect mechanism of price and in fact understands value semiotically, not as a relation of equivalence but in terms of "significant contrast or difference. Hierarchy, complementarity and inversion are all logically possible formulations of such difference."[47] The shift here is accompanied by a perception of value creation as a process, as a recursively constituted outcome of acts of substitution, juxtaposition, and transformation that effectively reveal persons and parts of persons (their capacities or attributes) and artifacts, animals, or other exchange items in particular ways.[48] In an analysis of this kind, value is not dissociable from broad and socially pervasive processes in which actors, objects, and relations valorize each other. At an abstract level, this may seem tautological or meaningless, but it is approximately the premise of some very rich analyses such as Nancy

Munn's *Fame of Gawa*,[49] which proceeds by identifying basic modes of value transformation, embodiment, and signification. While Munn's study is distinguished by its phenomenological terminology, among other things, other works such as Strathern's *Gender of the Gift* similarly construe value as a process constituted through a wide range of relations and representations; any specification of value in production or a defined "economic" sphere becomes unintelligible. Work of this kind has also been marked by extreme suspicion of the aptness of anthropological theories and what Strathern sees as "Western property metaphors" for the interpretation of Melanesian sociality. Although my analysis of Fijian ceremonies is not motivated by the same concerns as appear to be present in the symbolic literature and is necessarily more cursory than most accounts of that genre, I suggest that Fijian marriage presentations must be understood in part as recursive works that juxtapose and valorize partible entities, rather than as "transactions" expressing some relation between the things exchanged.

It is clear that this ethnographically grounded, processual, and symbolically complex analysis is most salient in fine-grained studies of particular societies or variants within a relatively small region; in a wider frame of comparison, something closer to a classical labor theory of value retains relevance, as a basis for making crude contrasts between types of systems or for providing terms that make exercises in finer comparison possible. The central assumption for such thinking is that shell valuables, domesticated animals, garden produce, and other things can be understood as objectified labor; the processes of conversion which such objectifications are subject to are then available for analysis. The aim is not to establish that noncapitalist transactions, such as barter or marriage payments, can then be interpreted as if "prices" reflected the labor embodied in the items exchanged, as has been attempted in some instances. My interest instead is in possible kinds of circulation, which in some cases permit labor to be transacted against a diverse range of commodities or services, and which in other instances insulate different spheres of value circulation from each other.[50] This perspective makes no attempt to grasp indigenous constructions of exchange and is obviously inaccurate insofar as those constructions actually give transactions their meaning and logic. A broader kind of comparative vision is, however, crucial and helps convey a sense of the distinctiveness of particular local forms. Recognizing a multiplicity of other economies and forms of sociality also permits difference to be envisaged among a plurality of others, rather than confined to a gulf between us and them.

I indicated in the Introduction that I aim to contribute to an intermediate level of theory and analysis that has been lacking, in cultural and economic anthropology: there seems to be a distinct cleavage between generalized discussion of "the" gift and a vast world of ethnographic intricacies, which are now extensively documented. Just as people in the United States or Europe know all about the subtle mutations of transactions with their friends or relatives, any anthropologist knows about the variety and specificity of prestations among the people with whom he or she has lived. But this knowledge has somehow not led to theories of particular forms of exchange and appropriation, or much analysis of the principles which generate ordinary as well as peculiar gifts; instead, numbingly familiar and dogmatic propositions extracted from Mauss are reiterated to the point of canonization.

There is a larger sense in which theorizing and to some extent even theory are avoided here. My strategy of discovering general propositions and issues through particular instances and stories is not intended to signal a return to empiricism, but instead arises from a sense that inquiry does not so much establish edifices as work through problems. Analysis can be seen as a procedure of engagement, a practice that cannot be differentiated into distinct levels of theory and description. But the kind of analytic agency that theorizing appears to presuppose also seems wrong or misplaced. I cannot pretend that the space of this text is a *tabula rasa* or vacant block to which I can freely import building material, where I can freely structure concepts, methods, and arguments. There is instead a superfluity of available material (verbal and visual as well as textual) which I react to rather than shape. My observations in this chapter thus constitute no novel synthesis but aspire to the status of derivative distortions or ways of rephrasing that help expose old questions in terms that happen to be salient now.

This is partly why, despite the extent of my disarticulation and specification of the categories of gift and commodity, I do not repudiate the dichotomy; in fact, at an abstract level a hard distinction between these transaction forms is sustained, while I attempt more concretely to demonstrate their coexistence in particular economies and the impossibility of speaking generally of gift or commodity economies or societies. Inventing new concepts, a new theory, or a new binary pair would not dissolve the exoticizing force of that opposition but simply make it available in superficially different terms: "To make a new word is to run the risk of forgetting the problem or believing it solved."[51] Perhaps writing "gift" and "commodity" would suggest the tensions in this effort to deploy and strain not only individual terms but also ways of seeing, "using the only available language while not subscribing to its premises."[52] (But my interest is in working through this distortion, rather than making a series of typographical gestures toward it.) The critique of Mauss—which many writers have curiously shied away from—does not, therefore, lead me to reject his theory in the categorical manner that its empirical inadequacy might demand. That is not the point; it is rather that we continue to be vulnerable to the same traps: on one side we fail to recognize what is different in other social regimes; on the other we tend to make radical alterity out of partial or contingent difference. Thus I seek to relocate and displace versions of these various theories and points of departure in ethnographic cases and historical narratives. Of course, beginning an account of exchange with negation and displacement is hardly a new move.

The hau *is not the wind. Not at all.*

2

The Permutations of Debt: Exchange Systems in the Pacific

Standing on Mauss's shoulders, we must chart more ideologies of exchange than the simple binary division between primitive and modern, status and contract. We have learned two lessons since the days of *Gemeinschaft* versus *Gesellschaft*: Firstly, probably all societies have their versions of "fetishism" of objects. Secondly, the manner in which objects and persons are intertwined and evaluated differs according to each society's cosmological design and cultural grid, in which social, divine, animal, and object hierarchies are mutually implicated . . . In such an enterprise, it is essential to concede that "alienation" is not solely a deficiency of capitalism and "participation" the sole glue of archaic society. All societies—with the exception of the paradisiacal and affluent pygmies (?)—surely have their own dialectical versions of alienation and participation.

S. J. Tambiah, *The Buddhist Saints of the Forest and the Cult of Amulets*, 1984

It is often supposed, in both conservative and radical thinking, that imperial intrusions have had such shattering and pervasive effect upon the dominated groups that the form of local, precolonial society is of limited significance for subsequent development; even when struggle and resistance are recognized, the responses of the colonized are taken to be merely reactive. While the real balance of forces at particular phases of colonial history requires specification, and there clearly are times when indigenous peoples cannot do much to shape the events which overtake them, I am committed to the view that local relations and representations are never totally encompassed or determined by the violence of colonialism, and that the distinctive forms of indigenous sociality and politics contribute in a crucial way to the dynamics of accommodation and resistance constitutive of colonial history. Critiques of Orientalism and associated colonial discourses need to avoid reproducing one of the central assumptions of those ideologies: that prospectively or already colonized places are *tabula rasa* for the projection of European power and European representations.

My discussion (in Chapters 3 and 4) of barter and the poetics of appropriation thus presupposes a context: the indigenous systems prior to this process of interaction. This chapter, in particular, aims to convey something of the distinctiveness of indigenous Pacific forms of value and exchange. But any such mapping out of Oceanic economic regimes must avoid the traps of anthropological space and time—the places of different people, the time outside our entanglement. It has been suggested that the ramifications of passing over history in the construction of culture have been "sufficiently denounced"[1] as if an effort to delineate an indigenous system could readily avoid the fabrication of a stable form outside the events of contact. The discussion here thus has a provisional character, attempting to suggest the principles of systems which elude our vision as they change. I am not harking back to a conventional style of ethnohistoric reconstruction, which seeks an authentic indigenous form out of time, but instead aim to set out the relatively autonomous preconditions for a variety of regional histories.

Although I refer to contrasting Oceanic regimes of exchange and value, the analysis does not attempt to encompass whole economic systems. That would require an examination of divisions of labor, production processes, and articulations of daily or mundane transactions, larger-scale ceremonial exchange, and external trade. Although these topics enter into the description, the argument is oriented toward a particular set of questions about inalienability, debt, and valuables. These problems, outlined in the previous chapter, seem central to the understanding of noncapitalist exchange; or perhaps it turns out that the project of transcending such terms is central. The approach privileges difference within Oceania, rather than features which can be generalized to a "clan" or "gift" economy. "Inalienability" is a central notion because it incorporates the sense of singular relations between people and things—in effect between people with respect to things. Although certain Fijian examples are used to challenge the accepted relationships between "gift," "debt," and "inalienability," something like the older concept remains applicable to particular heirlooms and valuables. This substantiates one of the more general claims here—that domains of transactions and kinds of things constantly need to be taken into account. A kind of alienability or attachment which applies to a particular sort of product, or to a certain sphere of exchange, will not necessarily be important in another context. The point that some things may be available for circulation but inalienable, or available and alienable, or unavailable for circulation, acquires great importance in the context of early barter and contact. The discussion of exchange regimes thus sets out a background for the transactions which were constitutive of world-system entanglement, although it must be remembered that such involvement, and consequent transformation, predates the moments of observing the indigenous systems outlined here.

Alienation in Melanesian Exchange

A Maussian conception of "the gift" has informed the general notion that Melanesian economies are or were gift economies. The Maussian concept, especially as it has been reformulated in some recent studies, is in many respects the direct antithesis of the notion of the commodity, and it is thus not surprising that actual prestations documented ethnographically or historically in island societies take more or less different forms. The discussion of Fiji later in this chapter aims to disconnect the idea of debt from that of the gift and recast the presenting subject as a composite created recursively through prestations, rather than an individual generator of debt. In a similar way, numerous ethnographic studies have specified transactions and associated social relations in great detail, but at the same time the idea that these are all essentially gift systems has been adhered to quite dogmatically. What has been done *for particular societies* has thus not been done theoretically. This is the trend in contemporary cultural anthropology; earlier studies, informed by formalistic economic theory rather than local cultural constructions, were strongly oriented toward generalization and far more open to the idea that Melanesian transactions were analogous to, or continuous with, capitalist types. Hence counterparts to "investment," "capital," and "credit" were identified, and various "primitive currencies" such as the Rossel Island shells which W. E. Armstrong made known to readers of the authoritative *Economic*

Journal,[2] were the subject of extensive debate in economic anthropology.

There could be no interest now in reestablishing a frame of discussion which excluded indigenous understandings of prestations, but there is an anomaly in the current approach. Terms such as "shell money" have virtually dropped out of use,[3] and the central point of John Liep's recent reappraisal of the Rossel Island case—which typifies the contemporary perspective—is that there is no market and that Armstrong's interpretation was therefore misdirected.[4] Though it provides new and valuable information, that clearly undermines Armstrong's views in a number of ways, his critique clearly resorts to a radical separation between gift-based and market-based exchange regimes; anomalously, however, extensive reference is made in Liep's ethnography and Melanesian studies in general to "payments" of various kinds, and especially those associated with marriage and death. It thus seems necessary (at an ethnographic level) to represent certain kinds of substitutions as "payments," but impossible (at a theoretical level) to acknowledge that these are sometimes effected through exchange media. And while the force of cultural ethnography is supposed to derive from its attachment to indigenous ideas, some of these figure more conspicuously in anthropological accounts than others. It is significant that the theoretical debate in anthropology about whether certain sorts of valuables should be described as "primitive money" is made irrelevant by the fact that islanders themselves equate introduced cash with their own "money" or—of course a rather different thing— incorporate the former into their ceremonial exchange. The Roviana extension of the word *poata* to cover European currency exemplifies widespread identifications which, as A. M. Hocart noted, were also made in Solomons pidgin.[5] Without entertaining the economists' argument that shells amount to a currency, there is clearly an indigenous sense that the analogy works the other way around.

The implication might be that forms of Melanesian exchange approximate commodity transactions more closely than can be generally acknowledged. The concern here is not to follow up the old formalist generalization of economic principles from capitalism: I am obviously not interested, for instance, in suggesting that the values of indigenous articles fluctuate on the basis of supply and demand in some imaginary market.[6] The point is rather that while alienation, commoditization, and abstract exchange media are most pronounced in capitalist economies, they are not peculiar to those systems. Capitalism is character-ized by social relations which bind worker to capitalist in exploitative transactions, rather than the facts of alienation and commoditization, which predated capitalism historically and which now exist in some forms in all societies. The identification of these social relations in societies which are or were supposedly dominated by "the gift" permits one to recognize the forms of inequality and domination that exist in such systems and to understand the particular kinds of material culture that take the form of "valuables" and exchange items in various con-texts. The transformations and contextual mutations of objects cannot be appreciated if it is presumed that gifts are invariably gifts and commodities invariably commodities.

Commodities are here understood as objects, persons, or elements of persons, which are placed in a context in which they have exchange value and can be alienated. The alienation of a thing is its dissociation from producers, former users, or prior context. Prior context may refer to a commoditized person's kin associations; these terms are deliber-ately vague in order to allow scope for the nuances of particular movements. As I noted in the introductory discussion, both inalien-ability and alienability must be imprecise terms which may refer to various bonds between persons and objects, or the erasure of such bonds. This is consistent with the emphasis here upon diverse eco-nomic regimes, in opposition to the categorical distinction between gift and commodity economies.

A series of dichotomies discussed in the anthropological literature on Papua New Guinea provide a starting point. Systems involving bridewealth have been contrasted to those involving brideservice in several influential studies. The importance of the distinction is not connected with classifying marriage, but rather arises from links which can be analyzed between modes of reciprocating for women and broader principles of political economy. Bridewealth implies that whichever goods or valuables are presented as marriage gifts figure, in some sense, as *substitutes* for the wife (and her future labor and child rearing). Brideservice, by contrast, is often associated with restricted exchange (where men take each others' sisters or classificatory sisters as wives), and with the notion that objects cannot be substituted for persons or for life; this often has the correlate in the context of warfare that valuables cannot be presented to enemies in compensation for killings—only another life can achieve balance and peace.[7] There are

The Pacific Islands, indicating colonial encounters discussed in the text.

MEXICO

Tropic of Cancer

Oahu

Hawaii

nds

THE PACIFIC ISLANDS

North Pacific
Ocean

Line

Islands

Equator

Cook

Islands

Cook	1774
Russians	1804
Porter	1813
French annexation	1842

Marquesas

Nukuhiva
Hiva Oa
Tahuata — Fatuiva

Tuamotu

Rangiroa

Society Islands Tahiti

Archipelago

otonga Rurutu Gambier Islands

Austral Islands

Tropic of Capricorn

Rapanui
(Easter Island)

ook	1774
ill	1838
rskine	1849

South Pacific
Ocean

0   2000 kilometres

Papua New Guinea, indicating periods of ethnographic field research. In most cases the dates

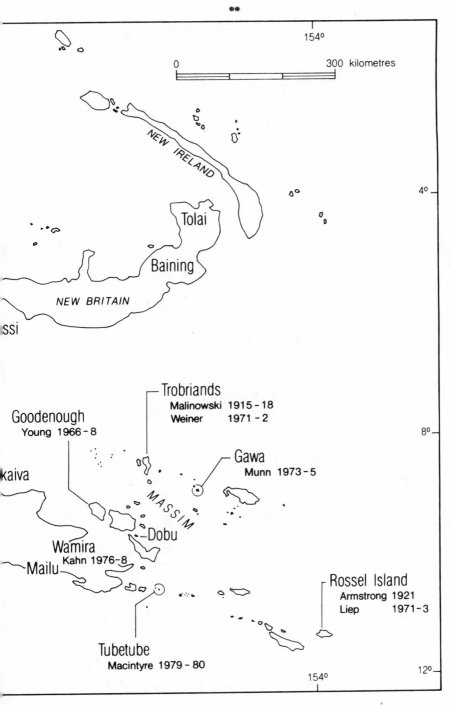

refer only to the first major period of fieldwork, not follow-up visits.

many particular studies which could be drawn upon to elaborate each case and, of course, the intermediate permutations:

> By far the most important [types of ordinary exchange] are transactions in lieu of individuals and their bodies. Culturally defined damage or major alteration to these, or changes in group association, should be accompanied by an exchange . . . the main ones are marriage and death . . . As women cannot move bidirectionally between subclans . . . wealth must be substituted for the bride. Married women, in other words, always create "debt."[8]

In this case it is clear that exchange is essentially concerned with recompensing groups for "debt" which functions, or is created, at some other level. What is conspicuous is the process of *conversion*. Yet there seems to be no tolerance for such value transformations among lowland Papuan societies including the Kamula: "Bridewealth payments are not considered by the Kamula as reciprocating for a marriage as this can only be achieved by an exchange of women. Rather such payments prevent affines from becoming 'angry'. . . A marriage cannot be revoked by the failure to provide bridewealth as it can be in the Highlands. Indeed, not all affines demand payment of bridewealth."[9]

As Strathern noted, "relations between people and things are characterized by nontransformability—things do not embody persons (labor)."[10] These types of societies could be seen to stand in a happy relation to the project of cultural anthropology: the brideservice case facilitates the argument—elaborated in its most radical form by Strathern—that Western property metaphors are wholly inapplicable to societies of this kind. The type of analysis which emphasizes difference, however, seems less comfortably situated with respect to bridewealth societies; here it seems that labor and people may take object-forms or be connected through relations of value conversion. Even Modjeska, arguing from something like a Marxist perspective, implied that it would be wrong to regard the substitutions enabled by the exchangeability of pigs as commodity transactions. But is it so clear that there is no "property" that can be alienated? I do not pursue the issue of what conceptual categories may or may not be appropriate for the highlands, and it would seem essential to deal more with the intermediate social cases in which a mixture of value conversion and nonconversion applies. However, accounts of some of the insular

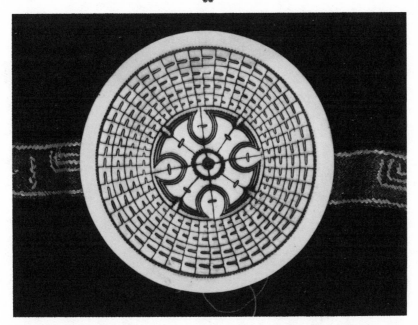

Shell with tortoiseshell open-work decoration, western Solomon Islands, late nineteenth or early twentieth century. This and the next illustration show typical trade articles.

societies to the east and southeast of mainland New Guinea prompt an analysis which does not place these Melanesian groups in a world of exchange completely divorced from our own: various transactions fundamental to the wider dynamic of social reproduction appear to have entailed value conversion and alienation.

The New Georgia exchange system, which perhaps resembled the kula more closely than anthropological stereotypes of the latter would initially lead one to suppose,[11] consisted in a dense network of links within a region which was relatively homogeneous culturally (and which roughly corresponds with the present Western Province of the Solomon Islands); these were articulated with trade connections to more distant parts of the northern and eastern Solomons. Various manufactured goods—barkcloth, baskets, mats, wicker shields, other weapons, and shell valuables—and foodstuffs, including pigs and tubers, as well as people described as "slaves" were regularly transported and exchanged by canoe. The shell valuables were of particular importance[12] for the articulation of trade and other activities of crucial social significance for prominent chiefly men *(bangara)*, such as organizing headhunting raids and building new halls for war canoes and cult houses. Shells could be converted into prestige by rewarding warriors who obtained heads and staging feasts at which pigs purchased with shells were consumed; they could be used in such rituals as offerings to deities and ancestors and payments to other ritual specialists who performed those services or other forms of magic on one's behalf.

Shell rings could be substituted for a wide range of articles through "barter" and were also used to alter the state of social relations—to obtain forgiveness or compensate for the deaths of enemies when making peace. But Hocart was being somewhat misleading when he suggested that they "served no other purpose" than functioning as a medium of exchange.[13] Unlike the cowrie money which circulated in parts of south Asia and Africa,[14] which was of much lower unit value than even any depreciated south Pacific shell valuables, *poata* and related types were closely associated with deities and ancestral power:

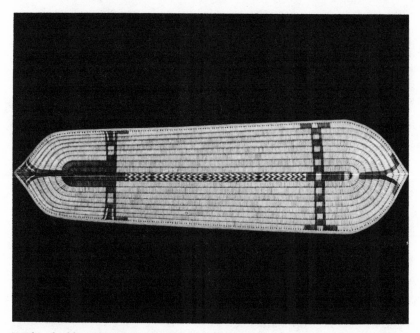

Wicker shield, western Solomon Islands, late nineteenth or early twentieth century. A small number of rare examples have elaborate shell decoration.

A *tomoko*, or canoe for headhunting and trading, western Solomon Islands, early twentieth century. This example may have been constructed under mission tutelage after actual headhunting canoes had been destroyed by the British colonial administration just before 1900. The Methodists encouraged the construction of "mission war canoes" used in races on sports days and perhaps attempted to appropriate some of the ritual significance and potency of the older canoes.

they are referred to in myths and used in the installations of chiefs; and ritual privileges were, in some cases, founded upon the control of certain shells.[15]

Hocart contrasted "sacred" shells with those ordinarily used in trade or routine exchange. His account suggests that there existed relatively standardized values which regulated such transactions:

1 pig = 4 to 6 *poata*;
1 shield = 1 *mbakia* = 20 *mbulau*;
1 canoe = 1 *poata* per rib;
19 eggs = 1 arm ring;
5 *olu* of nuts = 1 arm ring;
1 basket *(elaka)* of taro = 1 arm ring;
1 bunch of areca = 1 stick of tobacco;
1 small child in Choiseul = 20 *poata*, or one shield, two *mbakia* & 18 *poata*, this was considered expensive.[16]

It is not clear, of course, precisely how these ratios were conceived; they are unlikely to have been fixed and non-negotiable, especially since the qualities of particular goods obviously varied. It is also probably the case that the elaboration of scales of value took place in association with the activities of white traders in the area, who introduced various new articles (hatchets, calico, tobacco), sought to purchase others (such as copra and tortoiseshell), and themselves traded indigenous artifacts such as barkcloth, fishing nets, shell rings, baskets, and lime for betel (the sources of some of these being regionally dispersed).[17]

The extent to which interisland transactions in these various goods were embedded in longer-term exchange partnerships and took gift rather than commodity form is quite unclear; there are insufficient descriptions of actual transactions, which were, in any case, changing dramatically over the course of the nineteenth century. Nevertheless, it is apparent that people or their parts were commoditized in certain ways in New Georgia exchange. A direct analogy was made between the prestigious practice of headhunting and an activity which was normally associated with it—the seizure of captives. These people were "really supposed to be dead; that is why Muke speaks of having killed eleven in Ngerasi."[18] Subsequently the captive or "slave" might be exchanged for shell money with those from another group. In most cases involving children, the captive child was then adopted and would refer to the captor or purchaser as "my father"; other kin relations would be derived from that. They were incorporated into the group like normal members and not systematically forced to work harder than anyone else. But when sacrifices were required for the launching of new canoes or the inauguration of new canoe houses—around which headhunting and fishing ritual revolved—an unsuspecting captive would be clubbed and used.[19] The fiction of the captive's death and reconstitution as a member of the appropriating group seems to mark a definitive erasure of any residual associations with the place of origin. The moment of transaction or appropriation can be seen as a commodity phase in such a person's existence;[20] he or she is subsequently reconstituted within the appropriating group as a being similar to any other, except in the sense (no doubt important to the individual concerned) that the fact of foreign origin marks the person as a suitable sacrificial victim.

An aspect of the person was alienated in a more specific manner in practices reported in a number of sources:

> Whenever a temple or an altar or a war-canoe or even a rest-house was built, a custom called bibolo would also be held. Some young girls would be bought from their parents to be used for those special occasions only. There could be any number of girls—six, or five, or three, or even nine. Those girls would be taken to the place where the ceremony would be held. There they would be kept for one or two years . . . They would be cared for in a very strict way . . . The hair of the girls would be cut very short and their faces would be decorated with lime.
>
> When the time of the feast had come to celebrate the opening of the new temple or altar, the girls would be allowed for any boy to have sexual intercourse with them. It was more like a public show, but the girls must be paid by the ones who touched them. The money paid would be put through a dried stump by each girl to indicate the number of men who went to each of them. At the end of the feast the money was divided amongst the tribe.[21]

Hocart made it clear that the women were not always, or most likely to have been, captives; his account suggested that the transactions took place within the context of raising shell money to stage major feasts. The sponsor of a feast would secure the right to control access to the women's sexuality from their fathers through payment of rings; the women would be made up with lime, blue barkcloth, and many arm rings, and then would be made available over a period of months. The rings in exchange for sex were paid directly to the chief, but when the feast was held, the woman received "the head of the pig, one pudding, and two orange-stained rings."[22] The term "prostitution" is obviously misleading to a certain extent: the celebrated status of the woman and her capacity to choose partners are emphasized in some accounts, and the activity is clearly closely linked to larger ceremonial purposes, rather than being merely an individual sexual transaction. There is no suggestion that the encounters create longer-term relationships of any social significance; where women are "loaned" by their fathers for particular feasts, it is implied that they later return to their own group, and that (for most women) the practice is restricted to an adolescent phase in the life cycle. Although the accounts are not detailed, there is nothing to suggest that shells and women's sexuality alike were not alienated in these contexts.

Commoditization, or a condition approximating it, permits powerful people to own and control something in a more radical sense than gift giving allows: the residual interests of other people in things, people, or knowledge can be denied. Such an observation perhaps makes it clear that commoditization should not be conflated with the simplicity of the market, or with economic rationality as opposed to the mystique of the gift: a complex meaningful economy may structure the definitive appropriation of things, just as it structures their partial or qualified transmission in the form of gifts. If a kind of ceremonial prostitution was pivotal in the "financing" of festivals and communal projects in the western Solomons, then it is clear that we cannot understand these systems as unitary gift economies or, for that matter, as economies dominated by any particular transaction form. The analysis of transaction forms should take place at a different level of specificity to the discussion of regimes of political economy.

The importance of commoditization in New Georgia is apparent not just in obviously "economic" domains but also from the way in which special ritual powers were created. In most of the eastern Pacific these were associated with chiefly ancestor deities, transmitted genealogically, or with inspiration: people who exhibited certain capacities were recognized as shamans. In contrast, it is notable that in New Georgia ritual knowledge seems always to have been acquired through "purchase," that is, through an arrangement whereby an individual who wished to become a practitioner paid an established specialist in shells for knowledge and the magical treatment (stroking with leaves) which was presumably thought to ensure efficacy. Leoki, a prominent man on Simbo, who was one of Hocart's main informants, told him that knowledge associated with a particular hunting shrine had been purchased from a Roviana man "at a reduced rate of one shilling" because he was a relative of Leoki's. Diverse forms of medical knowledge were acquired in the same way; it was noted that one healer was said to have "bought his knowledge from Ngelevuru, his 'mother' for one ring and two arm-rings."[23]

Aspects of ritual agency can be said, in a strong sense, to have taken the forms of things. The empowering aspect of personal qualification has its origins elsewhere—often on different islands within the cultural area—but could be abstracted and appropriated. The sense in which this was effected through the substitution of another kind of abstracted value *and outside the determination of kinship relations* is manifested in what would appear to count as an exception, that is, the fact that Leoki received magic at a lower price because the donor was a relative. The fact of a relationship thus stands as an external qualification to a transaction of an essentially different character. Moreover, it could hardly be thought that the ritual capacities could be later taken away from a practitioner, and there is no indication that there was any subsequent debt. The practice of ritual may often have involved reference to the source of knowledge, to the empowering authority, but in such contexts the allusion to the name figures as authentication and validation, rather than as the expression of longer-term indebtedness. If the persisting attachment of the name is thought to express any residual inalienability, it is clearly of a limited kind, which does not actually entail any practical control or residual interest on the part of the original donor.

Matching accounts of these systems against Malinowski's kula might set up a polarity between the complex and diffuse combination of alienability and inalienability of the Solomons and the classic description of inalienable kula gifts—the "system-communal property," which is cited in so many textbooks. Reappraisals of Massim societies have emphasized the diversion of kula shells into other exchange networks and the importance of *kitomwa*—valuables which are not encumbered by debt and can therefore be used according to the wishes of the owner.

> On Tubetube, *kitomwa* are alienable in the sense that their ownership may be transferred. A man who makes a valuable and gives it as *maisa* [payment concluding a transaction] for a pig becomes the owner of the pig and his partner becomes the owner of the valuable. The original manufacturer cannot reclaim the valuable or specify its future uses. If his partner puts it on a shared *kune* [kula] path the maker may try to regain possession by offering its *mwaka* [match or price] but he would have no special claims over it . . . The only sense in which it was not alienated from him was that his name (as its manufacturer) would usually become part of the renown of the valuable.[24]

I am not arguing that these Melanesian systems are to be characterized generally as commodity regimes; both the Massim and New Georgia systems were probably dominated by relations of mutual entanglement effected and extended through flows of gifts, especially in the contexts of alliance and mortuary ritual. The point is rather that a succession of value conversions entailing both gift and commodity forms sustained a political process.

Objects might be introduced into a particular situation as commodities or gifts and transmitted into a particular domain of exchange in another form. Gift and commodity are not, of course, the only relevant types in this pattern of transformation: in Tikopia, and in certain other chiefly societies characterized by a coherent hierarchy, gifts reflecting social equivalence between ordinary people could similarly be transformed into offerings to chiefs which did not create debt because of the generalized indebtedness of people to chiefs.[25] In that case, the prestation form is specific to the social relationship, and since in any context there are various, qualitatively different relationships, it might be assumed that prestation forms would vary correspondingly. In some societies, such as the lowland Papuan brideservice societies of the type discussed by Michael Wood,[26] it appears that objects or pigs cannot be substituted for people in any context, and transactions within such groups may be characterized by inalienability to an extreme extent. Societies in which shell monies are used, however, do permit a broad range of transactions in relation to exchange media and standardized values. A number of Solomon Islands groups appear to be at an extreme point on this continuum, whereas Fijian exchange has been characterized by complex value conversions nevertheless generally embedded in alliance relations.

Sections of the discussion here and below draw upon the observation that people are sometimes multiple and divisible entities. In this respect and others, the present analysis owes a great deal to Marilyn Strathern's *The Gender of the Gift*, although my theoretical perspective is quite incompatible with one strand of her argument.

> The [Hagen] wife is not an owner of the pig who can transfer that ownership to someone else or who has it wrested from her control, because there is no one-to-one relationship between her and her working capacity or between her working capacity and the products of her work.
>
> Here is the crucial factor that makes it impossible to speak of alienations in the gift economy. Gregory stressed that it was particularly between exchange partners that a tie was created by the transfer of inalienable things; the point may be extended, with qualification, to spouses. Inalienability signifies the absence of a property relation. Rather than talking about "inalienable property," I prefer to sustain the systemic contrast. Persons simply do not have inalienable items, that is, property, at their disposal;

they can only dispose of items by enchaining themselves in relations with others. Whether between exchange partners, spouses, or between kin, the circulation of things and persons in this sense leads to comparisons between the agents. Items cannot be disposed without reference to such relations.

. . . The difference between gift exchange and commodity exchange is systemic; it is hardly admissible to decide that this particular transaction results in alienation, while that particular one does not. One cannot tell by inspection. [27]

This is abstracted from a section of *The Gender of the Gift* in which Strathern criticizes a materialist interpretation of gender relations in the Papua New Guinea highlands. It had been argued by Lisette Josephides that pigs, the products of women's labor, were alienated from them by men for use in ceremonial exchange;[28] Strathern suggests that this account could not be matched against local conceptions. The particular argument that there is no Hagen idea of property, and therefore no scope for speaking of the alienation of things, is logically coherent and may or may not be regarded as empirically correct for societies now profoundly influenced by the production of cash crops. However, it seems unfortunate that Strathern has chosen to project the critique in such generalized terms, since insofar as it is applied to "Melanesia" (which is in any case an artifact of colonial ethnology) there are problems at a number of levels.[29] While readers might or might not be sympathetic to the insistence upon what is said to be a local model, as opposed to Josephides's Marxist-feminist view, it is difficult to see why such totalizing claims should need to be made for a general system and a wide range of societies.

Strathern's argument depends upon a connection between a pair of premises (that people are partible and products multiply authored) and the proposition that there is "no one-to-one relationship" between a person and his or her working capacity or products. The effect of this conjunction is a condition of pervasive association, an inescapably general and binding field of person/object/person implications: "Enchainment is a condition of all relations based on the gift."[30] The fact of the first principle does not, however, generate a field of qualitatively similar relations unless it is supposed that all forms of work and ways of circulating products are conceived in the same fashion. This would eliminate the question of there being a degree to which a person's or a group's contribution to a product is acknowledged. But if contributions are not all of the same weight or substance, authorship is not merely multiple but may be different and unequal. In many if not all patrilineal or patrilocal societies it is recognized that there are debts to the mother's side; such links are frequently expressed in various life-crisis and mortuary ceremonies. It could not be disputed, however, that in general a child's association with his or her father's side operates at quite a different level: the mere fact that the group with whom he or she resides makes restitutions for debts underlines the separateness and disconnection between the mother's and father's sides. Dual or multiple authorship of the child is the basis or outcome of the whole series of prestations, but these similarly express the nonequivalence of parties and the fundamental fact of the child's residence with one collective rather than the other. If it is admitted that authorship and its implications may be differentially imagined, it must be possible that in some cases contributions may be appreciated and taken account of to an insignificant extent. These questions need to be explored if a variety of indigenous exchange systems, and hence a range of possible responses to colonial contact and intrusion, are to be visible.

Kinds of work which constitute a thing differ and may be entirely elided. Pandanus mats in Fiji are the exchange items which women present and which they are constantly working on or using. The fact that men contribute to mat production marginally by cutting the green pandanus and transporting it to the village has no bearing on this association.[31] Yet men present drums of kerosene which are purchased with money obtained from cash crops—that is, from the garden work of both women and men.[32] At presentations of property—the *solevu* described below and in Chapter 5—a long line of men bring one or two drums each and stack them up. They are followed by a line of women who throw one or two rolled mats on top of the drums or into a separate pile. The result is a totality which is then offered by a senior man who hands over a whale tooth. His speech and the supreme valuable encompass the gift as a whole, and it is clearly a collective offering—usually to affines. (The presentation thus recursively creates the distinction between the sides and the form of indebtedness.) The unity of what is offered depends quite tangibly upon its initial separateness: what people witness is a process of bringing together, of assembling, which always takes place in a formal manner once the attention of those present has been focused upon the event. Each socially competent adult on the giving side brings forward an equivalent contribution, those of men standing as a counterpart to those of women. This practice would be completely unintelligible if women and men were not construed as the providers of the items they carry. The recognition of the valuables in these terms diminishes, if it does not entirely elide, the male and female contributions to each. Hence, contrary to Strathern's characterization, it *is* as if "the work belongs exclusively to one of a pair."[33] In western Fiji, persons and some products such as various kinds of food are considered composite, multiply authored entities. But valuables for exchange are mostly not represented in this way, despite the fact that (in many instances) the work of various people of both sexes is drawn into their production. The separateness of male and female goods such as drums and mats is a precondition of the image of collectivity created at the moment of presentation.

Work is alienable in a rather different way in hierarchical regimes such as early Marquesan society. It would be true in this case that there was no one-to-one relationship between a person and a product, but agency was divisible and partial for different reasons than in the New Guinea highlands, Fiji, or the Solomons. Work of any consequential kind depended upon an active association with deities which was ritually contrived and sustained through segregation, through a state of being *tapu* or "off limits."[34] *Tapu* often bonded people, their artifacts, a place, a deity, and their products, but it operated in a fundamentally hierarchical manner, so that those who embodied deities or otherwise represented them (priests, chiefs, and certain others of particular rank) could absorb things upward through the extension of personal *tapu*. Any cloth which accidentally passed over a man came to be associated with him and could no longer be used by a woman; use by a person who was not *tapu* in some equivalent sense would endanger both the violator and the person with whom the thing was primarily associated. A tree overhanging the house of a chiefly child would be identified with that child, such that the fruit could be eaten by no one else. Through a great variety of analogous associations, food, houses, artifacts, gardens, and sacrifices came to be identified primarily with a user or consumer, rather than another person who might previously have possessed a thing or played a part in its making. The point here is not merely that certain articles may potentially be abstracted from associations with former owners, users, or producers, but that the logic of the system made it possible for things to be recognized through *tapu* rather than through a producer/product or donor/gift association. Hierarchical systems of this type draw our attention, in the first place, to the power mediated by cultural forms; it is this power, rather than reciprocity among transactors, that seems fundamental for the understanding of objects and exchange.

Whether the Polynesian instance, or any other particular example, represents alienation may of course be debated. The separation of a thing from a person may, in practice, be tantamount to appropriation, and there are many contexts in which objects that move through various transactions carry no enduring association with a donor, or retain his or her name in the absence of any practical control or residual influence.[35] This question bears directly upon the more basic theoretical problem of Strathern's argument. She suggests that the nature of prestations, and the question of whether or not work is alienable, is not to be investigated or determined on the basis of inspection. The properties of these relations are instead determined on the basis of the systemic contrast between the gift and the commodity. There are specific methodological objections to this, because the analysis effectively conflates the Maussian model with the Hagen ethnography and marginalizes other Melanesian evidence which is not consistent with the model. It is noted with respect to the Sa speakers of south Pentecost, Vanuatu, that contrary to the model of multiple authorship, pigs and yams "are seen pre-eminently as the creations of men,"[36] that is, the process "re-authors them in terms of production."[37] But this point is adduced merely to emphasize, through contrast, the claim that in Hagen "the work that women do in their gardens and tending the herds is fully acknowledged." The Sa qualification in no sense figures in the general model of the system characteristic of the region: "The Melanesian idea that work is evidence of and governed by the mind precludes its appropriation."[38] Exchange theories, in their emphasis upon reciprocity, have always marginalized, in a paradigmatically liberal fashion, questions of power; the intrusion of dominance and asymmetry might here and there be acknowledged, but transactions take place between partners in time and space; power was never taken as a further dimension in which they were necessarily situated. In effect, Strathern consummates this tradition by effacing the possibility of alienation in Melanesian societies, while domination becomes unintelligible through a succession of displacements which are characterized as "aesthetic."[39]

To reiterate my intentions in raising these questions, the aim is not to affirm simply that alienation was present for the sake of arriving at a more correct account of the diverse early contact or indigenous Pacific exchange systems: the interest is rather in establishing the range of local preconditions for subsequent colonial interaction. If connections between historical developments and earlier, relatively autonomous systems are to be identified, an emphasis upon the various forms of those indigenous systems is crucial. If we follow *The Gender of the Gift* in privileging what is taken to be generally "Melanesian,"[40] which can be construed as a primordial and distinctive cultural logic, then no sense can be made of the differing development of economic articulations and local representations from one place to another.

Strathern's notion that work or objects cannot be alienated in Melanesian systems is derived simply from the proposition that a gift regime cannot permit such transformations. The reference point is a reformulation of the Maussian model, not the array of variants which have developed historically or which may be documented ethnographically. She acknowledges that the construction of the gift rests upon that of the commodity and that this is a "fictional division—as though one could thereby characterize whole cultures or whole societies,"[41] but this qualification merely bypasses the issue of the utility and justifiability of the analytical construct. There is, moreover, a contradiction between an acknowledgment that such a fictional division cannot really encompass whole cultures or societies and the theoretical principle that exchange relations within the social or cultural region can *only* be generated by the theoretical principles specified in the model.

The most substantial problem with an argument that deploys systemic constructs which are identified with a pervasive logic of particular societies is that it distances these groups from our own sociality and represents them as being isolated from larger economic regimes. The implication of rigid distinctions is that no interpenetration is possible, but this is manifestly absurd, since all Oceanic peoples are to a greater or lesser degree involved with cash transactions, wage work, and markets. This fact of articulation does not mean that local exchange regimes are displaced by, or subordinated to a monolithic

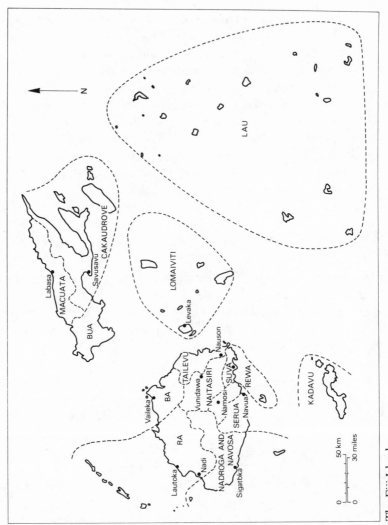

The Fiji Islands.

capitalist type, and there is abundant evidence that relations with outsiders such as traders and planters and internal relations involving wages or cash are adapted and in some contexts subsumed to local forms. This interpenetration has been, and remains, absolutely crucial to economic circumstances in the colonial Pacific, but the attendant transformations and contradictions are invisible from the perspective of any dichotomizing analysis of general economic forms.

Debts and Valuables in Fiji and the Marquesas

In early upland Fiji,[42] ceremonial exchange, as distinct from the wider array of casual reciprocity, or the routine sharing of food, generally took place at large-scale events known generically as *solevu*. These presentations of property were constitutive of marriage and certain other moments in the life cycle (including of course death). But they also marked other debts which might have followed the same paths of alliance even when interests in women and children were not directly at issue. Valuables thus mediated the father's and the mother's sides; they specified the debts inherent in reproduction and affinity and might also signal something like past assistance in warfare. At the same time they effected transfers of goods such as barkcloth, wooden articles, blocks of salt, and mats. Some administrators concerned to stimulate commerce among the indigenous Fijians thus took comfort from these occasions, which seemed to prefigure marketing and trade.[43]

Solevu were (and are) distinctly "ceremonial" in the sense that they involved large public gatherings and the ritualized transfer of actual property. *Solevu* had often been witnessed by earlier visitors to coastal Fiji;[44] the traveler Von Hügel was one of few early observers of such occasions in the interior (in this case, at the village of Nar-okorokoyawa), and was particularly struck by the elaborate manner in which substantial quantities of barkcloth were presented:

> The many hundred yards of stuff were first rolled into an oval ball and then unwound from the ball and wound again onto the body of one of their own men, so that he had a huge encasement of *malo* round him and looked as if he had got into a cask with the bottom out. One end of the stuff was fastened in front and the other hung in a long tail on the ground behind him. There was white *masi*, and some which on one side was silver grey, and also a thicker and wider sort, shiny and very dark, and mot-

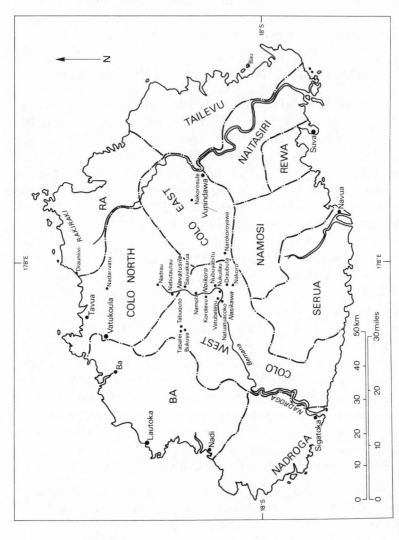

Viti Levu, Fiji, in the early colonial period.

tled with black. This last variety was put on to another man in a succession of loops which fell from his chin to the ground, and was so disposed as the back of his head as to look like a monk's cowl. When complete this strange garment made the wearer appear of enormous bulk, and the most extraordinary thing was that a single knot held the whole get-up together, which when undone allowed it to slip off in a mass to the ground. In the loop costume the man inside is to be considered as an animated clothes-peg, and in the "cask" as a reel or bobbin; he is in both cases merely a support to the offering. Altogether there were five of these cloth bearers.[45]

Von Hügel witnessed the formal manner in which the property was presented and gathered that mats were, at some point, to be given in return, but he gleaned little sense of the meaning of the ceremony or its context in prior relations between the groups. More under-standing—if less sympathy—emerges from some later colonial docu-ments, from the reports of district commissioners who were engaged in, among other things, the policing of *solevu:* in this benevolent system of indirect rule, Fijians could not travel from their villages, to attend ceremonies or for other purposes, without official permission. Resolutions explaining why certain groups wished to engage in ex-change were passed by provincial councils of Fijian representatives, although these were not necessarily endorsed by white officials. "II. That the people of Wailotua in the Tailevu district be allowed to come and make a solevu of mats at Burenitu, the chief village of Nasautoka, Colo East. III. That the people of Sautoka district be allowed to make a solevu of whale's teeth and mats at Vuravatu in the Sawakasa district, Tailevu province."[46]

The resident commissioner Joske thought that these proposals, put forward by people from the Wainibuka valley of the eastern interior, should be vetoed.

Generations ago the Sautoka men helped the Wailotua people in some almost forgotten cannibal war. It constitutes a debt on the part of the latter, who desire to discharge it with payment of mats. At the same time that they make these supposed payments they will receive large presents of food, in the shape of cooked pigs &c. which will equal in value the prop-erty presented at the Solevu. When the Sautoka people get the mats &c. they want for a similar reason to go off to Vuravatu . . . to wipe out a sim-ilar debt, & get feasted on pigs &c. in a like manner. I think to these ancient debts the statute of limitations should be applied. They are a waste of time, and no good results from them. They are in most cases payment for bloodshed and treachery and are excuses for gluttony and orgies of yaqona.

Despite Joske's hostility to these practices, their general meaning is clear enough: providing assistance in a struggle was not, apparently, compensated for by similar assistance at a later time.[47] Rather, a kind of imbalance was constituted, which was eliminated through the presentation of valuables. There is thus a strong implication that the whole system functioned through conversions—services once rendered became debts to be recompensed in another form.

Debts are also mentioned by the Marist ethnographer de Marzan,[48] who, in an essay called "The Cult of the Dead," mentioned the importance of "old debts" (dinau makawa). He noted that "in most cases" sickness or death was thought to have been caused by some unrestituted obligation arising from assistance in warfare, or from the fact that a chief died on alien land and had to be buried by another group, or from some other kind of help. If illness was occurring, divination was used to establish what prestation had not been made, what debt remained to be settled. De Marzan alluded to the "anger of spirits" and this is of course the cause which would be postulated in many ancestor-worship systems (or at least in such systems as stereotypically imagined). However, oral accounts (obtained in 1988) suggest instead that incompleteness itself and an associated kind of moral irregularity produce malaise. The word leqwa can mean a minor difficulty of any kind, but when used in a stronger or more loaded way it generally has the special meaning of some problem (or problems) with a deeper history. Whereas illness may have immediate and recognized causes, leqwa arise from something which has happened earlier, which often, but not always, is associated with the failure to make some proper presentation.[49] These ideas have been expressed in rather controversial ways in the context of the political instability since the military coups of 1987; the maladies of various politicians, and the death in November 1989 of the deposed Prime Minister Timoci Bavadra, have been seized upon as evidence for the error of their ways.

Although these are recent observations, a brief account of a dispute over another early solevu suggests that there has been a great deal of continuity in such understandings of the relationships among conduct, prestations, and malaise:

It appears that some 19 or 20 years ago the Noimalu tribe then residing in Colo West came over to Narokorokoyawa to join their relatives there. Because they did so without making a fuss over the matter & had strengthened the community there, it was thought to be incumbent that the portion of the tribe already resident at Narokorokoyawa should present the newcomers with mats for their houses. It constituted a debt that had not yet been liquidated. In consequence of this dereliction of duty the debtors were dying out . . . [Joske was opposed to the *solevu*]—The Noimalu people were considerably hurt at this & reiterated that the community at Narokorokoyawa had wasted and dwindled away because of their neglect of their obligations . . . I merely mention this to show that the ancient spirit still lingers on.[50]

"The gift" does not seem so much to create debt as to address it, or rather to address debt which was not created by gifts. A presentation of valuables—*iyau*—was always, or virtually always, countered by another prestation, generally of something different. The counter-gift emerged from the structure of ceremony and in no sense wrote off or negated the effect of the first presentation. Gifts had to be acknowledged, and the presentation of a feast is often the proper sequel to a presentation of property. Prestations of this type are thus not the origin points of debt, as models derived from Mauss might indicate, but are rather the points at which debts of relatedness are expressed or at which debts arising from particular services may be extinguished. In the modern system, land that has been transferred to a *vasu* or sister's son (who would have no strong or necessary claims under the usual patrilineal regime) will never really be his unless he makes a prestation of mats, or whatever, and *tabua*: then people say, *sa lutu na vanua*— the land has fallen. Since that has happened, there should be no *leqwa*. These concerns—and the context in which the source of trouble can be diminished—are expressed in contemporary ritual expressions used when formally receiving kava (or, in fact, other things). To do this is to *tabakia*, literally, to "touch" what is offered, and involves leaning forward from the respectful seated position to touch the edge of the bowl. The formulas always feature contextually appropriate wording, but two phrases which occur nearly always are "let illness be dispersed from your midst"—that is, from amongst those who have just made the appropriate presentation to the group represented by the speaker—and "let there be no *leqwa*."[51] The moment at which a transaction is formally constituted is thus also the appropriate one at which this exhortation or injunction may be expressed.

Villagers at Narokorokoyawa, eastern interior of Viti Levu, Fiji, in the early colonial period—perhaps some of the people Von Hügel met in 1876 or those subjected to the repression of the administration in 1901.

This reading depends too much on what is known from the present, but there are points in early sources which imply the same cultural logic. What emerges is in fact a disjunction between the gift and the debt; debt derives from things that people have *done* and also from kin relationships. These will be discussed in a subsequent chapter, but it may simply be stated here that although a woman is incorporated into the group into which she marries in a radical way, there is a long-term, irreducible association between her children and her natal group. Even more than something like assistance in warfare, the debt to the mother's side must periodically be evoked by substantial presentations of the "valuables of the land."

Valuables with and without Histories

In the Fijian case, the question of what might constitute "inalienable" property seems as destabilized as the location of debt. It is clear that valuables are not "inalienable" in any strict sense. Once the *masi* described by Von Hügel is taken away for distribution, once mats have been formally received and sent off to various households, there is no sense in which the donors retain any control or "lien" over them. Nor is there much sense that there is any significant association of any other kind, any continuing memory of the donor in the thing. Of course people remain aware that certain articles come from a particular place; a distinctive type of *iyau* is often recognizable as the produce of a particular village or locality. But the fact that something was transmitted on a particular occasion, for a particular reason, seems not to amount to an important thing to remember. A *solevu* itself, if large, is frequently considered to have been a significant event, but mats are not seen as special emblems of affinity. It seems reasonable to assert that *iyau* do not in general carry exchange histories.

There is a definite contrast with kula shells, or at least those postulated in anthropology. As Mauss wrote: "*Vaygu'a* are not indifferent things; they are more than mere coins. All of them, at least the most valuable and most coveted, have a name, a personality, a past, and even a legend attached to them, to such an extent that people may be named after them."[52]

The words "all of them, at least the most valuable . . ." betray a wider tendency in economic anthropology to project the properties of special, high-status gifts onto gifts in general. The failure to make such distinctions and misconstructions of "kula-ing" might be noted—the

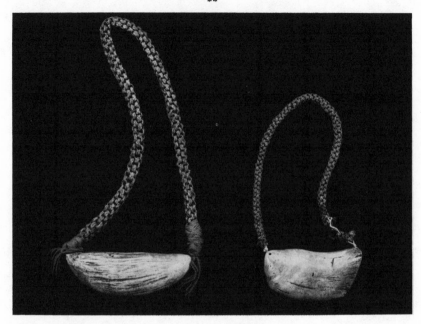

Whale teeth as Fijian valuables (compare illustration on p. 112).

inalienable properties of singular valuables are generalized to a whole system which did permit alienation in certain contexts—but there is no doubt that some shells do have histories and are made the subjects of biographies in the sense indicated by Mauss. However, while he notes that "Fijian money, cachalot teeth, is the same as that of the Trobrianders,"[53] it seems that in this respect there is an absolute contrast between the representation of whale teeth and that of kula shells. *Tabua* were and are constantly transmitted, and are usually not held by temporary owners for long periods. They certainly constitute what Jerry Leach called "system-communal property"[54] and in certain other respects are similar to kula articles and other forms of "shell money." But they are differentiated qualitatively—that is to say, adjudications are made about size, color, and so on—although they are virtually *never* linked with biographies. Nobody says, either formally or informally, anything like "before I got this *tabua* from your father's younger brother, So-and-So at Sauvakarua gave it to X because his people built a house for him and his wife." Nobody says, "this one we gave to the people of Nadrau when they brought Diana to be Jone's wife, and now it has come back." *Tabua* have a singular kind of attributed value, and highly polished teeth—which are presumably older—rank higher than smaller, newer teeth. But there is no naming of either individual items or ranked categories and no rank increment that derives from circulation itself; past transactions are not remembered and in no way bear upon the "weight" of a *tabua*. These articles have no histories.

This is not surprising, given the line of argument sketched out above. Prestations often express the conclusion of something, or at least a temporary creation, a temporary constitution of social propriety. They sometimes also express a request but do not then create a debt. It is the being or doing itself which has ramifications, which creates a debt. Being a *vasu* or sister's child entails debts of a behavioral kind; the obligation is not simply to visit the mother's natal place, but (for men) to make reasonably frequent visits and spend a lot of time talking and drinking kava. Assistance, whether in a crisis or through arrangement, creates debt. These practices thus have some of the characteristics normally associated with gifts. What takes place is, in a sense, inalienable. If something consequential has been done for one, or for a group, it exists as a consequence while other things in social life go on; or perhaps it is that other things in social life go on with this absence, the fact that some prestation or restitution needs to be made. And it is the absence, of course, which constitutes malaise; malaise expresses the failure to have done something about a persisting debt.

The objects which are presented in Fijian ceremonial exchange are thus not like gifts which generate the debt so generally postulated in anthropological theory. They are like a stone which makes a splash— for a moment—and then sinks quietly to the bottom of a deep pool. At the time of the transaction, everyone is thinking about how much *iyau* is presented, what fine pots and mats, what substantial *tabua*. But once these things move elsewhere, they carry no inscription. What does remain instead is something settled, the relationship, an agreement to provide assistance, or the acknowledgment that assistance was provided and recompensed. Certain practices, then, are like gifts. They endure, create a lien, and in that sense have "inalienable" ramifications.

Because *iyau* have this connection to *dinau* or *leqwa* which already exist, it is clear that we should never have expected them to create debt themselves, or to be inalienable. Rather, the whole function of *iyau* is to be alienated; with characteristic insight Hocart drew attention to the etymology: "lit. that which is carried or transferred."[55] There is, in fact, a radical sense in which valuables belong elsewhere. (This is explored through the analysis of a myth in the next section.)

The interpretation here depends in part on a different approach to subjectivity and the person than that embodied in the Maussian account. Irrespective of the extent to which the individual is qualified by other features of Mauss's work, the conception of the gift centers upon agency, upon the work of an actor to create debt. Within the context of certain "spiritual" or cultural conceptions of the force of what is transmitted, the accomplishment of the gift is fundamentally a result of the action of the giver. The general theme of much Melanesian anthropology, and particularly Strathern's critique on the basis of highlands materials, has been the deconstruction of the individual: persons are seen as the creations of various movements of substance and nurture, as divisible through exchange, as parts of social collectives, as constantly constituted through debts. The extent to which any particular cultural construction could be attributed to the whole range of Papuan- and Austronesian-speaking "Melanesian" peoples is debatable, but the implication for the Fijian case, that the person is recursively created through cycles of presentations rather than being their author, is powerful. In Fiji there is now (to my knowledge) no distinctively local theory of conception or nurture which postulates debts of substance on the part of individuals, but great emphasis emerges through ceremonial presentations on the obligations of children to their mother's side. In general, patrilocal groups are constantly engaged in planning presentations to the people to whom they or their children are *vasu*. Yet it would be wrong to regard people as behaving in a certain way in order to pay off debts which exist because of particular relations of alliance, as though the relations were somehow external to the process of ceremonial presentation and exchange. Rather, through such transactions, persons with particular debts to their mother's places are created, and the debts simultaneously advertised and partially recompensed.[56]

The effort thus far to destabilize "the gift" has drawn unavoidably on 1988 sources, on conclusions drawn from things said to me or in my presence by living Noikoro people. I am not suggesting that one can extrapolate backward because things have not changed—in fact, the context is very different, and Christianity, or rather Fijian Christianity, plays a significant part in shaping contemporary conceptions. But elements of the same logic are implicit in what Joske reported just "to show that the ancient spirit still linger[ed] on." The changes will be discussed later, but at this point the argument can draw some provisional justification from the unintelligibility of earlier *solevu* in the absence of something like the same analysis.

The Origin of Whale Teeth

The characteristics of Fijian exchange and value can be considered further through the examination of a myth which directly links the principle of exchange and the constitution of society. One can hardly claim anything about the social uses or salience of this particular text—there seems to be only one documented version. But, as Sahlins has noted, this is "perhaps because the story, once told, tells all."[57]

> The first man had three daughters but no sons, his wife was old . . . the man proposed to himself that his daughters should become his wives when the old woman died. One day the daughters found upon the beach a man half drowned, who had managed to swim ashore from a canoe which had been blown away from another land . . . they of course immediately fell in love with him, and at once set to work and cooked him some breadfruit and fish, oiled him, and made him very comfortable. When it became evening the girls took him back to their house . . . their father did not seem to like it at all, but gave the visitor food and a place to sleep. Next morning the visitor took courage and being warmly seconded by the girls made proposals to the old man for his daughters, promising to plant all the old man's food, and so nourish and cherish the old couple . . . The old man heard him to the end, and then said, "I never speak but once, and what I have to say on the subject is this. You came amongst us like a chip drifted ashore, you have no property, you have no tribe, and yet you ask me for my daughters, with the greatest impudence, as if women were of no consequence. However as the girls have set their hearts on you I suppose I can't refuse, but before I give them to you, you must perform a miracle, that will be your offering to me for my daughters."
>
> The visitor whose name (mentioned for the first time) was Tabua wandered about in a very disconsolate state . . . he suddenly recollected that as he was swimming ashore he had passed a dead whale . . . it occurred to him that the people of the land had never seen a whale and that he

could make some impression on the old man with the teeth of this one, with the value of which he was himself acquainted, whale's teeth having been in use a long time in his land . . . He found the whale high and dry in the next bay but one, and at once set about extracting the teeth, and as he was pulling with all his might to get out a most obstinate tooth, it came out with a jerk and knocked out four of his front teeth . . . it occurred to him that the accident would greatly help him to a miracle . . . He then gathered firewood over several days and burnt the whale, and then made a basket and putting the teeth into it took it to the old man, who was lecturing his family on the fickleness of young men . . . at the same time hinting that as the old woman was getting very feeble . . . it would be advisable to choke her that she might be at rest, and her daughters able to take her place.

Upon Tabua's appearance amongst them . . . he began his story . . . and told how immediately upon leaving them he had gone into the bush, cleared a piece of land, dug it like a yam bed, pulled out four of his teeth and planted them, and sitting down by them in eight days saw them grow and ripen . . . he had opened the mounds and found the teeth wonderfully increased in number and size . . . What could the old man do but give his consent? But he said that he demanded as a right to make certain laws, viz—that all property given for a wife was to be in part composed of large teeth like those grown by Tabua—that the said teeth were to be called Tabua after the man who first introduced them—that all strangers found drifted ashore were to be killed, and lest like Tabua's teeth they should grow in the ground, they were to be cooked and eaten.[58]

A myth of the foundations of a social order could hardly be more transparent. An initial condition of social isolation and endogamy is disrupted by the arrival of a stranger, who makes an improper offer of food and work for women. Their father, the indigenous owner, points out—with absolute justification in Fijian terms—that these things are incommensurable, that this is a great piece of impudence. Something remarkable must be offered against a woman. This is, incidentally, to echo contemporary women's explanations of why all these huge presentations are made: because here, in Fiji, a woman is a sacred or venerated thing.[59] Tabua is an ordinary man who cannot work a miracle but manages to produce large teeth which are then named after him. In accord with the "social contract" structure of the narrative, the native insists on a right to formulate certain laws before acceding to the historic inevitability of exogamy. The myth has complex ramifications[60] but also indicates something quite basic and important about *tabua*, marriage, and value.

Given the enormous and visible significance of whale teeth, an obvious line of inquiry would concern their symbolic content.[61] That is, what do the material items themselves mean? The myth, however, helps by displacing such a line of questioning. What is called for in the primordial transaction for women is a work of *mana*,[62] and the narrative offers us a fiction within the truth—that whale teeth represent magically transformed and grown human teeth. This is to entertain, in a sense, the notion that *tabua* can be substituted for women because of the divine power they embody. But behind this there is of course a trick and an absence of magic. What follows is the old man's specification that *tabua* must always form part of what is offered for women. Represented as convention, valuables emerge not as things which stand for anything in themselves, but rather as things created because of the prospect of exchange. They meet the need of the man Tabua for what is different and absent—something which can be substituted for women (a purpose for which food and the promise of nurture are inadequate). In this case, the classic structuralist tenet that things have no meaning outside chains of signification and exchange is sustained.[63]

Fijian barkcloth.

An oral tradition of an interior group further stresses the external sources of social value and the paradigmatic construction of marriage and exchange: "There was one very pitiable thing about Vunaqumu then,—the men had no loin cloths, the women had no dresses, and there were no pigs. After that, there came a chief from Navosa . . . who brought a roll of cloth and a pig . . . it was thus that they became possessed of pigs and of cloth, and the price of them was a woman, to belong to the chief who came from Navosa."[64]

Social value is thus constituted through sustaining transactions with external groups. It is no surprise, then, to find that metaphors connected with social paths *(sala; calevu)* have the same importance in Fiji, and the same associations with exchange, marriage, and the constitution of hierarchy, as in many other Austronesian societies. It is no coincidence either that the chief brought a roll of cloth; in Fiji barkcloth is an important exchange valuable that marks paths and alliance and that stands in a sense for the movements of social reproduction.[65]

This is the context in which other articles of material culture can be examined, to consider whether the concept of inalienability may be more applicable to classes of Fijian things which were not *iyau*. Very close association between people and some particular objects could exist. Wooden pillows (or rather headrests) were perhaps initially exchange items: they were probably produced by craft specialists in

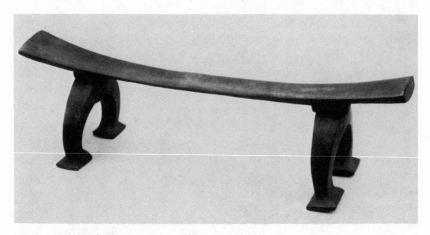

Fijian man's headrest.

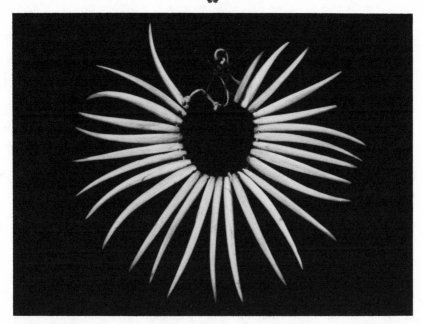

Necklace made of sawed pieces of whale teeth, Fiji, nineteenth century. These were also produced in Samoa and Tonga and traded into Fiji, or produced by Tongan and Samoan craftsmen in eastern Fiji and then traded into other areas. It is virtually impossible to be certain about the provenance in any particular case.

certain localities and may have been categorized as *iyau* and distributed through *solevu*.[66] However, once acquired and used by a particular person, association with anyone else seems to have been impossible, since headrests were often broken and thrown into the grave at death.[67] This instance brings out the sense in which objects, as Appadurai has argued, may be inscribed with a particular cultural biography, with a set of exchange possibilities. What is initially an article to be alienated—which may be part of the restitution for a woman or some kinship obligation—comes to be so closely associated with one man or woman that it cannot, at his or her death, be given even to a son or daughter. That represents an extreme on a continuum of exchangeability: some articles, and paradigmatically cash, can be given or transacted in a wide range of contexts for a wide range of things, while others can be appropriately passed on only in restricted ways or, in the case of the headrest, may not be transmitted at all.[68]

Restricted transmission is also evident in the case of certain chiefly ornaments. Breastplates made of pieces of pearl shell and sawed ivory were evidently of particular prestige value and were worn only by high chiefs.[69] Necklaces, also made from sawed pieces of whale teeth, were of high value but seem to have been somewhat more common. These were apparently associated with chiefly positions rather than individual chiefs: they were certainly not destroyed or buried at the time of death.[70]

It is significant that these singular, personal, chiefly artifacts were produced from pieces of whale teeth. As has been shown, *tabua* were definitely not singularized. To the contrary, they were things to be alienated, signifiers of the wife to come, and the facts of alliance. Individuals could not generally wear *tabua* as ornaments or hoard them (although some chiefs no doubt had substantial supplies). But the material abstraction of ivory from exchange directly mirrors the relationship between alliance and hierarchy. Chieftainship is founded upon constitutive transactions: asymmetrical relations between stranger and native which entail the substitution of a wife for objects of social value. The initial tussle with the stranger-chief brings mats and pigs and thus elevates people from a state of nudity and poverty to proper sociality (as the Tabua myth represents a shift from incestuous endogamy to exogamy). The transaction paradigmatically leads to a chiefly lineage, an established exchange relation, and the notionally ordered and hierarchical polity. Chieftainship thus stands as a stabilization and fixing in genealogy of the social value constituted through exchange, just as ivory is abstracted from transactions and stabilized in nonexchangeable chiefly ornaments to be transmitted from titleholder to titleholder.

These articles directly reflect the constitution of the Fijian hierarchical polity. They also exemplify some more general propositions about objects and exchange. Like the headrests, the breastplates (and necklaces) were initially transferred from specialist producers to high chiefly recipients. At this stage, they seem essentially to have been commodities: perhaps not inalienable in the radical sense of modern industrial products, but nevertheless extracted from the control of their specialist producers. In some instances they were passed between chiefs in recompense for services of unique importance: one example in the Fiji Museum was reputedly presented to a Wainimala chief by "king" Cakobau in the 1850s because the latter's life had been saved during a desperate war in the interior. Once associated with a particular high chief or chiefly line, it seems that such articles were not generally transacted any further.[71] They constituted a type of valued object which shifts from being an exchange article of a particularly prestigious kind to an "inalienable" thing—inalienable, that is, from chiefly holders of the thing and of the title.

Some articles of Pacific regalia were so closely identified with sovereignty that the possessor was effectively the ruler, and there were consequently military struggles to secure control of things such as the Tahitian feather girdles.[72] This was not true of these Fijian objects, but nevertheless Berthold Seemann's Eurocentric parallel with "the Crown jewels" is not really so misleading.[73]

Value Conversion versus Competition in Kind

If Fiji is taken to represent one kind of Pacific exchange system, its most important feature is perhaps the abstraction of values in differentiated valuables. Abstraction was conducive to systemic association between specialized local production and complex sequences of value substitutions and conversions entailing both persons and objects, which might be seen to create "value" in both. On the one hand, the particular importance of women is underlined through the prestations which compensate for their departure—piles of valuables which are themselves produced on the basis of alliance. On the other, the value of *tabua* was constituted through the fact that they stood for this fundamental transaction which at once creates sociality and hierarchy. *Tabua*, because they could be substituted for a woman, acquire distinctive value as "the stone of the land" (that is, of the polity), and the "most chiefly of valuables." This valorization of pieces of ivory enables a range of further prospective uses: payment for assassinations, for services, acknowledgment of "weighty" things. Especially in coastal and insular Fiji, there was much exploitation of the political possibilities of the accumulation of value, particularly in the "financing" of warfare (see Chapter 3).

Exchange was thus dominated by the substitution of different things, by coding of values, by asymmetry. In Papua New Guinea, systems of this type have been counterposed, as was discussed above, with those organized by brideservice, where there were few contexts in which people could be represented by things, where labor and nurture tended to be recompensed and reciprocated through labor and nurture. The early Marquesan societies of eastern Polynesia did not entail brideservice, but the prevalent forms of ceremonial exchange were very different from those in Fiji. The essence of these practices was the competitive exchange of quantities of food.

> A people always give a feast to another people; ordinarily a particular group feasts another particular group in another valley. Rarely the offer is refused; to refuse is to say that one cannot return that which is offered, this is a matter of shame . . . one tries to offer rare things and the largest number of pigs, so that those to whom the feast is offered will be unable to reciprocate; one especially gives plenty of breadfruit[74] and those who have accepted the feast must, upon their honour, eat it all; this may take them several months. For a chief it is a disgrace not to return, in his feast, what he had received, and especially not to finish the breadfruit which is given him; in this case one never refrains from reproaching him with having been defeated.[75]

There was also competition in dancing and chanting at these, or similar occasions.[76] There may have been some exchange of manufactured articles, and ornaments seem to have been included in marriage presentations, but the substance of major gifts was always food, and the process involved reciprocity in kind. Marriage feasts entailed a sequence of presentations from the wife's side, then from the husband's, and so on. What was given by the husband's side was the same, but the quantity was supposed to be greater. From a formal perspective alliance was restricted, as would be consistent with the lack of differentiation of valuables and the absence of a notion that wife-givers and wife-takers were systematically ranked.[77]

It is vital to note that what was presented was mostly prepared and cooked food. There was no scope for transferring what was received into some other circuit of exchange or into another form of value. What was presented was to be consumed; it created debt and a kind of social violence—shame—at the time. But its ramifications were worked out through the register of political competition, rather than a sequence of conversions and transformations.

The emphasis upon food as the medium of exchange created a series of constraints: what was to be given could be created only through production, and was thus subject to whatever constraints obtained upon production. In Fiji, what was to be given could be increased through the manipulation of exchange, while the production of exchange items was generally open to expansion through specialization of production (the discovery of new resources) and through drawing new foreign goods into the system. Fijian exchange was intrinsically generalized and expansionary, while Marquesan competition was limited to quantitative "upping the ante" between paired groups. This might be facilitated by agricultural intensification, but so far as the particular political process was concerned, local systems were basically closed. Goods from outside, and the development of a new trade relationship, could not directly alter the dynamic of exchange. The differentiation of Fijian exchange items into various kinds of food and *iyau*—cloth, wooden articles, *tabua*, and so on—enabled hierarchic difference to be expressed through exchange; this was especially manifest in coastal and insular Fiji, where *solevu* sometimes took on the character of tribute presentations, but was developed to variable extents elsewhere in the group.

The contrasting potentialities of categorically differentiated and in-kind systems do not, of course, relate to any evolutionary continuum of simplicity or complexity. As in Fiji, Marquesans produced and used a range of chiefly and priestly ornaments, and although the richness of museum collections is not matched by contextual information concerning the circulation and cultural construction of such items, it is likely that as far as the biographies of objects are concerned the same general processes of alienation and commoditization took place in both Fiji and the Marquesas. Items initially associated as a form of *tapu* work with their specialist producers no doubt became more profoundly associated with their high-ranking chiefly and priestly users. The important contrast does not, then, emerge from the possible uses of objects, from the available forms of association and transmission, but is notable more at a systemic level.

The discussion here has made extensive reference to the contrasts between systems which provide for the substitution of persons and things and those in which such equivalences are impossible. The tendency in the New Guinea debate about this variation has been to invoke an evolutionary progression, and it is perhaps necessary to reiterate that this is not the model adopted here. In fact, it could be suggested that there are readily identifiable historical, but not evolutionary, factors which partially account for the pattern of variation: the elaboration of value conversions is frequently closely associated with the presence of external trade, and those groups in which the most elaborate substitutions can be made, of valuables of various kinds for hostages, wives, victims, enemies, or slaves, are often also those which are most deeply integrated with regional exchange systems. This is so in the Massim and throughout the Solomons, for instance. By contrast, groups characterized particularly by brideservice and the nonconvertibility of life for things are often also those separated from wider exchange relations, where commodity barter is either nonexistent or negligible (such as the lowland Papuan Kamula and the Umeda of the Sepik).[78] For instance, there is some evidence that the Umeda were earlier a sort of refugee population forced out of more attractive environments and into a region which also excluded them from trade. By using this example my intention is not to set up a positivistic correlation but to disable any evolutionary optical illusion, since it is clearly the case that involvement or disconnection in a regional exchange system is subject to historical and political fluctuation, migration, intergroup conflict, changing trading networks, and so on. Lack of value conversion, bridewealth exchange, and big-man leadership based in competitive exchange, is not an original condition prior to the local evolution of these relations but a historical contingency.

There is a parallel in the Massim region to the contrast I have advanced between the elaborate degree of value conversion in Fijian ceremonial exchange and the necessity of like for like substitution in Marquesan competitive feasting.[79] Though the kula system clearly operated in a manner quite different from Fijian transactions (for instance, exchange took place between partners rather than through collective presentations), a general similarity existed between these cases in the sense that values were abstracted into various classes of goods which were then set against various debts in kin relations, other kinds of objects, other kula valuables, and services such as assassinations. In fact, other forms of Massim exchange, such as mortuary and peace-making presentations,[80] resemble the Fijian collective variety much more closely. But some exchange systems in parts of the Massim peripheral to the kula were much more similar to the Marquesan model in that these types of value conversions appear not to have taken place, and exchange was basically a competitive process entailing quantities of food which were, and are, substituted for one another. This is the pattern around Milne Bay, on the mainland of

Papua (described by Miriam Kahn),[81] and on Goodenough Island. Kalauna (Goodenough) society has been described in a number of fine publications by Michael Young, including the recent reflection upon *Fighting with Food*, his first monograph on the competitive exchange cycles.[82] The point of interest here derives from a linguistic parallel between such terms as *kula* and *kune* and the Kalauna cognate *niune*, which refers to gifts, apparently always in the form of food and pigs, that are received through certain forms of ceremonial exchange. The particular structures of the prestations need not be entered into here, but at a systemic level there are close parallels with the Marquesan types: debts incurred in different types of feasts cannot be repaid through others, and there is a general tendency for affinal hostilities to produce escalation into the major competitive events *(abutu)* characterized by "massive commitment of resources."[83] The point of relevance for historical transformations, though, is that archaeological evidence suggests that the kula network formerly incorporated at least some areas to the southwest, specifically the northern part of Goodenough Island and adjacent mainland.[84] Of course, it cannot be proved that the ancestors of those who now engage in *abutu* formerly practiced something more recognizable as kula exchange, but it is clear that there is a spectrum of forms of exchange across the region which are elements of a simultaneous system. It is quite possible that in areas geographically peripheral to intensive and complex exchange systems, the dominance of the process of competition in the exchange of quantities of food is a peripheral reflex of competition on the basis of the exchange of ranked valuables—the kula that you have when you don't have the kula. I am not concerned here to pursue such speculation about the deeper and longer-term dynamics of these patterns of regional variation; I simply want to stress that contrasts between Melanesian economic forms are easily beguiled by evolutionary connotations—it is hard not to think of brideservice societies as "elementary"—but must instead be situated in political histories. The groups not caught up in regional exchange relations may well have been forced out of them.

Rather than moving further into a typologizing project—to set up more oppositions, such as those between restricted and generalized exchange, between centralized and spatially dispersed trade, between competition on the big-man basis of "equality of opportunity" and the hierarchical exchange of ranked items—the rest of this book explores the encounters of these diverse systems with colonizers, and their manipulations of, or reactions to, foreign contact.

The necessity of such a perspective is revealed if the cases set up thus are considered further. It is most apparent that the Fiji interior of the last thirty years of the nineteenth century was different from the same region at earlier and subsequent dates. The differences derived not just from contact with Europeans, which in a direct form did not substantially precede Von Hügel's account. It would be easy to say that because he saw the *solevu* less than, say, ten years after white men first moved through the area, that any changes could hardly have been consequential. This would be to ignore the ramifications of the much longer history of contact with whites on the coast and, more significantly, would incorrectly suppose that whites were the most important foreign agents and stimuli for change. In fact, the most significant source of dynamism in the whole of Fiji during the eighteenth and nineteenth centuries was an intensification of contact with Tonga, involving military interaction, trade, marriage alliance, and extensive cultural transfer of customs and articles of material culture. It has been argued, in fact, that the "aboriginal" Viti Levu culture was completely transformed by the development of new Tongan-style hierarchies, whole new arrays of Tongan material culture, and secondarily by transformations associated with European trade with both Tonga and Fiji.[85] The question will be explored further below. The point is that, through the connection with white whalers and traders, the number of *tabua* increased considerably during the first part of the nineteenth century. Some writers suggest that *tabua* were originally restricted to high chiefly use and then became "democratized," but this is to restrict change to a quantitative dimension, to suggest merely that distribution became broader.[86] It also seems that most of the artifact types based on ivory were both imported from Tonga and Samoa, and only developed in those particular forms subsequent to the introduction of iron technology: before saws were available, it was not possible to cut pieces of teeth up into the sheets which were tied together with shell in breastplates. Although, in many instances, there were no doubt substitutions of new types for old, the implications for production and exchange must have been different. It is also apparent that the myth of Tabua the man and the Fijian transition from endogamy to sociality is very likely to have been an eighteenth- or nineteenth-century development. Reconstructing early Fijian society is thus like trying to look at people moving on a train that passes you. What one sees more clearly, at a slightly later moment, is not what first appeared.

Although concepts of transaction forms such as gift and commodity are analytically indispensable, it cannot be assumed that the logic of these particular types of prestations is pervasive within particular societies. The old notion of "spheres of exchange" is highly relevant to a more particular and partial appreciation of the logic of movements of people, their attributes, relations, and knowledge. Certain "logics" of alienability and exchangeability can be specific to classes of things as well as classes of relations. It is important also to break away from the notion that commoditization need be associated with anything like an institutionalized market. My emphasis upon the plurality of transaction types and constructions of artifacts should not, however, lead to a vision of an unstructured array of unlimited empirical variants. These economies were systemic, and their cultural figures and flows of value can clearly be imagined from various perspectives; I have chosen to privilege the scope for value conversion and substitution and could notionally have mapped a variety of societies onto a continuum with the Umeda, perhaps, at one end, and Fiji or New Georgia at the other. But my interest in all this is not classificatory; it emerges from the use of these distinctions in a more historical and processual analysis, which is part of the next chapter's agenda.

I have emphasized that the societies described were not traditional; they do not exemplify anything purely Oceanic or Melanesian uncontaminated by contact with Europeans. Insofar as they could be observed or described as developing according to local dynamics that were not drastically adapted to European domination, the cases are, however, suggestive about the autonomous local preconditions for colonial history—what was, after all, a two-sided or multisided colonial history. The Marquesan "system" prompts another qualification, arising from the need to be honest about how much is really known of late eighteenth- and nineteenth-century societies. Although there is a good deal of information which supports the propositions that have been advanced, there is also much that is simply unclear, for instance about the connections between marriage, exchange, and trade in the islands. The evidence about forms of marriage and associated prestations is sparse, late, and unsatisfactorily vague; there is no information as to how locally produced craft items were traded around and whether any of these transactions occurred in the context of marriage. Some interisland "barter" or "trade" certainly took place; it involved various things such as ax stone, feathers, prepared turmeric, and other items, and it is really only negative evidence, and a partly tautological idea of what would be consistent with what else is known of the system, that indicates that such exchange was not politically consequential, that the interpenetration of asymmetry created through exchange and political relations was limited. It has to be remembered that my ethnohistoric sketches are not only theoretically interested but also partial and insecure. Now, in the late twentieth century, both indigenous historians and metropolitan writers like myself can attempt to colonize the past through an interpretative scheme; but just as indigenous societies were never encompassed by colonizers' representations, or by the socioeconomic consequences of the world system, the past must remain refractory and partly intransigent before these projects.

3

The Indigenous Appropriation of
European Things

I already knew about Indians from having read about them in
school. Over and over we were told the story of how Peter Minuit
had bought Manhattan Island from the Indians for twenty four
dollars' worth of glass beads. And it was a story we didn't mind
hearing because it gave us the rare pleasure of having someone to
feel superior to, since the poor Indians had not known (as we eight-
year-olds did) how valuable a piece of property Manhattan Island
would become.

> Jane Tompkins in *"Race," Writing, and Difference*
> (ed. Henry Louis Gates, Jr.), 1986

Mr Hicks who was the officer ashore did all in his power to entice
them to him by offering them presents &c but it was to no purpose,
all they seem'd to want was for us to be gone.

> James Cook, on contact with the Australian
> Aborigines of Botany Bay, 1770

Historians of the relations between Europe and people said to be
"without history" have often described the process of European expansion—the sequence of demands for particular commodities and the
political violence—as though everything about colonial contact derived from the interests of the world market and imperial states. Such
a perspective can only fail to specify the reasons why particular "peripheral" societies became involved in international trade at all: it is
obvious that such involvement, which often developed initially in the
absence of any physical coercion or through an uneven combination
of acquiescence and resistance, cannot simply be regarded as an imposition of the West upon the rest. Although the ultimately exploit-

ative character of the global economy can hardly be overlooked, an analysis which makes dominance and extraction central to intersocial exchange from its beginnings will frequently misconstrue power relations which did not, in fact, entail the subordination of native people. The character of early contact was often such that foreigners were in no position to enforce their demands; consequently, local terms of trade often had to be acceded to; and even much later, when plantation regimes had been established, intrusive Europeans frequently found that they could not make laborers of unwilling islanders. The partial intransigence of indigenous societies in the face of both imperialism's sheer violence and its more subtle ploys must thus be recognized.

The underlying problems of interpretation are, however, cultural as well as economic. More localized and precise discussion of particular transactions might qualify the "world system" perspective but will not account for the significance of foreign trade in indigenous history unless the meanings of objects and the events of contact are interpreted culturally. For a long time, the assumption that intersocial transactions generally amount to "barter" has been an obstacle to cultural understanding. The problem with barter, as was noted in the Introduction, is that it has been regarded essentially as an asocial kind of exchange and has been subordinated to the founding narratives of European social theory. In formal economics, for instance, peripheral transactions provide the circumstances in which money must be invented; and a classic passage in Marx described the origins of commodity exchange in barter across social margins.[1]

The Allure of Barter

One of these just-so stories, about white men encountering native peoples, makes barter the constitutive transaction in colonial relationships. The central motif of this story, which takes much the same form whether the notional referent is in the Pacific Islands or Africa, is the gap between primitive tools and the manufactured things of white men: the magic and abundance of the latter are the source of asymmetry between powerless natives and dominant European colonizers. The indigenous people may be afraid of Europeans, as the Australian Aborigines depicted by Jacques Arago appear to be, but they are desperate to acquire European tools and trinkets—so much so that they are prepared to give away any or all of their own property to acquire things which were worthless or overvalued. They are, more-over, prepared to sacrifice their social relations and customs by working for whites or adopting Christianity to improve their access to such imported items.

> The white men have matches, leather shoes, hydrogen peroxide, razor blades and tinned food . . . Their cargo makes them the natural lords of all they survey . . . The god of the white men emerges as a bowler-hatted, black-waistcoated gentleman who manages an enormous factory in Germany where rice-in-bags and razor blades are produced and reproduced in ceaseless abundance. The people are often eager to please this high being. They give up their old customs, rituals and beliefs; they sing the new songs and build the new buildings; and wait for the moment when their period of initiation is over and they are rewarded with as much power and as many possessions as the white men now have.[2]

The narrative is also present in rather more sober sociohistoric accounts: "The fur trade forced the Inuit [of Canada] into a symbiotic relationship with traders: they forsook their traditional hunting ways (in which trapping was unimportant) to trap the furs that would get them trade goods—guns, bullets, knives, flour, tea and tobacco."[3]

Indigenous agency is represented in a contradictory manner: here the Inuit were at once "forced" and actively "forsaking." This sort of account can appear in works which convey a sympathetic attitude to the people colonized, but the fundamental implication is that their "loss" of their own culture and political autonomy is the result of the fatal attraction of European goods: the people are innocent but hopelessly greedy. Asymmetry is thus constituted in the nature of first contact rather than through a history of subsequent engagement, as a consequence of later imperial intervention and annexation. The power difference is recognized from the very start by the indigenous people themselves and is thus not an effect of the actual application of force or violence later on. Writers such as Julia Blackburn, whose description of the white men's appeal is quoted above, thus displace the blame for colonial violence in part onto local populations, who become to a certain extent authors of their own predicaments. A similar preoccupation has been apparent in interpretations of religious activity associated with contact, involving the representation and parody of white behavior, in terms of cargo cultism—the central feature being the desire to obtain European property rather than, say,

One view of early contact: exchange between Australian Aborigines and French mariners, 1818.

political subversion or appropriation. The theme of these histories is that the irresistible magnetism of white commodities compels their adoption and imposes a choice irrespective of the cost to culture and autonomy. This view takes the properties of artifacts and introduced items as self-evident: it is assumed that the advantages of new items are immediately manifest to natives. In reality, however, technology is dependent upon cultural knowledge: even relatively specialized tools do not have specific purposes inscribed in them, and purposes and uses are variously relevant and recognized. For instance, an object as useful as an iron ax will be appreciated in places where swidden agriculture is practiced or canoes frequently built in a different way than in places where neither of these tree-cutting activities are common. Without even considering the meaningful associations of an introduced article, it is hence apparent that the native interest in particular objects can be expected to be variable. But in any case, the cultural uses of some axes seem to have fallen beyond the obvious and intrinsic purposes that we would recognize: "They possess indeed some tomahawks of European make . . . These tomahawks however they prize too highly to put them to common use and generally keep as articles of special virtue, hung up in the part of the hut specially devoted to the gods."[4]

To question this story of the origins of dependency too much may seem perverse—not just because, at a general level, the superiority of iron and European technology obviously was important, but also because the general narrative is found in indigenous histories as well as the type of Western liberal writing that has been quoted. "The colonialists . . . took the best land from us in exchange for items like empty bottles, tobacco, soap, fishing lines and hooks."[5] One of the reasons frequently adduced in support of oral history has been its association with an "internal" perspective on the impact of colonialism; the indigenous side of the story can be recovered. But just as contemporary Christian Pacific Islanders cannot be expected to represent neutrally the customs of their "heathen" ancestors, in this case indigenous hindsight seems to partake of colonialist distortion in rendering the islanders of an earlier period as mere victims. Paradoxically, both Western liberals and local historians, while lamenting that native transactors did not understand the "real" value of what they gave away, pass over the counterpart to this question: what was the real value of what they received?

There is thus scope for a reexploration of the political dynamics of early transactions, aiming to establish not that islanders welcomed colonialism but that the early phases of their entanglement were grounded in local cultural and political agendas, rather than naïveté. The form of early entanglement moreover arose from existing political and economic forms—the permutations of debt discussed in the previous chapter—and in turn created preconditions for subsequent colonial intrusions. An adequate understanding of the latter, of the crudities of colonial violence and annexation, must thus refer both to immediately prior phases of colonial interaction and to the earlier autonomous dynamics of indigenous forms. My lens for these processes is the mutability of material objects, and my strategy takes things which are transparent—such as the value of an ax—to be opaque. Indigenous interests in trade are not presumed to be straightforward or predictable but must instead be contextualized in prevailing ideas of what foreign visitors and their goods represented. This cultural context is not easy to apprehend, especially since interpretation must be based mainly upon what can be discerned of indigenous reactions at the time; although all available material is taken into account, oral histories serving later perceptions of the past provide a less satisfactory approach than accounts of local statements and behavior in first-hand European descriptions of events, notwithstanding the partiality and ideology of these texts. But the analytic problems must not prevent us from attempting to give an account of the local ways of recognizing new strangers: these perceptions conditioned what was at stake in contact and exchange.

In about 1903 a Samoan mission teacher, John Lupo, wrote down (at the request of a foreigner) a history of the small and isolated island upon which he had been settled since the 1860s: "In the beginning this island now called Niue was nothing but coral rock," he began. He proceeded to describe how the lump had been fished up from the ocean by the god Maui, how it had been settled, how cultivated plants had been brought. Later, various wars and invasions had occurred; certain evil spirits had occasionally caused famine. A story which began with a primal world and cosmological forces also embraced later developments—the arrival of mission ships[6] and white men (*papalagi*). The response to the latter had been initially hostile, but the attitude changed when foreign goods were discovered:

When the people saw what great things the *papalagi* had in their ship—
the axes, the fish-hooks, the soft cloth—they were crazy to get them. At
that time the only axes the *Niue* men had were those made of black stone
. . . and of the big clam-shells . . . and they desired above everything the
sharp hatchets of the white man. They were very anxious to become
Christians, because they would obtain teachers, sharp axes and knives and
cloth. And peace ruled over this island, where once fighting and man-
slaying continually prevailed.[7]

Some kind of religious conversion, with its attendant social and domestic transformations, is thus represented as the outcome of this
hunger for Western goods. But had Niue people in fact been so crazy
to get axes, fishhooks, and cloth?

John Elphinstone Erskine was the captain of HMS *Havannah*
during its western Pacific cruise of 1849. Like most of the other ships
which had encountered Niue people in the preceding sixty-five years,
his did not land on the island, and his dealings were with men who
came out in canoes. The barter which took place between the canoes
and the larger vessel, and to some extent on deck, seems at first sight
to have been typically haphazard and straightforward. The islanders
were particularly interested in knives, fishhooks, and black bottles,
which were probably broken up to make glass cutting implements (of
the sort made elsewhere from flint, chert, or volcanic glass). Erskine
reported that "their articles of traffic are almost entirely weapons" such
as spears; they were evidently of considerable value; some were carefully wrapped in leaves.[8] Others were decorated in a way which linked
them distinctly with their owners: "all very nicely made, and or-
namented with a few feathers, the arrangement of which, we were
told, represented the owner's name, and enabled him to claim the
credit for a successful throw in battle."[9]

Erskine wrote that the "system of barter was not well regulated," it
being "impossible to fix definite values on the different articles on
either side." But the Niue men evidently had a precise idea of reciprocation, if not of definite equivalence. For Erskine, the morality of
the act depended not on the presence or absence of a return but upon
relative values, and he admitted that he was "somewhat ashamed of
the trash we had given them" for their weapons and therefore "repeat-
edly threw out of the stern windows black bottles with a few fish-hooks
attached, intending them as a free gift."[10] This gracious gesture was
regrettably either rejected or misunderstood by the islanders: "Invari-

ably one or two spears were thrust on me, whether I would or no; the canoes which had dropped astern to pick up their bottles paddling with all their might to fulfill their share of the bargain."

This insistence on immediate return is extremely atypical in the broader pattern of Polynesian-European barter. In the great majority of cases, at Hawaii, New Zealand, the Marquesas, Tahiti, and in other parts of the Society Islands, a more diffused, sometimes delayed pattern of transactions took place, involving sex, services, and a broader array of things including water, wood, local artifacts, and food. Even when the visit of a ship to an island incorporated periods of direct, organized exchange—often in a delineated space upon a beach—goods changed hands in various ways at other times. Chiefly men and women, or others who were apparently prominent, were often favored with special gifts; theft was not uncommon, and the goodwill of chiefs was sometimes used in attempts to recover valuable items. Participants in Bruny d'Entrecasteaux's voyage in search of La Pérouse found the Tongans hospitable; a high chiefly woman presented them with a chicken and "took good care to let us know that she did not by any means give them to us by way of exchange; affecting to repeat, with an air of dignity, *ikai fokatou*, and to announce to us, by the word *adoupé*, that she was making us a present. In fact, the chiefs never proposed to us to barter their effects for ours; they made us presents, and accepted everything that we offered them."[11]

In these cases, the indigenous interest was undoubtedly in expansive and open-ended contact (in some cases, islanders wept when they heard that their friends from previous visits, such as Cook, were dead). In Niue, by contrast, the desire seems to have been to restrict the relationship, so far as was possible. The islanders evidently wanted fishhooks and knives, as Lupo suggested; in return they did not supply provisions or favors but gave weapons. This was the experience of a number of earlier visitors—"Sent two boats on shore to see what trade the savages had . . . but got nothing but spears and warclubs."[12]

In day-to-day exchange, as well as on more important occasions (in tribute and in sacrifices) food was—and in general still is—the primary medium for the expression of social and ritual obligations and affiliations throughout the south Pacific, whereas weapons were not generally articles of exchange. Various other forms of material culture, such as mats, cloth, coconut fiber, canoes, and pots, were often used in ceremonial presentations, but the movements of such things as spears and clubs seem to have been distinctly restricted. Obviously they were often made by people other than their users, so that some initial transaction between a craft specialist and a warrior must be presumed; but beyond this, it seems that weapons became articles of personal property, perhaps to be transmitted between male kin on the death of an owner but otherwise outside circulation. The probability of this being so in Niue is strongly implied by the personalization of weapons.

The use of these things as trade goods might be seen as a solution to a difficult problem which the Niue people encountered: they had a strong interest in articles which could only be got through exchange with the whites, but for some reason they wanted to avoid the social relationship which was almost always an indissociable part of exchange—or the purpose of it—within their own system. The innovation that overcame this paradox was the disposal of things which were not exchange items, which could carry no debt or burden of friendship. They made free, unsocial commodities out of precisely the things they would not have exchanged among themselves.[13]

The strenuous desire to limit contact is also manifest in the fact that Niue women played no part in these events. Most travelers from Cook in 1774 until Erskine and after did not even see any women. Elsewhere, in the most-visited parts of Polynesia, such as Tahiti and Hawaii, island women were eager to enter into sexual relations with sailors.[14] The aspect of these encounters which struck members of Cook's expedition when they visited Hawaii was that no material payment seemed to be expected or demanded. Some observers attributed this behavior to the "licentious" or promiscuous disposition of Polynesians generally, and a stereotype entered the European mythology of Tahiti in particular and the South Seas in general.[15] As part of a denser cultural description of the encounter between the Hawaiians and the British, Marshall Sahlins has elaborated on earlier suggestions that women wanted to give themselves up to those who were initially recognized as gods, in arguing that the practice was an extension of "the offering of virgin daughters to a ranking chief by prominent commoners . . . in the hope of bearing a child by the chief."[16] A cherished kin connection was established—of negotiable if probably limited practical import in this flexible cognatic system—and the commoner woman would subsequently take another husband of her own class. Because the practice was seen by the sailors as prostitution, they turned it into an exchange, and once Hawaiians realized that sexual services could become a commodity, they continued to participate enthusiastically on these new terms. Foreigners were not regarded as "divine" for very long,[17] but there were associations between the chiefly, the efficacious, the divine, and the foreign, which must have continued to permeate the interests in sex and exchange for many decades.

It would seem unreasonable to assume that sexual liaisons with men from across the sea had a pan-Polynesian or pan-Oceanic meaning, but in fact the association of chiefs and strangers was widespread in this part of the Pacific and may provide the basis for a cultural and political specification of the Niuean hostility to foreigners and the interest in constraining barter. An apparently more immediate explanation for avoidance was offered to a number of Europeans. The consequence of one ship's visit had been some kind of epidemic; according to a Niue man who met the missionary William Gill in 1838, they therefore "conceived a dislike to intercourse with [the white man], or to have anything to do with his property. While on board his ship they had also seen him eat '*animal*' food,[18] and had concluded that he was a '*man-eater;*' and consequently they resisted every temptation to put themselves within his power!"[19]

This account, reiterated in other sources,[20] seems straightforward but fails to explain the attitude of hostility, since more or less severe outbreaks of illness were almost a universal feature of contact. In such places as Fiji, major epidemics had occurred in very early phases of interaction, and although the Fijians were often hostile, this attitude derived from an interest in seizing European ships and property rather than from a desire to avoid whites. In any case, the fact that strenuous resistance to contact dated from Cook's initial visit in 1774—hence his subsequently resented appellation of "Savage Island"[21]—suggests that the distinctive resistance of Niue people needs to be explained on the basis of the character of their prior representations and experience of strangers.[22] Much of the openness toward foreigners in Hawaii and elsewhere was clearly connected with the close associations between chiefs and foreignness: as was the case in many other parts of the world, and in the Fijian narratives discussed in the previous chapter, chiefs were seen as immigrants or invaders, as sources of extralocal powers and things of value, to be domesticated and incorporated into the indigenous order. Although these cosmologies embodied ambivalence about chieftainship or kingship, frequently expressed in myths of cannibalistic and rapacious despots,[23] the overall orientation was obviously positive and celebratory.

On Niue, however, the set of values was certainly different. The ritual structure of chieftainship identified the chief with harvests and abundance, and in many parts of the region failures of production arising from combinations of social and ecological factors led to a decline in chiefly fortunes, a reorientation of their activities (often toward warfare), or in some instances their outright rejection.[24] Given the insecurity of Niue's production system, it is not surprising that this set of values developed. There were various traditions concerning the rejection of a monarchic order: "The form of government was formerly aristocratic or feudal; but in a comparatively recent period, the chiefs were all slain."[25] As would be expected on the basis of other Polynesian examples, shamans—whose powers were seen as indigenous rather than imported—appropriated the capacity to influence crops and the weather. They seem also to have been particularly hostile to foreigners and mission teachers.[26] There had been a long history of resistance to invaders from Tonga (from which the chiefly line had been founded), who were regarded, like the white men, as "man-eaters."[27]

Hence the general associations apparent in other polities between externality, chieftainship, new valuables, and new white strangers, were found; but these associated values seem to have been categorically rejected rather than incorporated. In this case, although the "sharp axes and knives" were of considerable importance, the demand for them did not justify far-reaching adaptations of practice or custom. Rather, it occasioned a kind of marginal commodity exchange—not an absence of social relations but a relation constituted so as to constrain and minimize contact, which was seen as essentially dangerous. Its threatening character was manifest in post-contact disease, but the recognition of danger derived from earlier invasions and cultural values rather than from incidents similar to those which had taken place and which had been represented quite differently elsewhere. The local situation, not the foreigners's acts, gave the process of contact its singularity.

Niue was rather exceptional in its management of contact. Most other islanders found encounters with white voyagers less problematic and were in many cases keen to expand relationships into political alliances marked by various forms of cultural appropriation. However, there was no general subordination of indigenous values to European demands. As in the case of Niue, where the determining structure was the internal logic of the Niuean polity, prior social and cultural regimes were crucial. Relatively similar forms of exchange and interests in foreignness had profoundly divergent ramifications because the dynamics of indigenous polities differed. I develop this point later in the chapter in comparing the Marquesas and Fiji.

Values in the early stages of Marquesan barter were particularly fluid. When Cook first arrived (in April 1774) he secured quite a few pigs in exchange for trifles, but the situation changed after the crew had been permitted to trade individually ashore; the next day Cook came back from the beach with only a few small pigs, which he complained had cost more "than a Doz.ⁿ would have done the evening before."[28]

> What ruined our Market the most was one of them giving for a Pig a very large quantity of Red feathers he had got at Amsterdam [Tongatapu],[29] which these people much value and which the other did not know, nor did I know at this time that Red feathers was what they wanted . . . Thus, was the fine prospect we had of getting a plentifull supply of refreshments of these people frustrated, and which will ever be the case so long as every one is allowed to make exchanges for what he pleaseth and in what manner he pleases's.[30]

It was indeed a general feature that undisciplined barter engaged in by crew caused the prices of indigenous commodities to rise; this feature was accentuated by the noncorrespondence of scales of value. But the difficulty in obtaining pork endured well beyond these particular misunderstandings.

There was usually a good deal of sexual contact, and voyagers tended to be shocked that girls as young as eight or nine should be involved, and also that husbands should offer their wives, and fathers their daughters.[31] Urey Lisiansky, who with A. J. von Krusenstern undertook the first Russian circumnavigation, and who visited Nukuhiva in 1804, thought that "this proceeded from their ardent desire of possessing iron, or other European articles which, in their estimation, are above all price."[32] Though consistent with the general European idea that Western commodities exercised an irresistible magnetism, it is curious that Lisiansky should have written this, since both he and Krusenstern experienced extraordinary difficulty in obtaining any animal food in the Marquesas. It was their own pigs, rather than iron, which the Marquesans placed almost beyond price. Pigs were valuables partly because they were regarded as individual animals, to be named and nurtured like children, and also because they were reared and killed mainly for grand commemorative feasts for deceased chiefs and shamans, which were the most prominent and elaborate Marquesan social events. Certain animals would have been difficult to part with because they were *tapu* for some specific ceremony: to do something else with such a pig would offend the perhaps troubled and capricious spirit of the person being commemorated or detract from the significance of the birth of a first-born child.

Krusenstern had gathered that "very few hogs were to be procured" and therefore made it known that *only* pigs would be accepted in return for axes and hatchets, which he knew the Marquesans wanted. Given the circumstances of contact, and the fact that the Russians

The Russians in the Marquesas, 1804. Note the prominence accorded to exchange and sexual contact between the Russians and the Marquesans.

needed supplies of food, wood, and fresh water at least as much as the Marquesans wanted iron tools, it is not surprising that this imperialist attempt to dictate the terms of trade failed to bring in a supply of pigs. Some Marquesan attitudes toward exchange were so qualified that one wonders how any barter took place at all: The chief at Hakaui valley "was the only one who brought a hog for sale; but he could not prevail on himself to part with his treasure, and after having concluded his bargain four times, and at last on very advantageous terms to himself, he immediately repented of it and returned us our goods, though he was highly pleased with them."[33]

The only prospective exchange items the Marquesans seem to have been so attracted by that they offered their pigs in exchange were European sheep—which were regarded as a particular category of pig—and birds, which is to be expected since feathers were highly sought after for use in certain warriors', chiefs', and priests' ornaments. However, these transactions were mostly ruled out on the European side, as Lisiansky's description of one day's exchange indicates.

> About seven o'clock the traffic for cocoa-nuts, bread fruit, bananas, and different articles of curiosity, began, and was continued briskly until noon. Of the first three commodities, I obtained a considerable quantity, at a cheap rate, giving only, for seven nuts, and a bunch of bananas and bread fruit, a piece of an old iron hoop, not more than five inches long. At eight o'clock two canoes arrived, with the king in one, and his uncle in the other. They brought with them four pigs, which they wished to exchange for two of our English sheep; but finding me averse to this, the canoes took them back on their return. I offered, as a present, to the king, some axes, knives, and other articles; but he would only take a striped cap, observing, as he refused the rest, that such precious things could not be accepted till he had something to give me in return . . . while this was going on, another of his majesty's relatives came on board, and exchanged a large pig, for a cock and a hen.[34]

The reluctance of the chief, Keatonui, to take anything other than a striped cap, suggests that like the Niue men, he could not deal with the Europeans' occasional interest in separating "pure" gifts from commodities. In other contexts, islanders were happy to take things for which no specific return was requested, but they normally wanted to extend their association with the Europeans in question, and they saw something distinctly positive in a denser mesh of donations and obligations. Mostly the Marquesans did not resist this, but Keatonui was no doubt bothered by the pressure to supply pigs and did not want to become indebted.

Later, he brought out two pigs, which he offered for Lisiansky's green parrot, but found the captain unprepared to part with his pet bird. Various discrepancies in understandings of value and the attachment of people to their creatures thus made barter impossible, but the Russians failed to see any analogy between two kinds of noncommoditized animal. At another bay they saw many pigs and complained that the inhabitants were "equally avaricious," refusing to sell any. The choice of words—or what may be a mistranslation—implies that the islanders were merely rapacious and wanted more than could reasonably be offered for a beast. Given the Russian interest in obtaining a *quantity of livestock*, they could only have seen it that way, but what was so visible was absent, then, from Marquesan categories: pigs were singular creatures to be substituted, with difficulty, for other special things, or not substituted at all. This was essentially the experience of every visitor to the Marquesas before 1813. If pigs were obtained at all, they were obtained in very small numbers. It was often thought that this arose from scarcity, but, as a "clerk" on one of the Russian vessels discovered, animals had been moved inland, to create such an impression, presumably out of a fear that pigs might be stolen or trade imposed.[35] Just as intercultural relationships were understood differently on each side, here the matter transacted was construed differently, with the result that the Russians could not understand the Marquesan resistance to disposing of pigs.

As in the Niuean case, the situation also reveals intransigence on the part of indigenous people. Foreign trade was marginal in more than a literal sense. There was obviously an interest in iron and trinkets, but unlike the Niue men postulated in Lupo's story, Marquesans were not "crazy to get" axes or knives. They did not engage in much swidden agriculture, and their demand was perhaps limited to relatively few tools which would have been used in canoe building, house construction, and wood carving. If a number of hatchets were on the island, available for loan and use, the immediate demand had perhaps been largely satisfied. Within the broader cultural context, then, questions of supply and demand seem to have contributed to the comparatively low exchange value of axes. What Marquesans were prepared at this stage to give in return for further iron tools were mostly abundant foodstuffs such as coconuts and breadfruit, which in unprocessed forms encapsulated insignificant amounts of labor. The precise character of interest in European artifacts is not clear, but it is obvious that there was no overriding obsession with their acquisition.

Moreover, the Marquesans did not care about foreign contact to the extent that they attempted to monopolize it: they displayed no jealousy when visitors moved on to other bays, to people with whom they competed in feasts or fought with weapons. In 1791, Marchand was unable to get more than a few pigs at Vaitahu bay on Tahuata, so he went south along the coast to Hapatoni, where he did obtain some more. This seems to have been a matter of indifference to the Vaitahu people. Thirty years later things were very different, as we will see. But the earlier phase reveals the artifice of Lisiansky's view that European things were so highly valued: it did not often strike navigators that the things given out as "trifles" were sometimes received as such.

What made things different after 1813 was the intrusion of Captain David Porter of the U.S. Navy in the latter part of that year—or rather, the manner in which his intrusion led to a recognition of guns. Britain and the United States were at war and Porter, having captured several British whaling vessels, decided to take possession of the Marquesas (only one of a series of grand annexing gestures indulged in by mariners but studiously ignored or disowned by their governments). Porter constructed a fortified base by the large bay of Taiohae, and like some other visitors went through the ritual of exchanging names with Keatonui (the same chief who, nine years earlier, had not seen his way clear to accepting more than a striped cap from Lisiansky). In Marquesan terms, exchanging names notionally created a close identification, the property and interests of one becoming those of the other. Keatonui immediately used this as a pretext to draw the Americans into his own war: he told Opoti, as Porter was called, that he should help him repulse the Hapaʻa, a group occupying a valley a few miles to the east of Taiohae, with whom they habitually fought. Porter was initially reluctant to become involved but was unable to restrain himself in the face of obscene insults directed at him and his men by Keatonui's enemies. He humiliated the Hapaʻa and then became embroiled in another struggle with a more powerful tribe in Taipi valley (Melville's Typee); after an initial defeat his force fought their way up Taipi valley, destroying settlements, ritual sites and "large and elegant war canoes."[36]

Since it appears that political groupings and the balance of forces had been relatively stable in this part of Nukuhiva, such a clear-cut military outcome was an extraordinary if not an unprecedented event. To Keatonui, Opoti's victories "seemed incredible."[37] Porter's warrior style and (perhaps apocryphal) relationship with a twelve-year-old "princess" were conducive to the formation of a representation of him as a typically Polynesian invasive warrior chief; the presentation to him of numerous offerings is consistent only with such recognition. The hero perhaps became more significant as soon as he left, since his allies could exploit their association with Opoti in a manner unconstrained by the intrusive presence of the man himself. The connection seems to have become the focus for ritual practices which persisted until Marquesan polities in the area were disrupted after annexation by France in 1842. During the visit of the U.S. Navy ship *Brandywine* in 1829, the visitors learned that there would be a celebration: as one of them, Thomas Dornin, described it, "tomorrow there will be a great dance and feast in commemoration of Commodore Porter's victory . . . they think that Porter is king of all the world; they venerate his name." The feast no doubt took place while the Americans were in the bay because the Taiohae people wanted to engineer some repetition of Opoti's partisan engagement; Dornin in fact noted that their friends "are solicitous that we should join sides with them."[38]

Another American visitor had found that, in a more general sense, people at Taiohae stressed their links with Porter. In 1825 a chief told him "that his father had been a great warrior and a friend of Opotee. Before his door was a swivel and a number of shot, that he said he had obtained from Opotee. He prized them highly, although they could not be of the least use to him, except as they served to gratify his vanity."[39]

Europeans were shown many guns which—it was said—had belonged to, or been given by, Porter; in the context of this manifest preoccupation, the tables had been turned, as far as forms of prestations were concerned. Earlier, islanders concerned to obtain articles without entangling themselves socially with foreigners had refused to accept gifts as anything other than commodities. Now, articles of trade dispensed as commodities were reconstituted as inalienable gifts from foreigners by Marquesans. This was the sense in which an old gun was not merely useful but singular: the artifact embodied the narrative of Porter's alliance with the Taiohae people, and its possession stood for the continuing association between them and American power—not, needless to say, the kind of American power which had been deployed in war against the British, but the kind which these "primitive people" on the world system's extreme periphery had subordinated to their own military theater and their own ends.

Perhaps, then, the distinction between the "alienable" and the "inalienable" must be traced as specifically as this. What is at issue is presumably the way in which an object is socially consequential, the facts about it which account for the manner in which it can, must, or cannot be circulated. This is a matter not just of singularity or uniqueness but of context and narrative. Nor do the special features of these objects arise from either a system of circulation or relations of production—unless one is speaking of the relations of producing history, of dictating a story which constitutes a powerful relation and an enduring effect. It is a matter of cultural and political recognition: certain Marquesans set themselves up as the receivers of Porter's gifts: others might have disputed this, or claimed that other guns were given to *their* fathers. The cross-cultural prestation, through its perverse recontextualizations, exposes the mutability of exchange items. What begins as a commodity is transformed, not exactly into a gift, but into a historicized artifact, the sign of a former owner and his works.

The Musket Economy in the Southern Marquesas

The creation of a link between guns and Porter himself was probably made only in the valley with which he had been allied. But the distinctive events of 1813 seem to have prompted a new fear and respect of firearms through most of the Marquesan island group.[40] Ambitious chiefs and warriors began strongly to associate their prospects for advancement with personal links with foreigners such as ships' captains and even more strongly with their own access to muskets. Before Porter, ships experienced considerable difficulty in obtaining pigs; after Porter, almost anything could be exchanged for muskets or gunpowder. As early as 1816, a sandalwood trader noted that "firearms & ammunition [are] the staple trade at the Islds. and red broad-cloth next in esteem A variety of cutlery and beeds feathers & other articles & ornaments should be provided, & a few whale's teeth (the longer the better) may sometimes produce sandal wood & generally proove a good article for purchasing hogs & other provisions."[41]

The French trader Camille de Rocquefeuil, who visited both the

southern and the northern sections of the group in 1817, similarly
noted that muskets were the basic article of trade and were likely to
remain so, "given the continuous state of hostility in which these
people live."[42] The novel situation made this utilitarian connection
between warfare and a demand for guns eminently plausible, but there
had been no link to draw even five years earlier.

Muskets were exchanged as well as used and displayed by
Marquesans. They differed in a number of important respects from the
things which were circulated in the earlier indigenous system. As was
noted in the previous chapter, food—especially pork and breadfruit—
was the substance of presentations at major competitive and commemorative feasts, as well as at smaller-scale family or kin-group events.
There seems to have been a limited amount of interisland barter in
things which were not obtainable everywhere, but this was carried out
sporadically and does not appear to have been connected with marriage alliances or other politically consequential links. Production of
food was oriented toward competitive feasts, but there seems to have
been little production of wood or stone artifacts, ornaments, or other
valuables for exchange; there were, in most areas, craft specialists who
supplied local demand. Thus, in opposition to such cases as the shell
money systems of the Solomon Islands, or the regionally specialized
production of exchange goods in Fiji, local monopolization of particular kinds of artifacts was not a basis for any kind of asymmetrical or
imbalanced exchange.

In the Marquesan system, the competitive exchange of like for like
permitted indebtedness and temporary inequalities to develop on the
basis of unequal quantities of food. These status differences could
change relatively easily, if for instance one group experienced famine
or had its productive base damaged through warfare, and the system
did not constitute any stable hierarchical order at a regional level. But
the introduction of muskets could, and did, change regional relationships.

Given that most goods are ranked, and that despite a kind of quantitative equivalence between a more substantial amount of something
of lower rank and a limited amount of a high-ranking valuable, there
remains a sense in which the supplier of the higher-ranking article is
superior; there is clearly a basis, in the exchange of like for unlike, for
a distinct kind of social inequality. Muskets were obviously prestige
articles of a potent and relatively scarce kind, and the sociogeographic

character of contact between ships and the occupants of islands meant that they could usually be monopolized. European vessels, to a varying degree throughout Oceania, tended to return to the same harbors and bays, partly because these were sometimes the only safe anchorages, and partly because some places had established reputations as suitable ports, with friendly natives and documented navigational directions. In some parts of the world a similar funneling of trading relations was closely associated with the formation of small-scale states. This did not occur in the Marquesas, but between the 1820s and the early 1840s the chief Iotete of Vaitahu bay on the island of Tahuata substantially expanded his sphere of political influence. The southern Marquesas were not extensively visited in the 1820s, but whaling and trading through that part of the Pacific intensified in the 1830s, such that between ten and twenty vessels were calling every year; Iotete received a musket from each captain as a sort of harbor tax, and muskets, powder, and flints were received in exchange for food and firewood.

Iotete's attempts to stop traders giving muskets to any other tribes on Tahuata or the neighboring island of Hiva Oa seem to have been at least partially successful and to have provoked great resentment. A war in 1836 led to the consolidation of his position, and there are several accounts of his intervention in political affairs and disputes on the neighboring island which suggest that his influence, which derived directly from his capacity to supply firearms, was more considerable than that of any chief in the period of earlier contact.[43]

Although the information on southern Marquesans' perceptions of foreigners and of the nature of the changes over this period is extremely sparse, it is clear that Iotete saw himself as acting analogously to the Tahitian monarch Pomare I; for this reason he did not intend to adopt Christianity. Rather his son, like Pomare II, would remain untattooed, would become a convert, and would build on the political expansion initiated by his father on the basis of associations with Europeans and supplies of guns.[44] The narrative appears to have been both contested by some opposed to Iotete and more or less ignored by certain other southern Marquesans. Those on the more isolated island of Fatuiva to the southeast made canoe trips up to Tahuata from time to time to exchange muskets for pigs.[45] Fatuiva was not frequently visited by ships, and the people there cannot have obtained many guns, and so must have been less interested in their military potential and in the forms of foreign power they represented. This cultural and political circumstance might have undermined Iotete's monopoly, but it appears that since at least some of the Fatuiva people were friendly with him, much of the Fatuiva supply may have come into his hands.

Intercultural barter has been regarded as a starting point for the theory of commodity exchange. In such theory the issue of how other people are regarded is overlooked. If there is a fear or lack of interest in those with whom one trades, then the situation is perhaps straightforward: what is wanted is a thing which is valued because of its internal properties or what is done with it; it is not valued because of its history. If the links between the thing and its producers or former owners are erased, uninteresting, or inconsequential, then it can be considered a commodity. But where Polynesians drew Europeans into their own expansive games and made them underwrite their political risks, where the others were selectively constituted in a symbolic and socially powerful manner, the values of things became entangled with stories about their sources, about the great things that these outsiders did. A receiving group like this does not want commodities disconnected from their users; it wants artifacts which tell a story. Commodities were thus transformed into valuables with a heavy cultural burden and, further, into high-ranking exchange items or prestige goods. The Fatuiva sector of the southern Marquesan system illustrates that for some people who do not care about the stories, these special things may represent little more than the possibility of obtaining other things like pigs. But that commodity transaction is another local variant rather than a pure or fundamental form.

The Representation of the Foreign

Western commodities cannot be seen to embody some irresistible attraction that is given the status of an inexorable historical force. Indigenous peoples' interests in goods, strangers, and contact were variable and in some cases were extremely constrained. Nevertheless, preoccupations with certain trade goods and foreign associations were highly developed in some areas. How are these instances of fascination with imports and the sources of importation to be interpreted?

There are prior questions about more general processes of perception and classification. How does one deal with something completely novel? How does one categorize and value it? It would seem that there

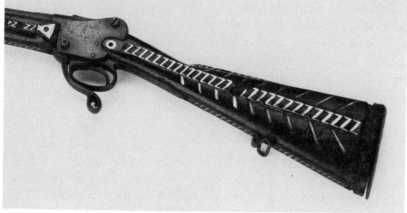

A nineteenth-century rifle, with inlaid shell decoration, from the western Solomon Islands, exemplifies a domesticated import.

are a number of ways in which new things—whether razor blades, Martians, or stimulants—can be dealt with conceptually and culturally.[46]

While the semiotic approach emphasizes difference and discreteness, it is also possible to look at signs and categories from their blurred edges, with respect to their ambiguities. The term "house" has a canonical referent but can also be extended to marginal cases such as a palace, a boat shed converted into a dwelling, or a garden shed which somebody sleeps in. Any of these, or something distinctly different, such as an apartment, might well be excluded from any strict idea of what the set of "houses" is, but the point is that usage has some mutability and a capacity to encapsulate dubious or problematic cases.

Something new can stand as subtype, a special form of something which is already known, or can be understood in terms of the properties of something more familiar. Sometimes terminological extension takes place in a superficial and conceptually uninteresting manner: the vocabulary of ships was transferred to airplanes and persists, despite the fact that the latter have displaced the former as the familiar method of international travel. The famous Stubbs painting of a kangaroo with rat-like features from Cook's first voyage provides a more apt example,[47] where representation evidently directly conveyed some categorical confusion or the lack of a prior template; the fact that the platypus was sometimes called a "duck-mole" illustrates another form of recognition in hypothetical hybridization (a thing being "a cross between" other types).[48] This case, though, alerts us to discrepancies between linguistic terms and cultural beliefs; presumably no English zoologist ever actually thought that the platypus was of such mixed descent. Nevertheless, some forms of categorical extension can exist in the absence of actual labeling: there were ways in which Marquesan guns were treated ritually like clubs and spears, but there was never any terminological inclusion.[49] I don't know whether this was so in the western Solomons, but the decoration of imported guns and hatchets

Iron hatchet in an ornamental haft, with inlaid shell decoration, from the western Solomon Islands.

with shell inlay exemplifies through physical modification the process of appropriation and assimilation that usually leaves no visible signs. In this case, at least, the theory in material culture studies of the objectivity of the artifact is manifestly mutilated. Of course, assimilation does not always take place: these diverse examples make it clear that the form of recognition and its cultural ramifications cannot be predicted in any way from general linguistic models—but that is not to say that there are no historical patterns.

The Tahitian polity, or rather some chiefly parties within it, seized upon European trade, the colonizing potential of evangelism, and some other features of new contact, which served political expansion well. It is perhaps not surprising, then, that Pomare II, like his father, was an enthusiastic consumer of alcoholic drinks, and that at some point he substituted these, which were known as 'ava Peretani or British kava, for the indigenous form. "Pohmaree left off drinking Kava, but he afterwards took to European liquors; and it was his delight to sit for long evenings together, along with his chiefs, over a bowl of grog, talking about Buonaparte, Captain Cook, King George, and foreign events."[50]

Here, the social value of alcohol turned upon what it replaced. Obviously, its intrinsic intoxicating properties were the basis of interest, but its particular meaning and attraction depended upon the broader political and ceremonial use of indigenous narcotic beverages. In Tahiti and eastern Polynesia generally, drinking was not especially ritualized—in this respect there is a marked contrast with the hierarchical ceremonies of Tonga and Fiji—but consumption was more or less confined to those of high rank. The flaky or "scrofulous"[51] skin condition associated with excessive use was a "badge of honour," in one observer's words.[52] British kava was the special, foreign form of this marker of rank, but it seems that the frequent and intensive character of trade with foreign vessels in the 1820s and 1830s made it impossible for the chiefs to sustain this elite signification. The popularity of alcohol was such that in 1834 Queen Pomare made its possession and exchange illegal, with the result that at least one trader had a useless cargo.

I understand also that the Augustus had on board a good supply of rum for this market—but it so happened that the Queen & head chiefs had prohibited the use of it a short time before the Augustus arrived, making a penalty of $5 for any person (native or white man) that should become intoxicated, & $18 for any man that sold ardent spirits or even had them in his house—However there was some bought and smuggled ashore in the night—but for all that the rum market was knocked on the head.[53]

There had been earlier instances of attempts sponsored both by chiefs and the missionaries to suppress drinking; "notwithstanding his infatuated love of strong drink" Pomare II had ordered every still in Tahiti to be broken.[54] But were the concerns of the missionaries and the Tahitian elite the same? Although chiefs themselves submitted to abstinence for short periods, their disquiet may have derived from the erosion of semiotic privilege as much as from the spectacle of dissolution.

These prohibitions were never of durable effect—it must be said that some of the missionaries did not themselves set a good example[55]—and the fact that drinking rapidly became widespread among the ordinary Tahitian population may have a bearing on regional cultural differences which are manifest in the present. There is now a dramatic contrast between the eastern and western Pacific: in Vanuatu, Fiji, Tonga, and Samoa, kava drinking does not merely persist but has arguably become more significant both as a "traditional" cultural practice and as a new male activity in urban bars, whereas in the east, the narcotic has long been completely abandoned.[56] Although various forms of home brew and toddy are made locally, drinkers in such places as the Marquesas and Society Islands rely almost entirely upon industrially produced alcoholic drinks. The early cultural shift explains at least the initial phase of the history which produced this difference. The Tahitian option itself probably reflects more basic cultural differences, although there was something similar in the early western Polynesian attitude to alcohol. In Fiji, when Tanoa, the paramount chief of the Bauan confederacy, said that rum was the "true drink,"[57] he was no doubt using the word *dina* in its broader sense: truth, efficacy, power, and even a kind of divinity were mutually expressive.[58] But alcohol was never adopted in anything comparable to the Tahitian fashion by the elite; nor was it in wider demand by ordinary people as an article of trade. This may well have been because the new liquor could not sustain the elaborate ritual burden of *yaqona* (as kava is known in Fiji); it could not be presented as roots or in the green form as an offering to the chief, to be reciprocated or acknowledged in the gift of the drink—and the ceremonial contexts which demanded *yaqona* are too numerous to begin listing here. Although Fijians also called (and still call) "ardent spirits" *yaqona ni vavalagi* (foreigners' kava),[59] they could not effect the same categorical play which the unritualized if not exactly "secular" drink of chiefs permitted in Tahiti.

Earlier I argued essentially that goods which were imported into the Pacific cannot be seen as unproblematic equivalents of whatever we take them to be. To say that black bottles were given does not tell us what was received. This is so partly because the uses to which things were put were not inscribed in them by their metropolitan producers, and partly because gifts and commodities could be variously recontextualized as commodities or gifts, as unique articles for display, as artifacts of history, or as a new category of prestige valuable, the manipulation of which sustained the construction of political inequalities.

The cultural burden of objects is not, however, merely a consequence of there being distinct forms of prestation which can be characterized through distinct possibilities of alienation, circulation or restriction. Further specification of prestation types such as the "gift," the "potlatch," the "commodity," or the "offering" cannot generate economic practices as they were witnessed. The military theater which Porter got himself entangled in was cited as an illustration of the consequences of a political narrative. This was not the only case when a superpower navy helpfully intervened in the sideshows of imperial history, and this type of event led to indigenous mythologizations of the uses and effect of foreign power.

One trader remarked upon the economic astuteness and political brilliance of Hawaii's Napoleon—Kamehameha—"in creating resources which did not before exist."[60] This was not just a matter of using guns, adapting to European interests in local resources, or expressing status in new ways with European-style houses and glass windows. It was also a matter of commanding a narrative, purveying a certain interpretation of events, and maintaining its salience. Sahlins has shown that certain Hawaiian chiefs established themselves as inheritors of the *mana* of Cook and the British.[61] The case of Nukuhiva between 1813 and the French invasion of 1842 exemplifies, perhaps even more definitely, the control of one group—the chiefly people of Taiohae—over the association with Porter and its implications for hegemony. The case of alcohol in Tahiti concerned the specific import rather than the historic narrative, but it reveals that attempts to recontextualize goods in a particular manner can founder if supplies are too considerable, or if distribution cannot be controlled.

Material expressions of the symbolization, and perhaps ritual manipulation, of the foreign were occasionally encountered. Commodore Wilkes, of the U.S. Exploring Expedition, came across "an odd amusement of the natives . . . in the forest . . . near one of the heathen villages":

> A fine large tree had been lopt of its branches (except at the very top), for a mast; around this a framework of timber, after the model of a vessel, was constructed; all the timbers were carefully fastened together with sennit, and with the requisite curvature; from the bow a large and long piece of timber projected, and at the stern a rudder was contrived, with its tiller; but instead of ordinary movements as with us, it was intended to act vertically, in the way to which they are accustomed in managing or steering their large canoes with an oar; vines and creepers were used for the rigging; ballast had likewise been placed in the hold.
>
> This afforded them great amusement, and showed an ingenuity in construction of this Papalagi ship, as they called it, which had cost them much time and labour.[62]

Papalagi ship in Samoa in 1839.

But I have no history which can encompass this: the form of contact which prompted the construction is not well documented; and the intentions of those engaged surely amounted to "amusement" of a rather serious kind but are even more inaccessible.

Given this background in an innovative process of cultural extension and appropriation, and specific, though variable, symbolic constructions of European power, we can turn to consequences of trading relations at a systemic level through a case history I present in more detail.

The Whale Tooth Trade and Fijian Politics

The interest of Fijians in iron and various articles of trade was such, in the first half of the nineteenth century, that the list of ships seized, or attacked with a view to seizure, is long.[63] Guns were one of the main articles of trade, but chiefs were also eager to obtain the whale teeth mentioned in Chapter 2. I have elsewhere remarked upon the fact that various ethnographies of twentieth-century neotraditional Fijian society describe the ceremonial uses of *tabua* as though these manifested a timeless indigenous customary order, but it is all too apparent that early trade and subsequent fluctuations of supply have produced a succession of dynamic but unstable exchange regimes.[64]

As was mentioned above, various sources indicate that valuables named *tabua* were formerly made from shell or hardwood.[65] Although this observation seems culturally motivated—stress being placed upon the arbitrary attribution of value—it must be the case that other valuables were in use earlier. Before contact with Europeans, supplies of whale teeth were probably extremely limited. Whales did not frequently wash up on reefs in the Fiji group; even in the 1830s a few Fijians on a trading vessel to Tahiti were astounded by the entirely novel sight of a whale, although they evidently knew that the teeth came from some large sea creature.[66] The relatively small number of teeth which were in circulation earlier presumably came from Tonga, where whales are occasionally stranded.

The wider system through which *tabua* were introduced into Fiji can be briefly described. There was very little significant contact before 1800, but after 1801 sandalwood was discovered and sought after intensively in the period up to about 1814, when it had essentially been exhausted. William Lockerby, who resided in the islands in

1808–1809 and who interpreted and facilitated trade, prepared a sort of guide to traders, including navigational directions, some Fijian vocabulary, and notes on reliable and not so reliable chiefs. This document is singular as a source of information and in its spelling ("the people on this island are a set of Rubbers").

> The Articles of Traid to pleas the Natives are Ivory Iron Work such as Tools the best plan is to carry a forge with you & make the tools to sute them knives & scisors Beads they are very fond of—White shels & Cloth the two latter are to be got At the Islands to windward of MyGoro [Koro] should you tutch their however Ivory is the Most Vallable Article Made in the form of a Whales Tooth and those of them that is possessd of any of them lays them up as graet riches as porshens for their Daughters & Making peace with their offended Supirurs etc.[67]

Lockerby's assumption here is that ivory in some other form would be obtained and cut to resemble whale teeth; later, when whaling was being conducted extensively in the Pacific, mainly by American ships from New England ports and some English vessels, it was easier to obtain the actual whale teeth (which were artifacts for European sailors as well as Fijians). After sandalwood was exhausted, trade contracted for a few years but soon developed again around different products for the Manilla and Canton markets—*bêche-de-mer* and tortoiseshell. But because the routes of these vessels rarely intersected with those of the whalers, the teeth were obtained through rather circuitous paths. Whale ships frequently called at the island of Rotuma to the northwest of Fiji for provisions, and although the Rotumans did not themselves use whale teeth as valuables, they took these to exchange with the traders active in Fiji ("This island is a great resort for whalers from whom the natives obtain their whales teeth"). Trade took place both directly and through white middlemen resident on Rotuma. Tobacco, which was conveniently light and compact in relation to its value, was given in return; it was said to be "worth almost its '*weight in gold*' at this place."[68] At about the same time Tahiti similarly became a port through which teeth were effectively transhipped: "I understand that Vandervort gave a great price for a few whales teeth here . . . The people here natives and all have found out that teeth are valuable & ask a monstrous price for them—one large tooth that might weigh say 2 lbs. they wanted a dollar for—the Emerald was well supplied with that article of trade which are in great demand among Feejee-men."[69]

This description is indicative of the manner in which individual transactions, perhaps made by some European desperate for a cargo, could transform the appreciation of values, but it reveals more generally the broad ramifications of trade on particular islands. Exchanging feathers, whale teeth, or tortoiseshell for some local product did not create new economic relations merely upon that island, but required further transactions in other areas to produce the articles demanded, as well as to obtain food and fresh water, sexual services, and so on. Since many islanders were employed as crew, there was also an early form of labor recruitment, which occasioned cultural encounters between the inhabitants of widely separated Pacific islands, sparking off a great deal of innovation in such areas as material culture and political practice.

To turn more specifically to transactions associated with *tabua* in Fiji, and their implications, it must be appreciated that the conduct and organization of trade was essentially upon Fijian terms to which

The whale tooth as European valuable, early to mid-nineteenth-century scrimshaw design. On the reverse is a poem reading, "Oh Great Jehova heed the prayers / Of we who hunt the whale / and speed our harpoons straight oh Lord / Each voyage that we sail / Make bold our hearts spread wide our fame / Throughout the Seven Seas / And blow our ships safe home upon / a fair and gentle breeze."

foreigners were obliged to adapt. This was apparent even at the level of language use: the owner of a ship could presume, in his instructions to the captain, to stress that "it should be your first object to acquire a knowledge of their language."[70] As far as transactions and the organization of collecting *bêche-de-mer* was concerned, the cooperation of chiefs was indispensable. *Tabua* were used not so much in payment for *bêche-de-mer* as in ritualized presentations to chiefs, made routinely upon arrival at a place and at certain other times. For example, when J. H. Eagleston (of the *Peru*) first visited the small chiefly island of Bau, which he took to be "the capital of all the Feejees," a ceremony was conducted, which in its general form appears to be essentially the same as modern *isevusevu* (offerings on arrival or in connection with a request).

> On landing I was conducted by the king and his high official, followed by a great crowd of natives to the [*bure*], which was large and spacious: all sitting down on the mats that covered the floor, myself near the king, with a space in front, and in a few words from his official speaker, received a savage welcome, when Mr. King [a Fijian speaker], taking a fine whale's tooth I had given him for the occasion, placed it on the mat and stated my business among them. It was received by the speaker who made quite a speech, bidding us welcome to the island, and hoped we would be successful in obtaining a full load of the articles wanted, as also all that had been saved from the brig [the wrecked *Glide*], and hoped we would bring them plenty of muskets, powder, lead &c. At the end of these sayings, Vinacka, Vinacka [*vinaka*—good], was repeated, followed by their usual slapping of hands and thighs. The drinking of Angona [*yaqona*— kava] closed the sitting.[71]

The American-Fijian encounter entailed both gift exchange and direct barter. Apart from ceremonial presentations of *tabua* of the type described, whale teeth were given on other occasions; chiefs and chiefs' wives also solicited and received a variety of other goods, such as red paint, fabric, and beads. These were often reciprocated with cooked food,[72] which was also sometimes sent off by "treacherous" natives who sought to falsely convey goodwill while designing to attack or seize a ship.[73] Trade was a two-level process: periodic high-value gifts to chiefs were a precondition for any economic engagement at all, while *bêche-de-mer* and tortoiseshell were reciprocated more directly to producers, usually with guns, associated supplies (such as powder), and iron implements.

Although it is difficult to estimate in any precise way the *total* number of muskets and other goods which were imported, lists from certain ships are available. Eagleston's trade, consisting of guns and many other "notions" (smaller articles such as beads) had cost $3,000; this included one lot of four hundred muskets, but it is not clear whether these were the only ones on board.[74] It appears to have been not uncommon to carry four to six hundred pounds (weight) of whale teeth, which, at about two pounds each, represented two to three hundred *tabua*. The profits from the sandalwood trade had been very high, and even for the later period Eagleston frequently noted the "small cost" of what was received—"I bought nine head of beautiful tortoiseshell weighing thirty pounds; worth in the States $360. I paid for same three muskets that cost $1.25 each."[75] However, the volume of what was given to Fijians was also considerable, and the consequences of the introduction of huge quantities of guns and other goods have occasioned debate. In most discussions so far *tabua* have been neglected; many earlier writers and a few recent scholars have emphasized the consequences of imports of guns, while others have stressed continuity despite contact and the persistence of "paths of the land." The issue of external stimuli versus indigenous agency and appropriation thus arises again.

As they were witnessed by observers in the first half of the nineteenth century, Fijian polities took the form of regionally extensive and highly stratified confederations. Tributary relationships brought vast quantities of food to elite centers, where the elaborate houses, canoes, and other forms of material wealth and ritual status were at a great remove from the living conditions of local chiefs in subordinate places, as well as those of ordinary people in general.[76] Warfare and ceremonies were conducted on an extravagant scale, and the fineness of chiefly ornaments, barkcloth, and weapons was much remarked upon. The paradoxical conjuncture of aristocratic refinement and the pronounced violence of warfare and despotism remained unresolved in many European accounts: here were savage nobles, rather than noble savages.[77]

This ethnocentric sense of inconsistency was reflected in claims that Fijians were not really the producers of their kingdoms; it was widely suggested from the 1840s onward into modern ethnohistorical literature that the hierarchical confederations (*matanitu*) were not autochthonous Fijian inventions but rather the products of contact, supplies of guns, and particularly the adventurism of a few European deserters of bad character. The most notorious of these was Charlie Savage, a survivor of the 1808 wreck of the *Eliza*, who was credited with introducing firearms and being personally responsible for the expansion of the Bauan polity. His story, often retold in historical asides in missionary books and travel narratives, retains currency in popular history in Fiji today. R. A. Derrick, the author of an official history which is still in print, places great emphasis on Savage's historical effect: "He introduced firearms to Bau, and the Vunivalu [paramount war chief]—Naulivou—was quick to see the advantage they would give him in his wars . . . his aim was excellent . . . [in] an attack on Kasavu, a village on the Rewa River . . . The victims were so numerous that the townspeople piled up the bodies and sheltered behind them; and the stream beside the village ran red . . . [such] bloody campaigns laid the foundations of Bau's political power."[78]

The hyperbolic and anecdotal approach to history does imply a cultural interest in a spectacular *Boys' Own* story—the fatal conjuncture of ambitious barbarians and wild Europeans producing the disorder that only British colonial authority could supplant—but the rendering of the Fijian past cannot be commented upon further here. The thesis that hierarchical confederations did not exist before contact collapses in the face of abundant evidence for both political expansion before consequential contact and similar earlier centralized states. The specific connections postulated between foreign involvement and political expansion have also been demonstrated elsewhere to be unsustainable: the particular hegemonies clearly existed before the alleged interference of persons such as Savage (although it may well be so that his intervention in some particular fights was effective).[79]

Historians' careful reappraisals of the evidence do make the important point that existing political processes became adjusted to, rather than overturned by, new weapons and new trade relations, but they overlook the fact that stories about Savage's involvement were told frequently *by Fijians*.[80] While there is no doubt that the historical significance of individual Europeans has been distorted and magnified, the Fijians themselves may have had some interest in mystification. Although the implicit conclusions concerning the significance of European involvement were obviously different, the narrative would presumably not have been repeated if it lacked political and cultural salience: there must have been some interest in linking conquest to the presence of foreign warriors in a king's retinue and to the use of guns. There was perhaps some parallel to the manifest interest of Fijian chiefs in associations with Tongan warriors, who frequently numbered among followers or attendants.[81] The appeal of such individuals as Savage would have been consistent with the broader interest in guns and warfare in Fiji but did not amount to a narrative which was manipulated by any particular group: although this story has something general in common with the mythologization of Porter, in that the excitement of warfare and competition was heightened through a connection with foreign power, there is no direct parallel with the Marquesan case, because Fijian chiefs were never considered to be the inferiors or successors to powerful invasive foreigners. It is clear that beachcombers such as Savage and William Diaper, who repaired weapons and provided other military services, were no more than the privileged servants of chiefs.

Whale teeth were—or came to be—used in a wide range of cere-monial contexts: in installations to chiefly titles, at mortuary ceremonies, at presentations of children to their material kin; and from the start they were were certainly used, as Lockerby noted, in marriage, which was indissociable from regional political relations. Tabua were also used to request and acknowledge assistance in political trouble and war, and thus figured prominently in exchanges between chiefs and those referred to as the "teeth" or the "edge" of the land—the warrior-subjects who stood in a protective but privileged relationship to the sacred titleholders. In 1834 George Cheever witnessed a cere-mony after a battle between Bau and Rewa where a Bauan man of chiefly rank had been killed. The warriors brought the body "or-namented with a white flag" to Rewa and after performing a chant seated themselves respectfully while the "king" presented them with spears, "about 100 fathom of Tapper [barkcloth]," and presented a *tabua* to the man who had actually killed the chief. After receiving their gifts the warriors reasserted their loyalty in a ritual manner by striking their clubs in the ground.[82] Ordinary relations of this type would no doubt have been consolidated by the capacity of chiefs—who were virtually the sole recipients of whale teeth from traders—to draw on new supplies of valuables.

The use of *tabua* in more singular cases of political upheaval is exemplified by two cases, both involving violent conflict within elite families. In the early 1830s bad relations developed between

Tabaiwalu, then the paramount chief of Rewa, and his son Koroitamana; ill-feeling was generated, as was typical, by rivalries between co-wives and their sons; the latter were, of course, potential and competing successors to the title. The conflict gradually escalated until Koroitamana, confident that he would be supported by a number of high-ranking men and warriors, assassinated his father. But the chief's principal wife, Adi Dreketi, successfully deceived the people of the town, leading them to believe that her husband was still alive, though very weak, and that he wanted his son killed. A meeting took place, at which the general opinion reputedly expressed was that Koroitamana's conduct had been justifiable and provoked, although many also "feared the wrath of the king, in case he should recover." Hearing of the uncertainty, the "queen" settled matters by taking "some whales' teeth and other valuables, and presented them herself to the chiefs, saying they were sent by the king to purchase the death of his son." Whether the general belief actually was that the king was still alive is not clear; in any event, it was not long before Koroitamana was clubbed. [83]

A case which had much wider ramifications for the polities of central and eastern Fiji in the 1830s was the "coup"—Fijians do make the analogy with the military takeovers of 1987—against Tanoa, the paramount chief at Bau. A faction based around his half-brothers seized power, and Tanoa was fortunate to escape assassination himself but was exiled to Somosomo between 1832 and 1836. From this base, and subsequently from Rewa, he began to build up his support among the people subject to Bau, but the process which was perhaps more crucial for his return to power was recovering the internal support of the Bauan clans. This was effected by his son, Seru (subsequently known as Cakobau), particularly through a steady stream of gifts of *tabua* to the Lasakau group, who played a crucial role in a brief but decisive fight which actually displaced the rebel side. [84]

It may have been significant that at least some of the traders were favorably disposed toward Tanoa rather than toward those who had ousted him;[85] but it is not clear that anyone ever refused to trade with the rebellious party, which certainly would have had some supplies of whale teeth and other valuables. The sorts of things done by Adi Dreketi and Cakobau were being done all the time but simply in a more timely, selective, and effective manner by some chiefs and chiefly women than by others. Because trade was generalized rather than monopolized, and because there was much circulation of articles once introduced, no individuals or chiefly factions were singularly advantaged to the detriment of others.

There are a number of parallels to this large-scale European introduction of articles already functioning as valuables within a particular system; in the 1930s, for example, prospectors such as Michael Leahy flew vast quantities of pearl shells up into the New Guinea highlands, which they traded for food and labor.[86] Some diminution of value obviously takes place as the quantities of these articles in a particular area rise over the years, but it does not seem quite right for anthropologists to suggest that the main process has been a "democratization" of the use of particular valuables.[87] It is unclear whether this interpretation relates to practices or to access to objects, and at one level it is quite misleading in implying that there is some overall reduction of inequality. In the Mount Hagen area there is evidence that a more rigid rank structure existed in the early contact period, but new kinds of inequality connected with cash crops have emerged. In the Fijian case, the introduction of considerable supplies of weapons and *tabua* clearly led to the intensification of existing dynamics and particular struggles. Warfare escalated, and there was a protracted conflict between Bau and Rewa in the 1840s, which entailed widespread destruction of dependent villages and greater loss of life than probably occurred in earlier wars. Insofar as there were shifts in the balance of power, they occurred at a wider level, in the sense that the coastal polities as a group must have increased their strength with respect to the inhabitants of smaller islands and various interior populations of the larger islands. In the second half of the century, guns were certainly traded throughout the interior of even the largest island of Viti Levu, but whatever access people there had probably was achieved through asymmetrical exchange relations which had not existed earlier.

Prior Systems and Later Histories

The remarkable capacity of the Fijian system—or at least of the chiefs of the first half of the nineteenth century—to absorb and put to use a new set of trading relations and imports might be taken to attest to a general theoretical principle about the capacity of local systems to appropriate introduced goods. It is certainly important to recognize the processes of selective indigenous recognition and use of foreign contact, and—in opposition to such views as those articulated by Julia Blackburn—to insist upon the historically particular character of the form of appropriation. But the singularity of the Fijian case must be taken into account, and assertions of indigenous agency which merely mirror the thesis of overdetermination by the world system cannot deal with the very different capacities of some indigenous exchange systems and polities to manage or seize upon the potential of foreign contact.

As I noted in Chapter 2, a feature which distinguishes the Fijian systems within the spectrum of Pacific exchange regimes is the possibility of a wide range of conversions between services, valuables, debts, assistance, and, not least, spouses. The fact that, paradigmatically, the whale tooth stood for a woman meant that it was a signifier for, and a means to, an open-ended kin path of debt and exchange. As in any other system, marriage created a broader set of relations, but in the Fijian case these had distinctive political potential. The system was essentially hypergamous, such that women from tributary places, or at least groups of lower status, were taken as wives to the political centers such as Bau and Cakaudrove. Their sons were sacred nephews (vasu) to their chiefly mother's brothers and could appropriate anything from the domains of the latter, as was amply attested to by such witnesses as Diaper and Eagleston. What was received was thus not merely useful in some immediate fashion but also could be placed into circulation, either to recompense warriors for their fighting services, to extend marriage alliances, to request assistance, to restitute canoes, or simply to redistribute goods to foster support and to develop the sense that the chiefdom was a fount of wealth and the ruler essentially generous.

Moreover, there was no contradiction between this positive process of deploying imports for political purposes and the production of what was to be extracted. The resources which the traders wanted were mostly not significant for Fijians. There is no suggestion that bêche-de-mer was eaten by Fijians; if so, it could only have been marginal to a diversified subsistence base. Curiously, tortoiseshell, which was used extensively in some Pacific material cultures, did not feature much in Fijian ornaments or regalia;[88] and sandalwood also was either not used at all or insignificant.[89] Although the preparation of bêche-de-mer did involve substantial commitments of labor, the activities were not unlike the collective efforts associated with certain projects such as canoe building, warfare, or preparing for ceremonies in areas away from one's home village. Fijians did not, in any case, agree to work continuously if there were other things that they wanted to do, and in some cases traders could do nothing but feel frustrated for days or weeks at a time when something exciting like a fight or a large ceremony took their workers away.[90] It was also, of course, necessary to provision trading vessels,[91] but their relatively limited demands were met by different groups over quite a wide area—the scatter of islands in central Fiji, the Lau group, and the coasts of Viti Levu and Vanua Levu— and could easily be accommodated. This was so because the ceremonial economy in Fiji was already developed to an enormous extent: there were many forms of intensive irrigated horticulture, and food was routinely produced to be offered up for ceremonial exchange—in some areas specifically for barter through specialized production networks. When accounts are read of feasts at which many thousands of yams or taros and dozens or occasionally hundreds of pigs and turtles were presented,[92] it is not difficult to imagine the smaller needs of ships being relatively easily dealt with.

This is not to say that there were not problematic longer-term ecological consequences; for instance, R. G. Ward has pointed out that the quantity of firewood required to smoke and cure the *bêche-de-mer* was enormous and must have reduced coastal forests around Bua and those other parts of Vanua Levu which supplied the "fish" considerably. Overcollection diminished supplies of *bêche-de-mer*, while sandalwood was virtually obliterated in a short period. From a shorter-term perspective, however, there was a good deal of compatibility between the interests of traders and the Fijians. The indigenous ceremonial economy did not depend upon goods which were being extracted to any excessive extent, while what was introduced was of considerable cultural and political use.

The point perhaps emerges more sharply through contrast with the Marquesas. In the later phases of the period discussed in the previous chapter, the trade essentially consisted in exports of pork and other food in return for guns and related supplies. Yet the Marquesan system did not function through value conversions in a manner at all similar to the Fijian system. Marriage seems to have been more a matter of direct exchange and although there was a certain amount of internal barter, this was not the basis for relations of prestigious social value. Inequalities were instead worked through and expressed in competitive presentations of food; these were connected closely with matters of the greatest ritual consequence, such as the commemoration of powerful shamans and chiefs. The estimation of individuals and groups was intimately connected with the capacity to stage such events and to consume what was received.

As was noted, supplies of muskets seem temporarily to have created another kind of socioeconomic asymmetry, where presentations of them created indebtedness on the part of the receivers, who had no independent access to monopolized supplies. But this form of exchange had limited political potential because there was no scope in the prior system for regional tributary relationships, seemingly no model for some kind of persisting regional domination. Had the trade relationship been tightly controlled over a longer period, it is possible that the hegemony of the monopolizing group might have been consolidated, but in the last years before the French invasion of 1842, when local chiefs were dismissively pushed aside in the course of many other acts of violence, it appears that the reverse occurred: certainly the military gains made by the Vaitahu people in the early to mid 1830s were not extended or consolidated over the following years. To invoke a rather crude market mechanism, it is probable that rising supplies of muskets led to some "debasement" of their significance as scarce prestige articles.

Guns thus lacked the potential of Fijian *tabua* to be converted into social projects or relations of alliance. Although they had broad cultural weight and were certainly markers of status, they did not actually help their owners accomplish other things. More fundamentally, there was a direct contradiction between what ships wanted to take away and the basis of the Marquesan competitive feasting system. Pork was not only a crucial element of this political "fighting with food" but was also, of course, of ritual importance: certain animals were raised specifically for commemorative feasts for many ordinary people as well as for renowned chiefs and shamans. And there may not have been much scope for diverting beasts from feasting to trade: the evidence is not good, but it seems that there never were considerable numbers of pigs in the islands. Supplying ships would thus certainly have undermined the other competitive and religious activities.

There are many travel books and official and missionary letters which convey a sense of disillusionment and apathy among Marquesans after the French annexation, and in especially intense and tragic terms in the late nineteenth and early twentieth centuries. Rather than repeating verbose and patronizing accounts of cultural despair, I aim to specify precisely what it was about trading entanglement—in addition to the drastic character of disease and depopulation[93]—which engendered such acute social and cultural decline. It may be that the conjunction of the form and purposes of indigenous exchange, together with traders' demands, made it impossible to conduct certain ritual activities properly, and at the same time diminished the status of the prominent people who had formerly focused their energies upon organizing such events. The decapitation of Marquesan hierarchy was of course accomplished through French assault, an external irruption that had no endogenous determination or logic. The dispersed and ineffective character of resistance can, however, be traced to the undermining of indigenous institutions and to some extent to the character of those institutions prior to contact.

These differences have ramifications even for later histories. It is striking that in Fiji the indigenous elite still retains an extraordinary degree of formal political power, which was reaffirmed by the military coups of 1987, while chiefly families are unknown or invisible in the Marquesas, as they are throughout French Polynesia. In the Fijian case, this has always been traced to the benevolent colonialism and indirect rule system of governors John Bates Thurston and Arthur Hamilton Gordon, but it is notable that the British policy elsewhere was different. Although the positions of individual chiefs such as King Cakobau were in some cases precarious and problematic around the time of Cession, it was precisely their strength as a class which made indirect rule feasible and desirable, just as the weak and partly discredited character of Marquesan chieftainship made it easier for the French to ignore and suppress traditional eastern Polynesian chiefs; their example was followed by the Americans in Hawaii and the Chileans in Easter Island.

Contrasts of a similar order can be traced through the recent histories and rather different societies of Papua New Guinea. The distinction discussed at length in the previous chapter between value-conversion systems, which substitute people for things and labor, and "brideservice" societies, in which such transformations are not possible, perhaps has some bearing upon differing histories of engagement with commercial farming (involving such cash crops as coffee and copra). In a well-known study entitled *Big-Men and Business*, Ben

Finney overlooked this axis of variation in New Guinea societies and asserted that a "wealth-prestige orientation" was general: most Papua New Guinea populations were said to "share the basic Melanesian values and institutions that link wealth, prestige, and leadership."[94] He proceeded to argue that they were thus *preadapted* for engagement in economic development; in making comparisons between the extent to which this had occurred in various societies, Finney derived the causes of variation in distinct colonial histories: in some cases Europeans had been more destructive than elsewhere. In fact, most of the groups discussed (such as the Tolai, famous for their shell money) would have to be categorized as "bridewealth" and value-substitution oriented groups anyway,[95] but there was no attempt to link variation in indigenous economies to different kinds of "preadaptation."[96] The actual colonial economic histories have, of course, been very important, and one could hardly expect to make precise correlations between prior systemic characteristics and the outcomes of messy, locale-specific, complicated events; but it is nevertheless striking that the societies which represent extreme cases on the brideservice end of the continuum (such as the Umeda, various lowland Papuan groups, and the Baining of New Britain) have almost always had difficult relations with outsiders and have displayed great reluctance to get involved with wage labor or cash farming. The notion of "preadaptation" is an unfortunate one in that it implies that these tribal systems *ought* to be oriented toward capitalism and that there is some internal fault if they are not; but the arguments of scholars such as Finney usefully draw attention to the mutual imbrication of indigenous and capitalist relations and raise the issue of the extent to which some economies are far less compatible with cash crops or related forms of development than others.

Something as simple as the movement of an object thus needs to be heard and said and talked about, rather than simply seen. The circulation of objects, especially across the edges of societies, civilizations, and trading regimes, is not merely a physical process but is also a movement and displacement of competing conceptions of things, a jostle of transaction forms. Global economies do not control the meanings of the commodities that their profits turn upon, even if the appropriation of these goods in the form of gifts, commodities, or prestige valuables inevitably entangles receivers in wider relations that are not easily shrugged off. The examples I have discussed confirm that precolonial systems could not determine subsequent histories but do reveal that the colonial process was influenced by the structures and events of early contact, just as these in turn were influenced by autonomous, precolonial cultural and social dynamics. Facts that may appear esoteric—the permutations of debt and prehistories of local exchange—are thus implicated in a global narrative of imperial history, which has remained unconscious of the peripheral representations and transactions that later made dispossession and autonomy, development and exploitation, more possible in one colony than another.

4

⚜

The European Appropriation of
Indigenous Things

. . . we were entertained with various new and striking objects.

George Forster, A *Voyage round the World*, 1777

All the others came empty in respect to refreshments, but brought
with them some arms such as Clubs, darts, &c which they exchanged away, indeed these things generally found the best Market
with us, such was the prevailing Passion for curiosities, or what appeared new. As I have had occasion to make this remark more than
once before, the reader will think the Ship must be full of such articles by this time, he will be misstaken, for nothing is more
Common than to give away what has been collected at one Island
for any thing new at a Nother, even if it is less curious, this together
with what is distroyed on board after the owners are tired with
looking at them, prevents any considerable increase.

James Cook, *Journals*, 1774

As socially and culturally salient entities, objects change in defiance of
their material stability. The category to which a thing belongs, the
emotion and judgment it prompts, and the narrative it recalls, are all
historically refigured. What was English or French, in becoming
Inuit, is reconstituted socially through indigenous categorization; similarly, what was Igbo or Javanese, in becoming American or Australian, now conveys something of our projects in foreign places and our
aesthetics—something which effaces the intentions of the thing's producers.

Museums are crammed with indigenous artifacts: stone tools,
carved bowls, clubs, spears, baskets, pots, barkcloth, mats, pipes, shell
money, *preserved heads*, anthropomorphic images, fishhooks, nets,

canoes, headdresses, feather cloaks, hatchets, garments, ornaments
. . . I have never quite understood why people want to look at such
things (although I often look at them myself). These museum arrays
are organized differently but are broadly similar from one metropolitan
or Third World institution to another. But the familiarity of such
displays may be misleading, if it permits us to think of these objects in
stable ensembles. We must ask why these objects were acquired and
what their collectors thought they were doing. And we must ask what
the genealogies of European representation are.

This chapter cannot attempt to grasp all the moments and styles of
Western interest. It is oriented mainly to collecting practices in the
islands and discourses of collection, rather than museum histories or
other primarily metropolitan developments.[1] The progression is
roughly chronological, and the focus of interest the distinctions between the perceptions of certain groups of foreign visitors and settlers:
explorers, missionaries, planters, colonial officials, and ethnologists.[2]

European interests in indigenous Pacific artifacts were manifest
from the earliest visits and observations. The three voyages of Captain
Cook are of particular interest because extended contact was made
with a wide range of Pacific islanders, which initiated a comparative
discourse of evolutionary assessments encompassing native physique,
temperament, and to some extent material culture; these questions
arose particularly for the ethnologist and natural scientist Johann
Reinhold Forster, who was accompanied by his son George on the
second voyage from 1772 to 1775. Interests in artifacts were also
manifest in a number of other popular travel works of the time, some
of which, such as Keate's *Account of the Pelew Islands* (the
Micronesian islands now properly called Belau),[3] are particularly relevant to the general problem considered here: the extent to which, in
this period, any unitary discursive project encompassed the interest in
tools and ornaments which were being apprehended by Europeans for
the first time. Later groups of colonizers were also sometimes unde-
cided, or inconsistent, in their purposes and evaluations, but lack the
singular indeterminacy of the eighteenth-century explorers.

Curiosity: Colonialism in Its Infancy

The artifacts of non-Western peoples were known over a long period
as "curiosities." Occasionally, this term, or "curios,"[4] also embraced

certain kinds of antiques and classical relics, and (in the absence of the qualifier "artificial") even natural specimens—coral, bones, and mineral samples. The connotations of such labels shifted, and in some contexts the words arguably do not tell us much about either the cultural construction of the things collected or the notion of the process of collecting. However, the literature of the famous late eighteenth-century voyages of exploration is suffused with the notion of curiosity,[5] both as a subjective attitude and as an attribute of things noticed. An attempt to map European interests in artifacts in the period could thus take seriously the idea that a collection of curiosities in some sense stood as an objectification of the culturally and historically specific form of intellectual and experiential desire which "curiosity" alluded to.

This is to express, perhaps in extreme terms, a tension between a scientifically controlled interest in further knowledge and an unstable "curiosity" which is not authorized by any methodological or theoretical discourse, and is grounded in passion rather than reason. A negative or at least ambivalent attitude to curiosity was explicitly elaborated in the opening section of Burke's *Philosophical Enquiry* (1757):

> The first and the simplest emotion which we discover in the human mind, is Curiosity. By curiosity, I mean whatever desire we have for, or whatever pleasure we take in novelty. We see children, perpetually running from place to place to hunt out something new; they catch with great eagerness, and with very little choice, at whatever comes before them; their attention is engaged by every thing, because every thing has, in that stage of life, the charm of novelty to recommend it. But as those things which engage us merely by their novelty, cannot attach us for any length of time, curiosity is the most superficial of all the affections; it changes its object perpetually; it has an appetite which is very sharp, but very easily satisfied; and it has always an appearance of giddiness, restlessness and anxiety.[6]

Although reference is made here to the active or vigorous character of curiosity, there is a more fundamental sense in which the condition places the subject in a passive relation to the diversity of the object world: a plethora of new things present themselves but are not subsumed into intellectual purposes. The curious person represented by Burke does not assert a classificatory rule or arrive at any idea of the import or origin of things; in his compelling image, curiosity is above all an infantile condition, and one which would apparently be disconnected from anything other than impressionistic judgment and from any analytical work upon phenomena, such as the classificatory project of natural history. The intellect is, as it were, overcome by desire, and rendered giddy by a succession of encounters with the novel.

But how could this child-like attitude figure in the context of major exploratory voyages, generally sanctioned by the state, the navy, and the Royal Society, which postulated the disclosure of the novel as a legitimate and noble endeavor? Of course, from an official perspective the project was prompted by particular scientific and practical questions, such as the existence of the great southern land; the outcomes of these inquiries took such unsentimental forms as accurate charts, coastal profiles, and tables of astronomical and meteorological observations. But Burke's observations accord closely with Cook's account of the "Passion" among sailors for novel artifacts, which was manifestly so extreme as to prompt local parody in Tonga: "It was astonishing to see with what eagerness everyone [the sailors] catched at every thing they saw, it even went so far as to become the ridicule of the Natives by offering pieces of sticks stones and what not to exchange, one waggish Boy took a piece of human excrement on a stick and hild it out to every one of our people he met with."[7]

The ambiguity of curiosity is more generally pertinent to the encounters with exotic peoples which, for everyone apart from the Admiralty, were certainly the most interesting feature of the expeditions. The introduction to George Keate's *Account of the Pelew Islands* (1788) justifies the work partly in relation to the importance and popularity of narratives such as those of Cook: "The relations of these several voyages having excited a great spirit of enquiry, and awakened an eager curiosity to every thing that can elucidate the history of mankind, I flatter myself, that no apology is necessary for my bringing forward the following work, whose *Novelty* and *Authenticity* will, I trust, insure it a favourable reception."[8]

The "double claim" is elaborated upon at some length, but there is an odd lack of specificity in the anthropological understanding that is offered:

Nothing can be more interesting to Man than the history of Man. The navigators of different ages have pictured to us our own species in a variety of lights . . . we observe a wonderful disparity; some are found under that darkness and absolute barbarism, from the sight of which humanity gladly turns aside;—whilst others, unaided, unassisted, but by mere natural good sense, have not only emerged from this gloomy shade, but nearly attained that order, propriety and good conduct, which constitute the essence of *real* civilization . . . The mind of inquisitive man, too eager after knowledge which his limited faculties can never reach, often idly asks - *Wherefore all the varied gradations of human existence?* But his question will remain forever unanswered . . . He will be far more wisely employed in feeling with becoming gratitude, that he was not destined himself to be an inhabitant of TERRA DEL FUEGO, or to add one to the number of the forlorn savages of the NORTHERN POLE.[9]

Keate proceeded to suggest that a more legitimate question, which (as he accurately predicted) might in the future be successfully investigated, concerned the peopling of the numerous islands, but this topic is clearly on quite a different level from the grand question concerning human diversity with which he begins. The more abstract philosophical issue is posed, and in a sense justifies the whole presentation, but readers are then told that difference—or perhaps its specific occurrence and distribution—cannot be explained by human beings. Since the evolutionary distinctions between contemporaneous but geographically separated peoples or "nations" were taken to be virtually axiomatic, Keate could not derive any general proposition about the "history of Man" from the information obtained on voyages. Instead, previously unknown societies merely further illustrated the diversity of the species; the author in fact felt "some satisfaction in being the instrument of introducing to the world a *new people*" who he suggested were "an *ornament* to human nature."[10]

This would perhaps explain why enlightenment evaluations from both British and French[11] voyages of south Pacific societies were frequently indeterminate or qualified: observations of barbaric practices conflicted with the acknowledgment that there were elements of civilization, and an idea that a particular people were generally ugly might be offset by remarks upon their intelligence.[12] This is not to dispute that there were essentially racist features of the discourse in general. A certain distance and attribution of inferiority is intrinsic to an evolutionary understanding, however qualified and disguised by positive local observations or ironic reflection upon the faults of Europe. The discriminations made between certain populations, such as the Polynesians and Australians, seem particularly invidious. But it is significant that customs, occurrences, and artifacts were frequently referred to by neutral terms such as "striking," "interesting," "singular," "peculiar" or "curious." In particular, such words were used to express the interest aroused by examples of indigenous material culture. As Bernard Smith noted, "to say that an object was 'curious' was to express an interest in it without passing an aesthetic judgement. Thus Parkinson speaks of New Zealand paddles as 'curiously stained,' fish-hooks and whistles as 'curiously carved,' and Maoris as 'curiously tattooed.'"[13]

There are many similar statements in the accounts of the second voyage. Cook found a Tongan coconut-fiber apron "curious," a Marquesan head ornament was "a curious fillet of shell work decorated with feathers &c";[14] for Johann Reinhold Forster, Maori wooden axes were "commonly curiously carved"; the dresses Tahitian women wore while dancing were "singular and remarkable"; the same Marquesan "diadems" remarked upon by Cook were "curious";[15] George Forster noted that bone arrowpoints at Malekula were "curiously and firmly united together by means of single coconut fibres," but he ambiguously described the Tahitian mourning costume as "whimsical."[16] Similar observations are made in what seems to be the only extant account by a common sailor: "Several of [the Marquesans] had caps very curiously wrought in shapes not inelegant, and composed of feathers interspersed with spangles of mother of pearl, that looked very gay and were very becoming."[17]

In the last case the proposition that a thing was curious could clearly drift into more definitely positive reactions. But most of the statements marked a novel or different thing which had just been observed as interesting (somewhat tautologically—only what was notable would be noted), while not characterizing in any manner the content of its significance. As Smith noted, with respect particularly to statements made on Cook's first voyage, aesthetic judgments were avoided; he adds that during the second and third voyages "comment upon the whole was more favourable."[18] This is to imply that there was a progression toward an attitude which could appreciate indigenous craftwork and art, a move away from the pattern whereby observers refrained from evaluation. This is certainly broadly discernible, but the indeterminacy may relate more to a certain inability, to a lack; for at this time there was no established anthropological discourse which actually linked propositions about artifacts to ethnological theory or political description in a systematic way. The notion that the whole array of artifacts and goods produced or used by a particular people could be construed as their "material culture"—a sort of physical counterpart to the totality of their manners and customs or social institutions—was the product of subsequent theory. This is not to say that there was nothing to motivate interests in artifacts in the 1770s, but there was a gap in the sense that there was no developed language through which their relevance to other things observed, or the purpose of the expedition, could be specified. Hence, observers either resorted to the vague and essentially vacuous terms quoted above or restricted themselves to strictly descriptive wording which conveyed no judgment and which effected no positioning at all. Among the "trifles" brought by Tongans for sale were "clubs which are Rhomboidal Pyramids below, with round handles above, & sometimes carved over & over; little sticks which they put in their Ears, which are perforated with two holes, & these sticks are of a reed filled with a red solid Substance or of Turtle Shell, or of a white Shell . . ."[19]

While there is a good deal of language of this sort, judgments about workmanship and the elegance or unattractiveness of items were also advanced though frequently not coherently. George Forster found Malekulan canoes "of indifferent workmanship," but the bows of the same people were "strong, elastic, and nicely polished," and their poisoned arrows "very neatly ornamented."[20] In some cases an ambivalent or ambiguous attitude toward particular pieces is manifest: "I observed a curious spear, whereon a curious face was carved in the grotesque manner"; "the heads of these canoes are commonly finely carved representing in a coarse manner a human figure, lolling out its Tongue, with Eyes of mother of pearl."[21] Reference to "the" grotesque manner almost implies that a style or form of stylization is posited, while the second quotation might be taken to separate the quality of the carving from the image carved. There is, of course, no reason why a visitor should not have had different reactions to different artifacts, or to technique and image, but the failure to arrive at any overall view underlines the extent to which the observation of manufactured articles was not subordinated to, or defined by, more general discursive projects. The point is not just that aesthetic adjudications are often absent, hesitant, or mutually uninformative, but that even when clearly expressed, they do not necessarily operate as a vehicle for the assessment of a particular people or their situation with respect to other

natives observed. There is thus a marked contrast between these observations and ethnographic remarks about the position of women in
particular societies, which are elaborated upon, quite explicitly, as a
direct indicator of relative social advancement. While descriptions of
Maori, Marquesan, Tongan, Tahitian, New Caledonian, and
Malekulan material culture all contain a certain mixture of positive
and negative propositions, the treatment of women as "beasts of
burden," and their postulated physical ugliness in the New Hebrides
(Vanuatu) and New Caledonia separated these groups sharply and
unambiguously from those to the east such as the Tongans and
Tahitians.

> The more debased the situation of a nation is, and of course the more re-
> mote from civilization, the more harshly we found the women treated.[22]

> In O-Taheitee, the Society, the Friendly Isles, and the Marquesas, the
> fair sex is already raised to a greater equality with the men; and if, from
> no other reason, from this alone we might be allowed to pronounce that
> these islanders have emerged from the state of savages, and ought to be
> ranked one remove from barbarians. For the more the women are es-
> teemed in a nation, the more it appears that the original harshness of
> manners is softened, the more the people are capable of tender feelings,
> mutual attachment, and social virtues, which naturally lead them toward
> the blessings of civilization.[23]

It is clear here that perceptions of gender operated in a very powerful
way as a sign for the grade of social advancement: Johann Reinhold
Forster in fact suggests that what was seen as relative sexual equality
in such places as Tahiti was the central and sufficient condition for
judging those people as standing on a higher level than the islanders
of the western Pacific. Although the formulation of distinctions which
separated the latter as "Melanesians" did not take place until later, the
differences noted in the eighteenth century carried precisely the same
evolutionary resonance.[24] As far as questions of migrations and "fa-
milial" relations among the populations of various islands and island
groups were concerned, language was referred to more frequently than
physique, and both more frequently and systematically than similarities or differences in material artifacts.[25] Hence, although there was
great emerging interest in the classification and hierarchization of
islanders, technology and material culture played a weak and minor
role in this major work of European representation.

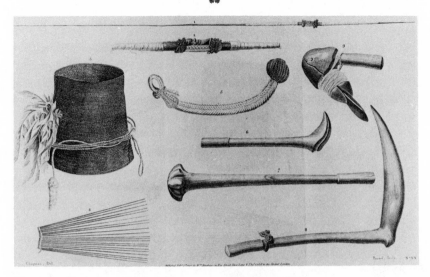

Tongan artifacts, from Cook, A Voyage toward the South Pole, 1777.

This is particularly clear from the fact that graphic representations of artifacts from diverse places such as Australia, Tahiti, and Micronesia look basically similar. While sharp distinctions are made in terms of physique and character and with respect to some aspects of material technology such as dwellings and canoes, other objects like baskets and weapons tend to be aestheticized through symmetrical layout and display of detail. Even in the case of the Aboriginal Tasmanians, where written and visual representations of people bestialize or convey ugliness in an offensive and profoundly racist manner, artifacts are depicted in the standard way.[26]

The images themselves manifest a combination of interest, qualified aestheticization, and indeterminacy in the setting-out of artifacts. Their balanced proportions are often manifest; in some instances the "grotesque" character of human representations is also conveyed, though not generally exaggerated. The plates which appeared with the official narrative of Cook's second voyage, convey predictable ambiguity in several assemblages of "weapons and ornaments." This combination of objects itself suggests a lack of specification about what particular vision is invited: ornaments are surely to be seen as more or less attractive decorations, while it might be expected that clubs and spears would connote savagery through the association with warfare

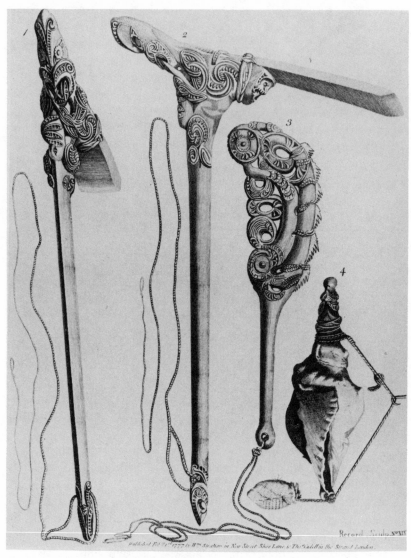

Maori artifacts, from Cook, A Voyage toward the South Pole, 1777.

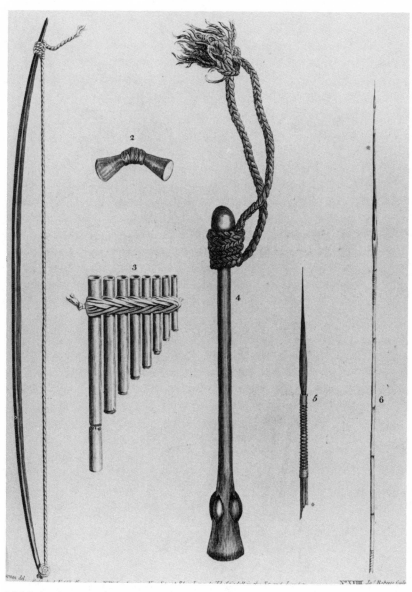

Malekulan, Tannese, and New Caledonian artifacts, from Cook, A Voyage toward the South Pole, 1777.

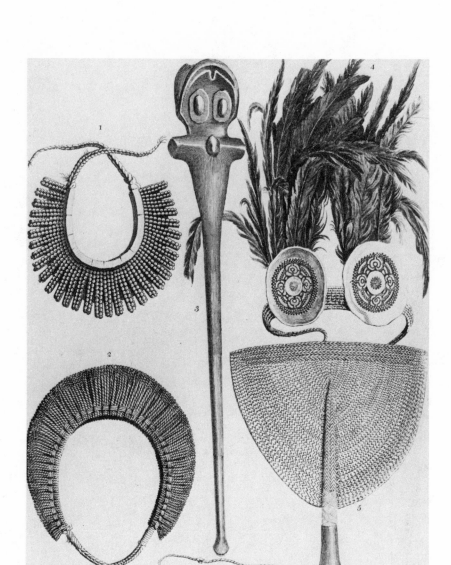

Marquesan artifacts, from Cook, A *Voyage toward the South Pole*, 1777.

and killing. However, the arousal of horror which is a systematic element of many later depictions of indigenous weapons is muted in both text and engravings: in fact, the conjuncture of such things as baskets, caps, and clubs marginalizes any interest in the functions of these things and is instead conducive to aestheticization or consideration of the lack of aesthetic merit. In general, depiction is consistent with the judgments expressed in the text. On the one hand, weaving and baskettry attract particular praise, and the representations bring out the intricacy and regularity of work; on the other, representations of human faces, which are routinely referred to as crude or grotesque, do seem to convey a sense of distortion, partly—in the case of the Tongan spear—through being seen from a difficult side angle. In another contrast, the nonrepresentational carving on the New Zealand adz suggests a high level of fineness, but it makes this intricacy complex and not easily apprehended: the effect of the succession of twists is in fact visually disorienting and perhaps manifests most directly the ambivalence of "curiosity." Adjudications of the relative quality of carving from one place to another also emerge, and the coarseness of weapons in New Caledonia and New Hebrides (Malekula and Tanna) is underlined by the thickness and the ragged ends of fiber and rope attached to a bow and a club, respectively. It might also be noted that the aesthetic properties of the Marquesan pieces are emphasized through the composition of the engraving—where both left and right and upper and lower halves are balanced—while in most other cases the eye is drawn to the individual artifacts.

The debatable character of these reactions springs from the complexity of the images themselves and the fact of their extreme objectification. What Norman Bryson says about still life—"it is the genre farthest from language, and so the hardest for discourse to reach"— seems even more true of these abstracted arrays that suppress proportion by placing artifacts of quite different sizes together; the engraved implements, moreover, seem to offer an "insult to the human subject" by depriving the viewer of any "bond of continuous life with the objects that fill the scene."[27] In this case, despite the fact that what is set out is not directly linked to a narrative or a classificatory scheme, the rationale for this evacuation of signification can be taken to be political, in the sense that a privileged investigative vision is implied by the analogies with the depiction of natural specimens. Artifacts are not tokens of a particular social condition, such as the heathenism created in missionary images, and are not used to mark social boundaries between populations;[28] instead, this decontextualized and—to be anachronistic—clinical form of presentation evokes the authority, precision, and disinterest of science.

A lack of specified interest is also apparent from the actual practices of collecting, in that the explorers did not make systematic effort to acquire either representative samples of a totality or artifacts of particular kinds. Although efforts were sometimes made to acquire ornaments which were striking and valuable, what was received was instead determined in most cases by the islanders, who (especially during brief visits) only brought certain kinds of goods forward. Examination of Cook voyage collections might lead one to suppose that the assessments of the savagery of the New Caledonians, Malekulans, and southern New Hebrides people were reflected in the marked predominance of weapons in material from these places, but in fact it is clear from the voyage journals that very little apart from arrows, bows, and clubs was ever offered to the visitors.

It was not long, however, before material culture was drawn more directly into an evolutionary hierarchization of the differences noted between western and eastern Pacific peoples. D'Entrecasteaux's voyage in search of La Pérouse followed Cook in visiting both Tonga and New Caledonia and sharpened the contrasts already noted between these populations. It was not suggested that artifacts were noticeably cruder or more primitive in New Caledonia than in the central Pacific, but artifacts were linked to narratives which established that, unbeknownst to Cook, the New Caledonians were cannibals. An "instrument which they call *nbouet*" was used to cut up those killed in battle:

> One of them demonstrated its use on a man belonging to our ship, who lay down on his back at the other's request. He first represented a battle . . . he shewed us that they began by opening the belly of the vanquished with the *nbouet* . . . He shewed us that they then cut off the organs of generation, which fall to the lot of the victor . . . It is difficult to depict the ferocious avidity with which he expressed to us that the flesh of the unfortunate victim was devoured by them after they had broiled it on the coals.[29]

The material illustrated in a series of plates effected a more definite contrast between a diverse array of Tongan things—bowls, baskets,

bags, fans, skirts, combs, and weapons, which were described as
"Effets des habitans des Iles des Amis"—and the "Effets des sauvages
de la Nouvelle Calédonie,"[30] which were almost exclusively weapons.
Another figure depicted "Deux cubitus humains taillés et bien polis,
destinés à arracher les intestins des malheureuses victimes que ces
peuples dévorent" (Two human ulna, cut and well polished, designed
to extract the intestines of the unfortunate victims these people de-
vour).[31] While the Cook voyage representations made New Caledonian and New Hebridean weapons conspicuous, they were not articulated to the quintessentially savage practice of cannibalism in this way.
In each case, the fact that weapons were acquired was probably determined more by the islanders than by those on ships, but the later
voyage recreated the material as a marker for what separated the New
Caledonians from the more civilized Tongans in a much more decisive way. The still unnamed Melanesia/Polynesia division was taking
firmer shape.

There is thus a progression discernible within the corpus of exploratory voyages: in the later accounts, artifacts and narratives associated
with artifacts sustain sharper judgments and the imputation of hierarchical difference.[32] The argument here, which applies in a stronger
form to the early encounters, is essentially that there was a tension
between an unstructured apprehension of diverse things and a scientific and imperialist project which affirmed certain relationships between Europeans and indigenous people and made it possible to clas-
sify and differentiate those who might become the objects of
colonization. It is not surprising, of course, that a literature which
rendered indigenous populations visible and legible developed only to
a limited extent in the writings associated with the voyages. The type
of practical project which the voyages represented was not an interven-
tionist one in any immediate sense; although various goods and supplies were demanded, there was no attempt to reshape local social
relations, no attempt to draw on organized labor in any significant or
extended manner. What was demanded of indigenous populations was
thus limited, and a combination of ethical precepts and practical
constraints largely precluded exploratory ships from forcing unwilling
people to work or surrender goods.

Just as later colonial engagement took quite a different form, depictions of people, customs, ethnological discriminations, and artifacts
were subsequently much more burdened by adjudications and larger

political projects, as is discussed in later sections of this chapter. While the categorical separations which emerged from the French voyages and the more expository discourse exemplified by Johann Reinhold Forster's *Observations Made during a Voyage Round the World* (1778) did make artifacts carry something of the burden of ethnological discriminations,[33] the lack of elaboration of this exercise is notable.

Such investigations might be taken to mark a discontinuity between distinct interests in the material goods of Pacific islanders. On one side there was curiosity: an infantile attitude which was excited and aroused by things but which had no assertive intellectual framework within which the objects could be classified or hierarchized; on the other, there was a more theoretical discourse which sought to define objects as scientific specimens and set up a way of discussing them that was authorized by rational criteria of some kind. In the activities of particular collectors on the voyages, this was expressed in a rather complex way. The natural scientists and philosophers, though often manifestly merely curious themselves, asserted the privilege of their own interests in specimens and regarded the acquisitive and commercially motivated behavior of common sailors as illegitimate. The issue arose in several disputes among those on board the *Resolution,* and Johann Reinhold Forster was quite bitter about the manner in which his trade for both artifacts and natural specimens was inhibited and prices forced up, by others.

> Today a Saylor offered me 6 Shells to sale, all of which were not quite compleat, & he asked half a Gallon brandy for them, which is now worth more than half a Guinea. This shews however what these people think to get for their Curiosities when they come home, & how difficult it must be for a Man like me, sent out on purpose by Government to collect Natural Curiosities, to get these things from the Natives in the Isles, as every Sailor whatsoever buys vast Quantities of Shells, birds, fish, etc. so that the things get dearer & scarcer than one would believe, & often they go to such people, who have made vast Collections, especially of Shells, viz. the Gunner & Carpenter, who have several 1000 Shells; some of these Curiosities are neglected, broke, thrown over board, or lost.[34]

Forster invoked the authority of the state in establishing the consequential and legitimate character of his own interest. There was an effort to define specimens of various kinds as something other than mere articles of traffic, which any European had a right to deal in, simply on the basis of an ability to purchase; the control and handling of material was thus colonized by those who would not capriciously neglect objects or throw them overboard. It is notable, though, that back in Europe the scientists also sold artifacts and did not, in any case, do much with the material collected, apart from making occasional presentations to museums. Hence the naturalist Anders Sparrman donated a collection to the Swedish national institution, and Forster presented material to the Pitt Rivers and Gottingen museums; but published catalogues of specimens or other forms of scientific evidence all dealt with botanical or faunal material, and such things as astronomical observations.[35]

These points suggest that what was important about collecting, was not so much what could be said about or done with the specimens collected but the way that collected material attested to the fact of having visited remote places and observed novel phenomena. In itself, the practice substantiated relations of knowledge and power that were distinctive to the period of exploratory voyages, although there are parallels with later academic disciplines such as anthropology, which privilege the primary fieldwork experience. In this context, sources of information for the study of the human species were placed at a considerable remove and accessible only to the very restricted number who had made extended travels; those who speculated without having engaged in direct observation were rendered unreliable by the special claim of a few to direct knowledge. Hence, in the prefatory rationalization for the discussion of the human species in Forster's *Observations*, he criticized those who studied "mankind only in their cabinets" and who relied upon untrustworthy secondary accounts.[36] The evolutionary temporalization of space not only made it possible for certain populations to be equated with the more or less distant ancestors of Europeans but also permitted a new claim to descriptive authority on the part of those who had actually witnessed the "anterior" groups. Just as the establishment of modern anthropology much later entailed the dismissal of amateur ethnology, the argument for empirical ethnography in this period entailed a claim to write about the real, a claim which excluded, or aimed to exclude, both those who had not traveled and those who had traveled but who lacked a philosophical interest in natural history. The interests of the common sailors in specimens— whether shells or artifacts—were motivated merely by capricious passions and a base desire for financial advantage.

Joseph Banks.

Curiosities brought home could also represent the accomplishment of the voyage in more personal and diffuse terms. Just as the knowledge of Europe and of the sites of classical literature obtained through a grand tour was sometimes expressed in the acquisition and display of classical relics, indigenous artifacts virtually became trophies which reflected the broader experience and mastery of a passage around the world on the part of a traveler. This use of material is typified in a portrait of Joseph Banks in which the subject is surrounded by a variety of weapons and ornaments: a comb and an adz are on the floor, and his own garment seems to be a modified Polynesian barkcloth cape. A sense that these are not mere ornaments, but the products of a scientific voyage, arises from the folio of botanical drawings behind the adz: the man depicted is associated with the cataloging of nature, rather than mere personal entertainment. The picture exhibits a conjuncture of things which were often represented but usually separate: peculiar and different "curiosities" normally appeared in larger scenes, around or in the hands of natives in some ethnographic vignette, or otherwise as decontextualized specimens; and, at the same time, the portrait typically conveys the attitudes of composure, refinement, and learning. If there is also a suggestion of excessive ornamentation, or feminine vanity, the enduring impression is of assurance with respect to the periphery of an expanding world, a world not familiar to most viewers of the picture, which hence separates the breadth of Banks's knowledge and command from their own. "The riches of Banks's collection, drawn from a dispersed variety of cultures, are organised to display his cosmopolitanism, their exotically random incoherence, as well as to indicate authenticity, the first hand and intimate experience that informs knowledge."[37]

This exemplifies the point made in the Introduction, that objects can have singular personal meanings at odds with their systemic significance. From the latter perspective, what Banks owned were commodities, things which were often bought and sold and were no less *recherché* among the bourgeoisie at the time than antiques and tribal art are today; but for him the things performed the more particular operation of standing for a voyage and the work of science.

This is of course a matter of prestige and social status, a point which occasions comment upon an analogy that might be made between this aristocratic display of material wealth and the tribal "prestige" which is often seen as the aim of Melanesian exchange. From Malinowski's text to the present, the preoccupation of transactors, and the accomplishment of acquiring certain shells or effecting certain presentations, is understood in terms such as "renown," "prestige," and "status."[38] I do not dispute that this is an indigenous model: informants from the Massim, in particular, are frequently quoted insisting upon the centrality and worth of names, fame, and renown,[39] but perhaps it needs to be made clearer that in both European and Pacific societies these words do not refer to entities—one cannot point to a thing called prestige which both Banks and the kula operator has—but are instead moments in a political process. In each case, the dual or multiple character of wealth items permits them at once to function as commodities and as "valuables," expressions of relationships, artifacts of a biography, or elements of some other singular fashion. Shell valuables in the Massim and in New Georgia could be alienated to acquire canoes, the assistance of warriors, heads, women's services, pigs, and a range of other things: their use was above all *a technique of power.* Similarly, Banks's material was not only expressive but also convertible into wealth, and although his collections seem mostly to have entered national museums—augmenting the cultural capital of the state— others made a great deal of money out of the trade in these commodities. Paradoxically, artifacts collected in the course of eighteenth-century voyages would now realize very high prices on the basis of their "original" character, yet this value is actually proportionate to their distance from their indigenous origins and measures a succession and duration of recontextualizations.

Descriptions of other people always embody some commentary— which might be approving or critical—on social circumstances at home, although the extent to which debate concerning dominant values or political questions actually motivate particular images and moral evaluations clearly varies considerably. Melville's *Typee* is, for instance, far more determined by the critique of metropolitan society than missionary publications, even though reflection upon immorality at home, and the need for domestic evangelism, amounted to a significant undercurrent in missionary works; by contrast, more "practical" texts such as official colonial reports were obviously oriented toward the circumstances they immediately described and purported to master.

The voyage literature of the late eighteenth century at once affirms

the distance between European civilization and the social condition of
Pacific islanders and—to a varying degree—relativizes the advancement of the former. As Johann Reinhold Forster wrote:

> We think ourselves much superior to these Nations in regard to Arts &
> Trades, & what is still more than all this, in regard to our sublime Sci-
> ences, & the use of letters. I will by no means say they are as far as we
> in regard to all these things, or even as far as any of the least civilized
> nations, but let us only give them their due, let us consider the difficulties
> they are under, let us examine their Ingenuity, their contrivances, the
> Simplicity of their tools, their Arts, their manufactures, their cultivation,
> their fishing, their Navigation, their Shipbuilding, their knowledge of the
> Stars, & all this I believe must convince us, that they have more civil-
> ization than we at first outset think. Our Poetry, Music, Dramatic Perfor-
> mances, make a vast addition to the refinement of Civilization: but these
> Nations are not without their Songs, which seem to be well measured &
> adapted to their Music, & allways accompanied by Dances, the most of
> which are of the Dramatic kind. The civilized Greeks were Musicians, &
> had a Flute of several Pipes of reed, which we found again in the Isles of
> *Middleburg* and *Amsterdam* [Eua and Tongatapu].[40]

Forster's demand here was for a fuller contextual appreciation of the
achievements of islanders such as Tongans and Tahitians and recognition of the parallels between their customs and practices and those
of the ancient civilizations. Such analogies were frequently made in
travelers' accounts of various parts of the world but here drew
specifically upon the observation of material artifacts, which moreover
could be brought home to be witnessed. The similarity of accomplishment between Greek and Tongan music was attested to by the instrument itself, while in other areas manufactured things were to be
compared favorably: "The fine fish-hooks made of Mother of Pearl, &
sometimes with hooks of TortoiseShell, are really the proofs of an
ingenious nation. The Nets they make are no doubt most excellent in
their kind & far superior to such as we make, both for materials and
workmanship. The structure of their Canoes, both of the common &
those intended for war, are Monuments of their Skill, & ingenious
contrivance."[41]

In this rhetorical passage, the relative uncertainty which often characterized adjudications was set aside, and the degree of taste and
elegance evident in various artifacts was emphasized. But this relativist
assertion of the merits of the islanders was by no means the only

message of these texts, and was in fact associated with a contrary proposition. One of the points constantly made was that wood carving (in particular) was especially fine and regular *given* the lack of iron; this at the same time reinforced the significance of the distinction between those who used, and those who lacked, metal tools.

Voyagers generally made the assumption that there was an intense indigenous desire for iron, as if the people perceived this to be their most crucial lack. Keate asserted that for the Belau people "the *English* possessed what was in their estimation of the highest value—iron and arms."[42] Although there is, indisputably, an objective difference between the effectiveness of iron and stone tools, such a difference is not necessarily recognized by, or relevant to, every social group. The European observation was often made even when it is apparent from specific accounts of barter that islanders did not in fact value iron to such an extent that they would surrender their own valuable property for it. Such a discrepancy was noted above (Chapter 3) in the Russians' rendering of Marquesan interests: while it was asserted that iron was seen to be "beyond all price," the unwillingness of the Marquesans to exchange anything substantial of their own for it was constantly manifest. The statement often prompted by the sight of islanders at work expresses the difficulty of various tasks such as cutting and clearing in the absence of metal tools: "We heard one of the men at work cutting down a tree with his hatchet of stone, and observed him through the bushes a long time. The tree was not so thick as a man's thigh, and yet it was a very laborious undertaking, with such a tool as this hatchet, to cut it in two."[43]

Apart from the occasional lack of indigenous interest in iron,[44] remarks of this type were often inconsistent with other observations— "Uncouth as their hatchets might appear to our people, it was a matter of surprize, to observe in how little a time the natives were able to fell a tree with them."[45] These inconsistencies, however, reveal the broader discursive significance of references to the limitations of so-called neolithic technologies. The symbolic burden of burdensome labor is most apparent in a remarkable reflection of George Forster's upon the small camp set up from the *Resolution* in Dusky Bay, in the far south of New Zealand:

> The superiority of a state of civilization over that of barbarism could not be more clearly stated, than by the alterations and improvements we had

made in this place. In the course of a few days, a small part of us had cleared away the woods from a surface of more than an acre, which fifty New Zeelanders, with their tools of stone, could not have performed in three months. This spot, where immense numbers of plants lived and decayed by turns, in one confused inanimated heap; this spot, we had converted into an active scene, where a hundred and twenty men pursued various branches of employment with unremitted ardour . . . We felled tall timber-trees, which, but for ourselves, had crumbled to dust with age . . . Already the polite arts began to flourish in this new settlement; the various tribes of animals and vegetables, which dwelt in the unfrequented woods, were imitated by an artist . . . the romantic prospects of this shaggy country, lived on the canvas in the glowing tints of nature, who was amazed to see herself so closely copied. Nor had science disdained to visit us in this solitary spot: an observatory arose in the centre of our works, filled with the most accurate instruments . . . In a word, all around us we perceived the rise of arts, and the dawn of science, in a country which had hitherto lain plunged in one long night of ignorance and barbarism![46]

Here the distinction turns upon the transformative power of a Western presence: the manner in which a whole array of forms of industry are embarked upon is contrasted with a condition of stasis, neglect, and nonproduction which is associated with barbarism. Such observations could not have been made in Tahiti and Tonga, where evidence for human use and modification of the landscape was far more immediate than in the cold, sparsely inhabited far south of New Zealand; and the remarks made on the basis of Tongan and Tahitian circumstances were generally different. Here the connection between the basic work of clearing and remaking the landscape as an area around a "settlement" and the arts and sciences that were diagnostic of civilization indicated also that the absence of adequate tools, and hence the lack of any means of transforming what was assumed to be virgin forest, precluded the development of these expressions of refinement. The comment upon technology thus made the gulf between the Maori and Europeans absolute: it suggested that there was no basis in the native inhabitants' relationship with the surrounding world for advancement and denied the kind of continuity elsewhere asserted (for instance by Forster senior with respect to the Tongans and Tahitians).[47] In emphasizing the failure of the Maori to carve any social or economic accomplishment out of the landscape, George Forster also prefigured the representations which were later significant in discourses of dispossession: the "parasitic" character of (for instance) Australian Aboriginal hunting and gathering was unfavorably contrasted with the constructive and transformative work of white settlers.

But at this stage this was less a systematic historical narrative than one of a number of figures in enlightenment workings of the exotic. Johann Reinhold Forster's discussion of the need to appreciate Tongan civilization on its own terms included a familiar reflexive criticism of Europe—that civilized or pious people often acted in an uncivilized or unchristian manner: "Let a foreigner, or only a Stranger, try our civilized European countries, let him experience what charity can do for him . . . We reckon these people among the Gentiles; but their Charity is preferable & more warm, more sanguine than that of the professors of Christianity."[48]

Keate's work on Belau—which was in no sense an official account—takes this ironic comparison much further. Most of the remarks made about both the islanders and their artifacts are positive, and he suggests that the only fault of the people is their propensity for theft. Here, again, the absence of iron plays a crucial explanatory role. Keate implies that the want for it is so acute that leaving a nail or bolt around is like dropping a diamond before a European peasant: in such circumstances no one would expect the peasant to refrain from taking what was of such overwhelming value. But Keate's principal suggestion is that such a criticism is in any case foolishly advanced, given that stealing and dissimulation prevail so widely in civilized society and cannot be prevented by the police and that an elaborate legal apparatus is lacking in Belau. The inhabitants of civilized society had to acknowledge that "all which prudence can resolve, wisdom plan, or power enforce, is frequently unable to protect their *Property* by night, or their *Persons*, at all times, even under meridian suns.—They will reflect, that every bolt and bar is a *satire* on society . . ."[49]

The point is thus not merely that "it becomes us to view with charity those errors in others, which we have not as yet been able to correct in ourselves"[50] but rather that the Other was an ironic, destabilizing force. The example of a people in one sense savage and in other respects an attractive "ornament to nature," characterized by social harmony in the absence of a repressive state, draws attention to the faults of Europe, to the absurdity of a system which establishes so much and rests upon such a long process of evolution and yet cannot accomplish elementary security of people and property.[51]

Although these propositions did not make direct references to artifacts, positive descriptions of Belauan products along with a sequence
of engravings constitute an important element of Keate's project to
depict these islanders as an ingenious and generous people. This is
accomplished, in particular, not just by the favorable presentation of
particular objects—some of which, carved from tortoiseshell, are said
to be very fine[52]—but also by accounts of the presentation of particular
valuables to the temporarily marooned Englishmen. A large bowl in
the shape of a bird, decorated with shell inlay, although unique and
exclusively for ceremonial use, was presented to Captain Wilson on
his departure; this "was an additional proof of the liberality of these
people, who were ready to divest themselves even of what they most
valued, to give to their friends."[53] Here, the fact that a thing can be
brought away, exhibited, and illustrated may be seen to attest materially to the claims made in writing. The sentimental and manifestly
unscientific character of interest is also apparent from differences between the ways in which ornaments are engraved in Keate's book and

"A large tureen, made of wood, in the shape of a bird," from Keate, *An Account of
the Pelew Islands*, 1788.

Artifacts from the Pelew Islands, from Keate, *An Account of the Pelew Islands*, 1788.

the superficially similar images of the Cook voyage publications. Radical decontextualization is produced in the latter partly by incongruity in the scales of different pieces and a general sense of abstraction and remoteness; the Pelew Islands pieces, by contrast, are made much closer and more tangible by attention to texture and the extent to which a few, rather than many, fill the framed space; the presence of much clearer toning and shadow also implies a source of light and a viewer, absent from the vacuous object world of scientific specimens.

To a large extent, the movement of all these articles from indigenous to European exchange circuits was a movement of commoditization. As Johann Reinhold Forster complained, one of the main reasons why common sailors were anxious to acquire things was the anticipation of profit through the curiosity market. But the singularity of exotic material culture gave it a special status, and the claims of the natural philosophers that articles were of scientific importance implied a broader movement that restricted their circulation. There was an attempt on the part of official scientists to monopolize the legitimate ownership of such rarities, although subsequently these claims have generally been more ignored than respected. On the part of some, such as the Banks of the portrait, there was certainly an appropriation of objects which manifested the breadth and command of the person. From his own perspective the thing did not so much become a commodity as a marker of personal history, an expression of the person's accomplishments.

In general, however, the explorers took artifacts to express something about the people who collectively produced them; they did not attach much importance to the singular histories of particular articles. The use of things to signify narratives, which was more important for some islanders and other sorts of later colonizers, was manifest in Keate's story about the drinking bowl: what remained important about the vessel was the fact that it had been a gift. It retained the name of the king and was a reference point for an assertion about the good relations established between the English and the Belauan people. The gift produced a social relationship, for Keate; and who knows?—perhaps the high chief himself saw it that way.

Converted Artifacts: The Material Culture of Christian Missions

> The Missionaries rightly judged that the natural productions of the distant countries in which they reside would be acceptable at home . . . The efforts also of natural genius, especially in countries rude and uncivilized, afford another class of interesting curiosities; whilst they prove how capable even the most uncivilized of mankind are of receiving that instruction which it is the study of Missionaries to communicate. But the most valuable and impressive objects in this Collection are the numerous, and (in some instances) *horrible*, IDOLS, which have been imported from the South Sea Islands, from India, from China, and Africa; and among these, those especially which were actually given up by their former worshippers, from *a full conviction of the folly and sin of idolatry*—a conviction derived from the ministry of the Gospel by the Missionaries.
>
> *Catalogue of the Missionary Museum, Austin Friars*, 1826

In George Forster's imagination, the sojourn of the *Resolution* in Dusky Bay was a moment of enlightenment. The work of clearing the forest and the exercise of polite arts and sciences were displayed in contradistinction to "one long night of barbarism." But the contrast is poignantly brief: it was as if the spot was illuminated by a shaft of sunlight which broke momentarily through heavy cloud. In observing that the visible space of the settlement would soon revert to chaotic forest, Forster affirmed the great distance between southern New Zealand and civilized Europe: the progressive development of the former place seemed remote to the point of being impossible.

The evangelical missionaries who began work in the Pacific in 1797 were dedicated to a kind of enlightenment which they understood in very different terms. [54] The argument with respect to the voyagers was that their interest in artifacts derived from a conjuncture of "curiosity" and the lack of a project to intervene in or restructure islands societies. There could hardly be a greater contrast than with most missionary efforts. The mission was not merely to change religion, to substitute Christianity for paganism, for it was conceived in broader social and moral terms: customs which were barbaric or inconsistent with Christian life were to be abolished. Both in campaigns in the field and in domestic propaganda missionaries dwelt on practices which seemed manifestly abhorrent: infanticide, human sacrifice, widow-strangling, and cannibalism; but there was also an interest in suppressing polygamy and sexual irregularities and modifying numerous features of social and domestic organization. As in missions to India, sexual segregation was regarded as a form of oppression from which women could be liberated by Christianity. The extent to which mission agendas were compromised in practice, or thwarted and appropriated by indigenous "converts," was of course considerable, but the interest in intervention was certainly in theory very broad.

What collecting practices and attitudes toward indigenous material culture did missionary projects engender? Those who regard missionaries as the worst disrupters of aboriginal Pacific societies might expect a nasty and pejorative attitude toward all elements of local culture to be exhibited, but this would ignore essential presuppositions of the missionary endeavor. Although hostility to heathenism was central, missionaries also believed, of course, that South Sea islanders, Australian Aborigines, and other tribal peoples were worth saving. It would not be correct to claim that missionaries genuinely regard Polynesians or Melanesians as their equals; evangelism did, however, presume a shared humanity and entail an interest in the incorporation of the other, rather than the imagination of a savage condition which was necessarily separate and distant. The concern to convert also imputed a certain instability and mutability in islanders: they were dissociable from the darkness which shrouded them.

The heathen condition was characterized in various ways; particular ritual observances or customs were represented as being central to it, and the adoption of Christianity was expressed through the dual step of repudiating these emblematic customs and professing adherence.[55] It particularly suited missionary discourse when the local religion could be characterized as idolatry, because this meant that "idols," as objectifications of the false religion, could be abstracted from their context in native worship and destroyed or displayed. The implication, of course, was that the removal of these artifacts, or even the abandonment of the particular spirits associated with them, reflected a broader repudiation of the underlying beliefs.[56] The ancestor or deity images which were described as "idols" also served the useful purpose of exhibiting the absurdity of pagan ideas: the fact that a figure which was small, crude, or grotesque could be equated with a spirit or supreme being was held up to ridicule. Although such arguments were especially prominent in publications associated with the zealous missionary colonialism of the first half of the nineteenth century—the period when Christianity was being established in the Society Islands and elsewhere in Polynesia—the theme was perpetuated in the more ethnographic accounts which missionaries later in the century (operating mainly in a secure Christian environment) could engage in. In 1885 William Wyatt Gill published an engraving captioned "Native worshipping a Post." "The god (will it be credited?) is *the central side post*, stouter than the rest, and crooked! Like the other posts, this god helps to sustain the roof, and yet is an object of daily worship! To the crooked post—utterly destitute of ornament—three green cocoa-nuts and a sacred leaflet were offered morning and evening."[57]

In earlier mission work in Tahiti and the Austral Islands there were several occasions when the conversions of chiefs or whole populations were marked by the surrendering or destruction of "idols." John Williams recounted that a boat returned from the inaugural mission to Rurutu "laden with the trophies of victory, the gods of the heathen taken in this bloodless war and won by the power of the Prince of Peace. On reading the letters which accompanied them, and seeing with our own eyes the rejected idols, we felt a measure of that sacred joy which the angels of God will experience when they shout, 'The kingdoms of this world are become the kingdoms of our God and his Christ.'"[58]

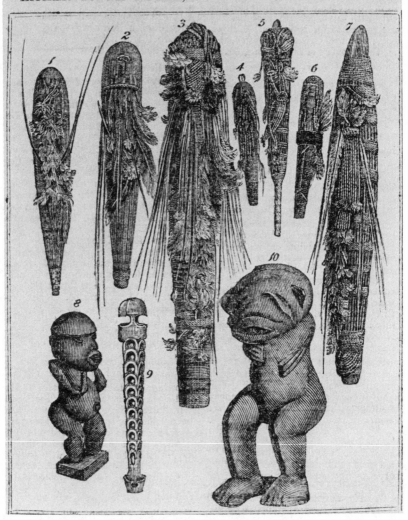

Missionary Sketches, No. III.

For the use of the Weekly and Monthly Contributors to the Missionary Society.

THE FAMILY IDOLS OF POMARE,

Which he relinquished, and sent to the Missionaries at Eimeo,

EITHER TO BE BURNT, OR SENT TO THE SOCIETY.

Pomare's family idols, from *Missionary Sketches*, 1818. This type of image was reproduced in popular missionary works as late as the 1890s.

Figures were thus recontextualized as tangible evidence of their repudiation: the evening that this vessel came back to Tahiti a special service was held at which "the rejected idols were publicly exhibited from the pulpit." The trophies of success were similarly used to arouse the sentiments of Christians back in Europe. They were displayed in the Missionary Museum in London[59] and extensively depicted in the popular *Missionary Sketches*.[60] One issue covered a set of "idols" presented to the London Missionary Society by King Pomare in 1818. The names of these, where known, were listed: one was "the son of the great god Oro," another "Temeharo, the principal god of Pomare's family."[61] Appended was a letter from Pomare, in which he affirmed his faith in the Savior and dissociated himself from his former deities: "If you think proper, you may burn them all in the fire; or, if you like, send them to your country, for the inspection of the people of Europe, that they may satisfy their curiosity, and know Tahiti's foolish gods!"[62]

This point was made central in the heading over the engraving: the idols had been relinquished; their recontextualization made them the relics of a great transformation. Some images were preserved so that they could attest to the former state of idolatry; others facilitated a more definite expression of its rejection in being burnt. Depiction of the moment of incineration similarly expressed the historic event of enlightenment.

As Bernard Smith has noted,[63] this particular picture, others of the

Burning idols, from *Missionary Sketches*, 1819.

genre, and engravings of the period made from earlier sources usually depict "idols" in a particularly distorted form, as is manifest in the huge eyes and star-shaped hands of the central figure about to burn. The representation of Pomare's "family idols" is less notably grotesque but instead conveys a threatening complexity and obscurity in the figures. They are composed of long spines or feathers and wicker or coir work and are visually perplexing in that the relation of different elements suggests no manifest form. The images thus imply a rather insidious and unknowable false god or spirit which presumably aroused disquiet and fear in the viewer. The accompanying text at once deprecated the figures and emphasized their strangeness:

> The public will no doubt feel much disappointed on the view of these de-
> spicable idols, and especially of this representation of them, as they cer-
> tainly form a very insignificant picture. The idols themselves, except the
> Tiis,[64] Nos. 8 and 10, bear no resemblance whatever to the human form,
> and differ from any thing we remember to have seen or read of, which
> has been used by idolaters for the purpose of worship. In general the idols
> of the heathen, however rude, have been designed to bear a resemblance
> to something, "in heaven above, or in the earth beneath, or in the waters
> under the earth;" [cf. Exodus 20:4] but these convey no idea whatever of
> an animated being, and we are totally at a loss to account for their form.[65]

"Idols" thus provided an extremely powerful mechanism through which the fact of conversion could be materially expressed and displayed. An indigenous object became an artifact of history for missionary discourse, an artifact made to speak at once of its original purpose and the transaction through which it had been detached from that purpose. But in some islands such as Fiji and Samoa religion was not regarded as idolatrous;[66] artifacts which materially condensed the beliefs, practices, and objects of heathen worship were thus not available for appropriation and depiction. In these cases, the burden of heathenism was displaced to other savage practices such as widow-strangling and warfare. Accounts of "exceedingly cruel" native wars were often illustrated with fearsome pictures or written descriptions of clubs and spears,[67] and Fijian forks allegedly used for the consumption of human flesh attested materially to this emblem of barbarism. Richard Burdsall Lyth, a prominent Methodist in Tonga and Fiji, made a "List of Curiosities" which linked these general associations with biographical incidents: "No 5 Tui Viti's club—presented me by himself—he is without doubt the most powerful and influential chief in Feejee. No 15 Tanoa's Yangona cup—presented to RBL by Tanoa."[68]

The fact that the missionary had been presented with weapons and other items by warrior-chiefs or priests said something both about the changing attitude of those individuals and attested to his own accomplishments in what was perceived as a difficult mission field—that the confidence and friendship of powerful savage chiefs could in fact be gained.[69] The focus upon idols thus gave way to a more generalized account which might refer to a variety of types of artifacts; any ritual object, however, could stand in the first place for the foolishness of indigenous beliefs and secondly for the islanders' willingness to abandon them. Thomas Baker, a Methodist in Fiji, noted in his diary in 1864 that he had

> purchased a small shell that had been with them for many generations, its use was singular. The priest of the town said "In time of strong winds we build a scaffold some sixty or a hundred feet high, and I ascend with this shell hung round my neck . . ." the wind was evidently the object of worship or fear. His prayer was that he, the wind, would retire into this said shell and rest there, and not blow, lest their houses and bananas should fall, and, of course, he assured me that it was always effectual. He however believed a butcher's knife to be of more value to him than the shell and accepted the offer.[70]

In this case, the disposal of the thing does not reflect the Fijian's passage to a Christian state but instead denigrates the priest's capricious subordination of his faith to desire for an article of trade.[71] Baker did not mention the scarcity of iron in the period and thus obscured the issue of precisely how valuable the knife actually was. It is also entirely possible that the Fijian man had previous experience of barter with missionaries and realized that the attachment of such a history to an ordinary ornament might dramatically enhance its value.

I suggested earlier that the missionary project needed to postulate a certain instability and ambivalence in indigenous society and character. On one side, it was essential for fund-raising propaganda and the overall rationale that barbarism and the darkness of paganism appeared to be shocking and arbitrary; on the other, the indigenous character was not totally repugnant, not totally devoid of the seeds of improvement, and indeed already had commendable features. The need for positive imagery generates a discourse quite at odds with that of the "disappointing idols." Other forms of material culture, such as baskets, cloth, pottery, and wood carving are adduced in the sympathetic constitution of indigenous aesthetics and creativity. The discontinuity between the meaning of these crafts and the shock value of savage practices was not disguised but explicitly invoked as the point of a descriptive rupture. Lengthy accounts of indigenous politics and war in Thomas Williams's *Fiji and the Fijians* were followed by a chapter on "industrial produce," which commenced with direct reference to the disjunction: "It is pleasing to turn from the horrible scenes of barbarous war, to the gentler and more profitable occupations of peace . . . At this point there is observable one of the strange and almost anomalous blendings of opposite traits in the Fijian character. Side by side with the wildest savageism, we find among the natives of this group an attention to agriculture, and a variety of cultivated produce, not to be found among any other of the numerous islands of the western Pacific."[72]

The forty-page chapter proceeded to appreciate the various forms of Fijian horticulture, barkcloth, mats, grass skirts, "the art of basket-making," nets, sennit, pottery, salt, canoe building, the carving of wooden vessels such as "fancy oil dishes," house building, fishing, and the forms of trade through which these articles were distributed.[73] The division between the discussion and the preceding account of Fijian barbarism was manifested in two discussions of weapons—the first in the context of warfare and the second in the section on carving.[74] The former emphasized the effect of various clubs and spears upon the body,[75] while the latter abstracted the things from their uses and made them the objects of aesthetic evaluation and ethnographic curiosity. Some clubs were said to be

> the result of days and weeks of patient toil. The handles of some, and the entire surface of others, are covered with fine and elaborate carving; a few are inlaid with ivory and shell. A very fine and beautifully plaited braid of white and black is made for wrapping some of the clubs, scarlet feathers being worked in with it . . . The knob of the small *ula* is often cut with exact symmetry, and the projections sometimes inlaid with ivory or human teeth. Some clubs are made merely for scenes of amusement, and not for war.[76]

The mention of the use of human teeth preserves an undercurrent of negative characterization, but this passage otherwise destabilizes the fabrication of the savage. This is conspicuously effected in the last

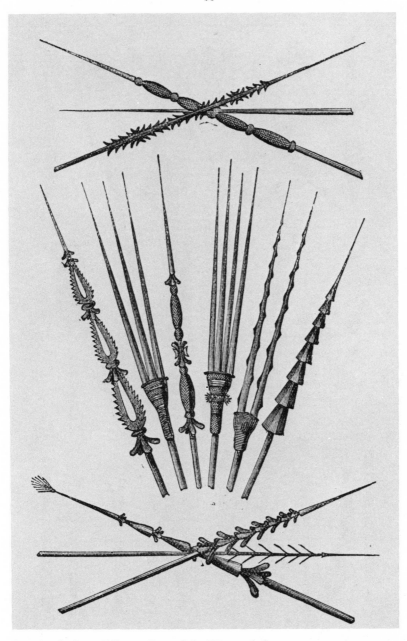

Spearheads, from Williams, *Fiji and the Fijians*, 1858.

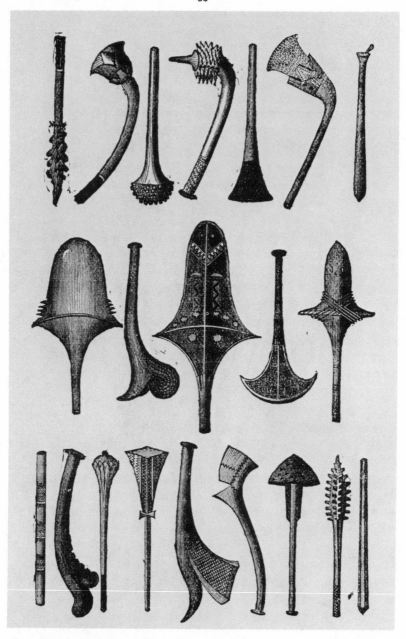

Clubs, from Williams, *Fiji and the Fijians*, 1858.

sentence, which asserts that many of these handsome artifacts were not really weapons anyway. The distinction between the earlier discussion of spears and that of clubs as manifestations of creative and skilled workmanship seems also to be expressed graphically.[77] An engraving accompanying the former emphasizes the sharpness and destructive effect of "Spear Heads"—as it is captioned—while the picture of clubs sets out a much larger number of pieces. Their balance and repetition of shapes and curves overshadows detail and the implication of violent effect. Both illustrations, however, tend to aestheticize the objects through symmetrical layout and call attention to form rather than function.

An analogous division between positive and negative constructions of indigenous material culture appears in a much later corpus of missionary representations. The propaganda produced about the Methodist mission to the western Solomons in the early twentieth century referred to a number of faults of heathenism, such as the treatment of women as beasts of burden, but placed great emphasis upon head-hunting. A film concerning the passage from barbarism to Christi-

"A study in black and white"; Australasian Methodist Missionary Society postcard, ca. 1910.

anity, *The Transformed Isle*, juxtaposed a long sequence of a staged headhunting raid with the images of an orderly, industrious, properly clothed, and sincerely Christian people, rhetorically asking, "Was it worth while?"[78]

Weapons such as clubs, hatchets, and shields are prominent in the headhunting footage, which is then succeeded by scenes of a domesticated life. The same transformation is reflected in the inclusion of weapons in photographs which are obviously not of heathen natives but of occupants of the new Christian social order. As with the Tahitian "idols," the shield and the paddle-shaped club are *converted artifacts* which express the distance of the people from their former uses. In these instances the weapons are not paraded as ugly or frightening things but are instead domesticated as mere ornaments, as innocuous relics of a former epoch which are now—but only now—available for aesthetic appreciation.

Other types of material culture express the constructive and artistic side which indigenous life is shown to have always had. Certain ornaments of tortoise and pearl shell are "marvels of patience and design"[79]; other products reflect not so much the native sense of beauty as simple industriousness. The popular Methodist magazine illustrated a "Solomon Island Paddle Maker, showing the various stages of production. The second on the right shows the thickness of the wood."[80] While different missions had suggested that other heathens, such as the Tahitians, were "indolent,"[81] in this case, and in Fiji, the prior dedication to work of various kinds marked the ambivalence of native character—an instability amenable to conversion and rebirth under missionary guidance. In the early twentieth century the Methodists placed great emphasis upon the doctrine of the "industrial mission"—whereby religious improvement and character formation were associated closely with disciplined work and the development of commercial activities such as the production of copra. In each case, particular features of the indigenous way of life came to figure as markers of—on one side—a barbarism which could be superseded, and—on the other—the underlying humanity and potential of the people being evangelized.

Murder Stories: Settlers' Curios

Theories of material culture have often privileged the issue of group identity and the process through which particular artifacts or arrays of

styles are appropriated as badges by cultures or subcultures. In transcultural and colonial contexts, this identification can also be made by
outsiders: things to which people attach no particular importance
themselves can be regarded as locally distinctive or as resonant of
national character by others. As I have stressed in the previous sections, it is also possible for artifacts to be associated in a much more
singular way with events and transactions. These identifications may
manifest a kind of inversion of the inalienability of the gift: in some
formulations the donor is said to retain a lien over the thing, or the
outcome of the gift is the relationship between transactors. But a
commodity transaction does not predict future mutations of an object.
A former owner may have no further interest in either the article
transacted or the relationship, but a subsequent user can regard the
thing as being interesting and valuable primarily because of its exotic
source or because of the renown of the producer. There is thus a
retrospective construction of the thing as something definitely connected with a name of a place or person. It was noted that Marquesans
and some other Polynesians generally treated guns, whether received
through purchase, through barter, or as gifts, as though they conveyed
elements of the person and the power of foreign warriors. In a similar
way George Keate regarded the bird-shaped vessel as important primarily because it attested to the generosity of spirit of the Belauan
"king"; and Pomare's repudiation of heathenism was manifested in the
exhibition of his "family idols." In all these cases artifacts were the
visible and tangible proof of certain events or dispositions rather than
signs of some part or whole culture.

Missionaries made weapons the evidence for both the barbaric past
and the disconnection between it and a new Christian society. The
ambiguity of their interests has no counterpart in the subculture of
another group of Europeans resident among Pacific islanders, whose
concern was not to reform indigenous people. Insofar as they wanted
to do anything with natives, they conceived of them as a market or a
source for articles of trade, but in general their own capitalist agricultural projects conflicted directly with indigenous interests.[82] Before
1860 the number of settlers permanently resident in Fiji was small—
perhaps less than fifty—and most were involved in trading rather than
activities which required land alienation. In the early 1860s, however,
there was a surge of interest in the cultivation of cotton, and prospective planters, mostly from Australia, poured in, with the result that
there were about three thousand whites in the group by 1871.[83]

For those interested in establishing plantations, native Fijians were an obstacle. Their attachment to their land created difficulties, and labor could generally only be obtained with the cooperation of chiefs, which had a variety of unsatisfactory consequences. It was also found that Fijians mostly wanted only to do "short jobs" at comparatively high wages. The prosperity of planters in the 1860s gave some room for mutual accommodation, but by 1869 it was generally believed that the problem of labor could only be resolved by importing workers from the Solomon Islands and the New Hebrides.[84] The fact that Fijians did not even represent a labor supply, and a steep decline in cotton prices in the early 1870s, led to the development of trenchantly racist attitudes, along with a bitter sense that the protectionist colonial administration placed native interests before those of white men.[85] Far from recognizing the more "civilized" features of Fijian society, such as its elaborate chiefly hierarchy and aristocratic etiquette, planters instead saw the Fijians merely as unattractive obstacles to development. The gap between this perception and that of others was symptomatic: the first governor, Sir Arthur Hamilton Gordon, noted that contrary to the desires of the settlers, he did not "mean to clear out the 'damn niggers' who by the way are not niggers at all, but of a warm light bronze colour."[86] The different camps of European opinion were in fact reflected in this usage: the word "nigger" was virtually never used by either missionaries or administrators but was the standard term among settlers and some traders.

The account of Anatole Von Hügel, a traveler who arrived in the group shortly before Gordon took up his commission, indicated how a certain view of artifacts accorded with the planters' attitude:

> Many of the planters . . . showed a rational interest in the plants and animals of their districts, but as to the human inhabitants of the islands no-one appeared to have any information to bestow. As soon as conversation turned upon them everyone's interest flagged, indeed many seemed to feel that "a set of lazy niggers" covered all that could possibly be said on the subject. What struck me as stranger still—no-one had thought of making a local ethnological collection. A few scattered native weapons or implements might certainly be found in the settlers' houses, but they were kept as "curios," often for the sake of some sentimental history which the owner could attach to them. Every dish was a cannibal dish, every club had been the instrument of some atrocious murder, and every stain on either was caused by blood.[87]

Under the circumstances, it would have been strange if anyone had attempted to assemble an "ethnological collection." While the attitudes of individual planters no doubt varied considerably, their overall situational interest was in denying the worth of the indigenous Fijians in every possible way. That material evidence for barbaric proclivities should have been the only form in which artifacts were appropriated was entirely consistent with the conflict of interests inherent in frontier settlement. The indifference and hostility of settlers has had the effect that their own extant observations on the matter are virtually absent, and indirect documentation, such as Von Hügel's unsympathetic description, provides our only view. However, a number of travelers with commercial interests seem to have shared the planters' perspective. W. C. Gardenhire, the author of one of many polemical pamphlets of the period in favor of development in Fiji and critical of government policy, went on from the islands to organize a "Fiji Cannibal Exhibition" on the American West Coast. This included not only Fijian weapons and "cannibal forks," but also the "Hand of the late Lovoni rebel king, killed in battle with Thakombau, present King of Fiji," and three live exhibits who were to perform war dances and sham fights. The emphasis here hardly requires elaboration.

The articles which were singled out by this interest in appropriation were the wooden forks termed *iculunibakola*, which have always been known as "cannibal forks" and supposed to have been used because the flesh of victims was sacred or *tabu*. Fergus Clunie, following A. M. Hocart, has pointed out that those killed were not *tabu*, and that confusion has arisen because the personal *tabu* of persons of high rank prevented them from touching food at all. Apparently they were usually hand-fed by servants, or used forks; commoner people, in contrast, ate human flesh without using any implements.[88] The cannibal fork "misnomer" corrected by Hocart was not, however, an unmotivated misinterpretation or contingent error. The transformation from a partial connection to a complete identification between the artifact and the practice best suited the European fascination with anthropophagy: it provided objects which could be appropriated and handled, which did not merely represent cannibalism but which had actually been used to consume flesh. As a later visitor to the Fiji Museum observed: "A group of cannibal forks interested me very much. Here was 'the real thing,' used over and over again to eat

THE
Fiji Cannibal Exhibition

WILL VISIT ALL THE

Principal Cities on the Pacific Slope

During the Fairs,

Then Proceeding East, via Virginia City and Salt Lake.

Two Celebrated Fijian Chiefs,

KO RATU MASI MOA, KI NA BOSE YACO, and

General Ra Biau, the Dwarf,

Thirty-five years of age, and only 3 feet 4 inches high, all regular Man
Eaters. They will perform National War Dances, Sham Fights and Songs
in Native War Costumes, with Fijian Weapons, consisting of Spears,
Clubs, &c.

Also, a great variety of

FIJIAN AND NEW ZEALAND CURIOSITIES,

CONSISTING OF

Cannibal Knives and Forks, used for eating human flesh; 50 kinds of
Wood, including the celebrated Sandal wood, used for burning before
Chinese Idols; 50 different sorts of Clubs, Spears, Bows and Arrows, and
other Implements of War.

Malay War Mask and Creese, Fiji Shark's-teeth Swords, Model of War
Canoe, Fishhooks made of human bone ; Tapa, or native Cloth, made from
the bark of tree; Head Dresses and Mats; Native Ladies' Powder Boxes,
Necklaces of whales' teeth, Fans, Bracelets, Combs; Spirit Houses, where
they suppose the spirits go after death, Idols, Crockery, Baskets, Kava
Bowls, used for making the grog from kava root.

Vampire or Flying Fox, all the tropical species of Fish, Snakes, Lizards,
Tortoise-shell Turtle, one half eel and half snake (Babirrussa), and a large
collection of Lava Formations from the Hawaiian Islands, and 200 different
varieties of Ferns.

ALSO THE

HAND OF THE LATE LOVONI REBEL KING,

Killed in battle with Thakombau, present King of Fiji, and presented to
W. C. Gardenhire on the day before sailing, June 17th 1871.

Some superior specimens of Fiji Sea Island Cotton (the best grown in
the world) and Tobacco.

Photographs of Kings and Chiefs, &c., on Sale at the Exhibition.

Back page of W. C. Gardenhire's pamphlet *Fiji and the Fijians*, 1873.

humans, for in all other feasts they ate with their fingers . . . To be actually looking at these carved cannibal forks and to possess at the same time a vivid imagination—really I felt I must be about to attend one of these horrible, loathsome functions."[89]

The demand for these utensils was such that the ethnological collector J. Edge-Partington, writing of the late 1880s, warned that "special care" needed to be exercised in buying forks "as when I was in Fiji they were being made by white men for sale to travellers."[90] The preoccupation has endured: passing reference to forks is made in many travelers' books, and even now they are conspicuous in Fijian handicraft stalls. Though tourists no longer imagine that the items they purchase have actually facilitated the consumption of human flesh, the persistence of interest in the cannibalism of the "other" reminds us of the extent to which modern perceptions resemble the partial, racist vision of the nineteenth century.

Not all travelers interested in weapons and forks had the same attitude to Fijian material culture as the planters. The planters' view represents an extreme point, characterized by highly motivated hostility, which produced a restricted and unambiguous interest in a particular class of things. The artifacts of murder stories simply betokened the relative inhumanity of the Fijians and were not, for the planters who told the stories, polysemic objects.

Ethnology and the Vision of the State

Let us return to Von Hügel's surprise that "no-one had thought of making a local ethnological collection"—which of course prefaced his own intention to do precisely that. Anatole Von Hügel was, in 1875, a twenty-one-year-old of Austrian and Scottish parentage who had undertaken a South Seas voyage for his health, and who had, as a result of a quarrel with the missionary-anthropologist Lorimer Fison, been ejected from the Methodist ship in which he had been traveling and found himself in Fiji. His father had been a traveler and a collector of natural and ethnological specimens, and this background had obviously impressed itself upon the son.[91] His arrival in Fiji coincided with the crucial moment of the formal establishment of colonial state power: seven months earlier, in October 1874, the islands had been ceded to Britain by a group of leading chiefs. Governor Gordon arrived just after Von Hügel to establish the administration which was initially based on Levuka on the island of Ovalau, for many years the center of European settlement in Fiji.

Von Hügel was preoccupied almost from the start with indigenous artifacts and proceeded to make several trips into the more remote parts of Viti Levu. Although he was interested in seeing the country-side, encountering Fijians he took to be less acculturated, and col-lecting ornithological specimens, the principal purpose of these jour-neys seems rapidly to have become the collection of Fijian artifacts.

Von Hügel's approach to collecting was obviously quite different from that of any previous visitors, missionaries or settlers, because it was self-consciously scientific: Von Hügel made note of native names, raw materials, and the significance of some articles in indigenous trade. The formation of "a local ethnological collection" was some-thing definitely removed from the *ad hoc* acquisition of pieces grounded in narrative, and although Von Hügel never expounded a theory of collecting in an abstract way, it is clear that he attempted to obtain a wide range of material: from mundane items to ornaments and weapons, in standard forms as well as unusual or bizarre variants. It would be going too far to claim that the assemblages of things he acquired were actually representative of the totality of Fijian material culture in a strict sense, and there was certainly some bias toward things which were obviously indigenous valuables. However, because he found that barter proceeded best if he accepted everything that was offered, he inevitably received a broad range of objects:

> So as to encourage trade I bought everything, consequently a good deal of trash, that was offered to me tonight . . .[92]
>
> Trade now came in fast, *yaqona* [kava] bowls, some fine combs, whale tooth ear ornaments, etc. and prices were not ruinous, as for one pretty bowl the owner asked a fish-hook . . . The best thing I got was a fine black wig, which I took off a fellow's head, giving him a fathom of cloth for it at his own request.[93]

Von Hügel made adjudications apparently based on aesthetic criteria: some clubs were "good," others "very fine" but a few ornaments merely "indifferent." Initially he also ranked categories of things and was much more interested in ivory ornaments of the kind discussed in Chapter 2 and carved wooden items such as clubs and spears, than in pots or baskets (which happened to be women's products). Early on, he noted with regret that on one occasion he could obtain "only" women's fiber skirts *(liku)*.[94] But as this first collecting trip proceeded up the Wainimala valley and its tributaries in the eastern interior of Viti Levu, he rapidly modified this attitude; especially as he became aware that different types of *liku* were worn by women at different stages of their lives (as is, or at least was, broadly the case in Melanesia): "This variety . . . seems to be the distinguishing dress of girls from the time they have obtained womanhood till they become mothers."[95] He also began to recognize variation from place to place and later expresses not disappointment at being offered nothing other than skirts but satisfaction in having obtained some "good" *liku*.[96]

Von Hügel happened to travel into the area at a particularly fortuitous moment from the perspective of acquiring these skirts, since the people had just adopted Christianity, a change which was expressed— by both men and women—in the wearing of European fabric rather than local clothes. In oral histories conversion to Christianity is still referred to by the phrase "taking the *sulu*," that is, wearing a sarong-like strip of cloth (in the case of women, so as to cover the breasts) rather than local clothing. In fact, since Von Hügel was exchanging fabric for a variety of indigenous artifacts including skirts, the transactions were central to the consolidation of local conversion—although Von Hügel himself was Catholic not Methodist and, far from having an active interest in assisting mission work, he seems to have been concerned to seek out less "acculturated" Fijians. The most significant point, though, is that although the acquired skirts marked a moment of social transformation, and could have been read as artifacts of the history of conversion, Von Hügel had no interest in associating them with the events of the moment. Unlike the missionaries, who often grounded "idols" and other things in narratives of social change, and unlike the planters and travelers, who made clubs and cannibal forks the material expressions of murder stories and savagery, Von Hügel had no interest in singularizing the things he collected in such a manner. The historical context is mentioned only in passing in Von Hügel's journal, and when, as the founding curator of the Cambridge University Museum of Archaeology and Ethnology, he labeled and catalogued the Fijian specimens, he mentioned various ethnological points but not the context of acquisition (although I restored this myself when I prepared captions for new displays there).

Another kind of context was important, however: the development of Von Hügel's interest set up a relationship between objects and ethnographic facts whereby the latter could enhance the interest of the former: an article of clothing came to express distinctions in a domain which was seen to be more complex and significant than that of simple material entities. Tribal life and locally peculiar customs were of interest and their attributes surfaced in the differentiation of material items. There was an extension of the tangibility of the objects to the social facts that they were taken to stand for. Just as the casual visitor might want a "cannibal fork" because it attested to the factuality of the key symbol of savagery, someone with a more scientific and less immediately pejorative interest in indigenous life might seek out the things which embodied customs and social differences of various kinds. The scientized approach produced not just an ethnographic context but a wide array, an array which could be regarded as a totality and turned to the purposes of the state.

Von Hügel returned to Levuka at the beginning of August 1875 and found the new governor to be intensely interested in what he had seen on his trip into the eastern interior. Gordon invited Von Hügel to stay at the Government House (called Nasova), which he did; the main topics of discussion at dinner on the first evening included "Fiji and collecting."[97] In fact a number of those at the governor's establishment became deeply preoccupied with Fijian artifacts, as is clear from Von Hügel's general account of life at Nasova:

> Sir Arthur keenly appreciated the scientific value of ethnological collections, and interest of this kind being contagious, it was not long before fresh centres of attraction were formed, around which samples of native art amassed themselves. Soon, every room at Nasova had something of the Museum look about it, and the trade in "curios" became so flourishing that one small general business at the farther end of town expanded its premises and blossomed forth as a "curiosity shop" of fashionable resort.[98]

The obsessive character of interest was described by another of Gordon's guests, the typically Victorian "lady traveler" Constance Frederica Gordon Cumming, who noted on her return from a tour around Rewa and other localities:

> Great was the excitement of unpacking my canoe-load of curiosities; for we are each trying who can make the very best collection—Sir Arthur, Mr. Gordon, Captain Knollys, Mr. Maudslay, Baron von Hügel, and myself. Our daily delight is to ransack the stores in Levuka, where the natives may have bartered old things for new, and great is the triumph of whoever

succeeds in capturing some new form of bowl or quaint bit of carving. All our rooms are like museums, adorned with savage implements, and draped with native cloth of beautifully rich patterns, all hand-painted.[99]

In some respects, this enthusiasm was motivated by the singularity of things and aesthetic interests, but it was distinctly rapacious, and this feature linked it with the singular colonial project of the British in Fiji.

For colonial forces it was of course always possible to act or attempt to act without regard for indigenous relations, to ignore or pension off local leaders, and to deny indigenous sovereignty (as the British did in Australia, the French in New Caledonia, and the Americans in Hawaii). Gordon's approach was different: it depended upon hegemony, consent, and the fabrication of shared meanings rather than violence and the denial of identity between colonizers and colonized. Of course, the Crown Colony of Fiji was not a theater state, like Geertz's Balinese *negara*, oriented to symbolic display rather than government, or a persuasive expression of imperialist ritual that lacked violence— there were many forms of intrusive regulation and harassment, and an 1876 rebellion in the Viti Levu highlands was forcibly suppressed. The logic of colonial expansion makes it almost inevitable that collaboration and compromise with an indigenous elite, or with the population of one region within a colonized country, will engender resistance and hostility on the part of subaltern groups or traditional enemies in other regions. Gordon, however, went as far as he could in co-opting not just high chiefs but village chiefs throughout Fiji into the new elitism and bureaucracy of colonial society; and since the local roots of indigenous hierarchy had mostly endured warfare and turbulence of the kind described in the previous chapter, this was an effective strategy that mostly made the extent of resistance and disaffection among common people invisible.

The system of indirect rule celebrated Fijian chieftainship and chiefly customs but also established the Crown and the Crown's representative as the apex of the hierarchy. The project demanded more than the establishment of certain political and administrative mechanisms; it had a cultural dimension because of the status it ascribed to what was recognized as Fijian custom and customary government. Ethnological interests expressed not only the need to understand a system which was being reified and stabilized but the more general approbation of Fijian folklore, craft, and custom. As was appropriate to those who placed themselves at the top of an indigenous hierarchy, there was an enthusiastic and self-conscious but only partial "Fijianization" of the British administrative elite. Local people of high rank were frequently admired or appreciated: Lady Gordon described King Cakobau as "a fine dignified old man, with a most commanding manner, and perfectly at his ease."[100] She virtually acknowledged that this positive attitude reflected cross-cultural class solidarity: "One has a curious feeling of equality with the ladies of *rank*, they are so different from the common people—such an undoubted aristocracy. Their manners are so perfectly easy and well-bred . . . Nurse can't understand it all, she thinks we are all *silly* about natives, and looks down on them as an inferior race. I don't like to tell her that these ladies are my equals, which she is not!"[101]

Gordon identified himself as the paramount chief, and the high Fijian chiefs seem to have acquiesced and actively supported this identification. Although the concepts of permanent allegiance and the absolutism of the state were quite inconsistent with the fluid and contested character of Fijian hierarchical polities, those in power at any particular time were naturally in favor of rigidification of the relationships which privileged them: it is now very difficult to establish what divergences might have existed between the chiefs' affirmations and their unreported perceptions and motivations. But if the transformation of the governor into the paramount chief was founded upon mutual co-optation and mystification, the new order rapidly acquired a life of its own through practice. Gordon was frequently welcomed and respected with modified or transposed versions of Fijian ceremonies; he even received "symbolical first-fruits—ten yams from each province."[102] At Government House a kava ceremony took place every evening; those present were served in order of rank, and the native constabulary often performed chants and dances. Gordon found the ceremony "always picturesque and in its way solemn."[103] These words express the duality of the vision of the state: Gordon appreciated a spectacle of which he had a detached view, but he also participated in, and felt moved by, a ritual in which he was a privileged figure.

In September and October 1875 Lady Gordon, with the help of others, made an elaborate display of artifacts in the dining room at Nasova.[104] Lady Gordon herself said little about the rationale of the exercise but did mention in one letter that "such beautiful and artistic patterns can be made with clubs, spears, bowls, arrows, axes, paddles,

End wall of the dining room in Government House, Levuka, Fiji, about 1876. The photograph was taken by W. A. Duffy, a notable photographer of islanders who also worked from a studio in New Caledonia.

etc.," a remark which locates artistry as much in the ordering of the indigenous products as in the artifacts themselves. A photograph of the exhibit shows only one end of the room: all that we know of the rest of the display is that the room had nine doors, above each of which a large kava bowl three or four feet across was hung with a club on either side.[105]

The motivations in the arrangement perhaps did little more than play with morphology: shapes took on complementary relationships to produce symmetry and variation. Aestheticizing a spear or club is inevitably a political act that presupposes some denial of former context and of the capacity of indigenous producers to perpetuate their own uses and construction of things. That is true of all of the cases I have so far discussed: appreciation entailed appropriation. But this array differed from earlier aesthetic arrangements of Pacific artifacts in the volume of material, the context, and the great emphasis on balance and order which is not apparent, for instance, in eighteenth-century engravings. The assemblage in this case reflects a setting-out and rigidification of Fijian culture: the manipulation of the diverse objects implies the apprehension and ordering of the totality they represented, that is, Fijian society in its parts and aspects. The apical position of the governing elite gave them the vantage point from which the totality could be recognized. Fijians "at cross purposes" could never stand as subjects in relation to the detached object of their whole society. But the laying-out of clubs and other articles expressed the duality of the administration's stance. The interest in, and common appreciation of, the things expressed the empathy of one moment, the sense of culture shared with the Fijian aristocrats and "ladies of rank," but the effect conveyed something different—a moment of privileged vision and appropriation.

It is intriguing that the anthropologist A. M. Hocart later questioned the Fijian administration's use of Fijians in the inquiries which determined the functioning of the landholding system in the various parts of the island group: "When will govts. realize that a native is not the best authority on native customs? He is the worst for he knows nothing outside his tribe and sees everything in the light of his own customs."[106]

Hocart was in part advancing well-founded criticism of an inquiry which imposed models from parts of Fiji upon the rest, but he also revealed a sense that the detachment of Europeans from custom enabled them to transcend any locally inflected vision and instead apprehend the totality. Hocart was in no sense a government anthropologist, but this sense of ways of knowing is precisely what the setting-out of the array of variants in the dining room expressed. The assemblage did not merely imply a perception which transcended that of those seen as culturally bound natives; it also set out the aspects of the entity to be acted upon. The initial moment embodied curiosity and empathy, but this enabled the fixture of a totality which one was then in a position to alter, disarticulate, and adapt. And although much was made of preserving Fijian institutions, Gordon made it apparent from the start that certain features of Fijian society were to be changed. State power was to be pervasive, like "a net of very fine meshes" which covered the land; Gordon also emphasized that indigenous district and provincial officials were to write to him frequently, "at all seasons and at all times."[107] The omniscience of official vision with respect to the objectification of Fijian culture was thus expressed in the space which, more than any other, symbolized British colonial control in Fiji.

Artifacts as Tokens of Industry

Gordon's setting-out of Fijian material culture was not an isolated occurrence but reflected a broader trend in the organization of ethnological specimens in museums: these expressed the imperial state's vision of other parts of the world in a more generalized way. They also documented the technical advancement of the West through contrast with the rudimentary tools of various savage cultures and expressed, in particular cases, many other things. These representations did not, however, exclude differently motivated uses of tribal artifacts.

Gordon's policies of perpetuating the authority of chiefs and maintaining what was seen as the communal native system were adhered to and developed, and settlers continued to protest against this approach on various grounds. Traditional landholding and chiefly requisitions were said to stifle native enterprise, and it was claimed that the administration did nothing to train the Fijians industrially: they "are not taught to produce anything," wrote one colonist.[108] The cynical view of some of those in the administration—that settlers were really interested in cheap land and freeing up Fijian labor which they could then exploit—is entirely plausible, but it is interesting in the context of these complaints that native Fijian products were included in displays representing the "Resources and Progress of Fiji" at International Exhibitions in Sydney and Melbourne in 1879 and 1880. European products such as timber samples, cotton seed, cigars, bricks, and nut oil formed the bulk of what was displayed, but space was also devoted to exhibitions of Fijian cloth, mats, bowls, pottery, and fishing nets.[109] Expositions of this type, which often included dwellings, fake streets, and live specimen natives, made an entire colonial world visible and tangible:

> The Colonial Exhibition of 1886 has impressed many useful lessons on the public mind. The concrete and palpable realities connected with the English Empire have appealed to every type of mind, among colonists as well as among the untravelled population of Great Britain and Ireland, and the value of our Colonial Empire is realised to-day as it never has been before. One cannot help feeling that the thought and power which conceived and successfully carried out the magnificent idea of the Exhibition are capable of greater and higher work. The bringing together of articles from the various colonies for exhibition, inspection, and comparison, implies healthy and effective co-operation throughout the whole empire for one specified object.[110]

This is to remind us, once again, of the crucial role of material culture and of the optical illusion that it constantly offers us: we take the "concrete and palpable" presence of a thing to attest to the reality of that which we have made it signify; our fantasies find confirmation in the materiality of things that are composed more of objectified fantasy than physical stuff. Not that this mystification is a veneer of falsehood; the dialectic of reification and consumption is as necessary and fundamental as anything else constitutive of human sociality,[111] but the truths are truths of seduction rather than presence. The plausibility or justice of inferences derived from specific cultural objectifications are, however, available for assessment; I need add nothing to the view of the writer quoted, that the Colonial Exhibition demonstrated the feasibility and desirability of unified imperial federation governed through an imperial parliament.

While much can be said about the effects of these expositions and world's fairs as total displays, and their assumptions about audiences,[112] it is also important to consider the ways in which the products of particular countries are presented. The striking feature of the selection of the Fijian material in these cases was that, out of dozens of items, there were very few weapons in Sydney and none at all in Melbourne. The difference between what was presented on these occasions and Gardenhire's "Fiji Cannibal Exhibition" was thus vast: the array of native material culture had been wholly reformulated, and the central element of cannibalism replaced by an innocuous and commendable propensity for craftsmanship. This meant that Fijians might be drawn into economic enterprise and the colony's advancement and (for those aware of the politics at the time) implied the government's neglect in the area. The differences between these displays was of course as much contextual as historical: only eight years separated the Sydney exhibition from Gardenhire's show, and the discourse of cannibalism was perpetuated through such media as staged photographs of Fijian warfare for the titillation of travelers. The use of material to emphasize industry did not displace this preoccupation but served distinct purposes in the particular institutional domain of the advertisement of the colony; more broadly, it reflected a distinct "modality of colonialism"[113] that displaced the negativities of savagery and abrupt civilizing transformations with a discourse of improvement, suggesting progress and development within an existing fabric. Fijians were already available for, and suited to, commercial development; in the settlers' imagination, the obstructions were mainly at the level of administrative conservatism, but the administration also partook of Victorian ideologies of improvement in seeking to order and clean up the Fijians' persisting blemishes through programs of sanitary regulation and reform.[114] A similar depiction of indigenous craft and work as a basis for regulated native industry under settler colonialism is manifest in an early twentieth-century photographic tour of German colonies in the Pacific (published shortly before Germany lost the colonies as a result of the 1918 defeat).[115] These parallels reveal the projects of particular colonizers to be crucial in generating particular representations of indigenous peoples and material cultures: as was suggested by the constant figures of missionary discourse, these situational interests produced continuities across historical periods.

The Name of Science

The European exploration of the Pacific was a protracted affair; it persisted well beyond the period of Enlightenment voyages discussed in the first part of this chapter. But by the early twentieth century, the masculine thirst for penetrative pioneering was exhausting the scope for discovery, except in the interior of New Guinea; given that the demand for unexplored places exceeded the supply, it is not surprising that in the early 1920s the popular Australian photographer and filmmaker Frank Hurley should venture into parts of Papua well known to patrol officers, while representing himself through the Australian dailies as the leader of an intrepid party which had opened up, for the first time, the mysteries of a lost world, a prehistoric landscape inhabited by entirely untamed and ferocious savages. Although Europeans had long been discovering places already known to their indigenous inhabitants, it thus became necessary for them to discover places which were already known to other Europeans.

In terms of exposing rather than initially detecting, Hurley did "discover" the Papuan world to mass audiences through journalism, slide shows, lectures, films, and a book; in so doing he was producing representations of a colonial settler state (Australia) in a period when interests in further settlement and expansion in Papua New Guinea, the Solomon Islands, and the New Hebrides were conspicuous.[116] Many in his audiences imagined that there were tracts of land to be opened up; the pervading motif of the film Hurley made of his trip through the rivers and lakes of lowland Papua is of the pith-helmeted party hacking their way through dense vegetation or striding through grasslands, establishing that spaces existed.[117] The very humanity of the owners of these prospectively colonized areas was placed in doubt: women who were smeared with clay as required by mortuary observances were "so filthy and hideous it is difficult to believe them human."[118]

Frank Hurley was anxious that his expedition be regarded as more consequential than a mere tour, and he sought to legitimate it by taking Alan McCulloch of the Australian Museum with him. A considerable number of specimens was acquired, and on one occasion the task was facilitated by the absence of the occupants of a longhouse.

> Everything was inexpressibly crude and primitive. We had entered the Stygian homes of prehistoric swamp-dwellers living by the shores of a primeval sea . . . [their] belongings hung from the rafters in countless bags, and, though feeling compunction for our actions, we ransacked them. In the cause of science, McCulloch allows that even an unfair exchange is no robbery; so we collected and exchanged to the great advantage of the owners and to our supreme satisfaction.

Skulls, human bits, and tit-bits filled our bone-bag, while axes, knives and fabrics were substituted. Surely, indeed, Father Christmas had visited the house! Iron and steel replaced bone and stone, and a million years was bridged in a day![119]

The science which made the generosity of Hurley and McCulloch so manifestly distinct from theft appeared to consist in the delight of the chase, the pleasure of acquisition, the denigration of former owners, and the assertion of absolute distance between the European self and the Papuan other:

From a dim alcove I gave a yell of delight! We had discovered treasures beyond bonanza! Human heads! Stuffed heads! What luck!

Skulls painted and decorated had grinned from every niche, but heads—stuffed heads! Glorious beyond words! Had we raided a bank and carried off the bullion we could scarcely have been more pleased than with such desirable objects.

This is, of course, scientifically speaking, for I can scarcely conceive anything so gruesome as these hideous human trophies of the head-hunters. The heads had been severed from the victims, preserving the neck as long as possible . . . The stuffing process distorted the face longitudinally, whilst the mouth which was forced open excessively was stopped with a ball of clay. The eyes were likewise treated and decorated with red seeds. The whole gruesome object had evidently been subjected to a lengthy smoke-curing process which mummified it and stopped decay . . . a large seed was found in the brain cavity, which evidently caused much grim amusement when shaken as a rattle during their death dances.

I have never seen objects more ghastly and horrible than these grim trophies.

What sort of people could these be that so callously made toys of their victims? Infinitely barbarous, ferocious, and cruel, with no feeling nor thought for human agony and suffering, and I shuddered to think of the ghastly scenes that had taken place in the small clearing by the gloomy bamboos.[120]

What is perhaps most telling about this discourse is the physical absence of the native people: "It was a deserted world."[121] Orientalist writing has often created the absence of particular people through anonymity and stereotyping: nameless Polynesian women are merely bearers of breasts and alluring dark hair, nameless Melanesian men are headhunters with clubs and axes. This passage from Hurley's text takes this effacement of humanity a step further by imagining people who

McCulloch of the Australian Museum, with preserved heads, from Hurley, *Pearls and Savages*, 1923. These are not the same set of heads as those described in the passage I quote.

are never seen, whose million-year distance from civilization places them beyond representation. In this operation material culture performs a crucial mediating function. Just as one tribe was ironically presented as "welcoming" visitors and manifesting their savagery with a display of skulls, the crudeness of the general array of artifacts was "inexpressible"; the stuffed heads testified in a more specific manner to horrifying and murderous propensities of those with "no feeling nor thought for human agony," implying a lack of feeling or thought *per se*. Yet while the nature of the Papuans is explicitly represented to be beyond comprehension,[122] Hurley could confidently infer that the head would be shaken as a rattle during dances, and that this shaking would cause "much grim amusement." This would seem to establish conclusively the promiscuity of the artifact: the racist imagination roamed freely across these objects in the absence of their makers and users.

"Science" was (and is) of course a contested term, and Hurley's slippage and self-correction—"this is, of course, scientifically speaking"—marked the deployment of this authoritative cover for a characteristically colonial prurient tourism, which was as morbidly curious about heads and skulls in one part of the world as it was about foot binding and cliterodectomy in other parts. Hurley's claims were disputed on this occasion because his style of collecting material was too much for the Papuan administration: an assistant resident magistrate forwarded allegations to Port Moresby, and the collection was impounded while "irregularities . . . in securing certain curios" were investigated. Photographs of the "stuffed heads" in question appeared in *The Sun* amidst an acrimonious series of articles by Hurley under such headings as "Hurley—Not a Pirate."[123] Most of the specimens, including the heads, were in fact released, but a number of bullroarers and a shield were apparently returned to their owners. Hurley claimed that this would have been "far more valuable amongst the records and treasures of a museum than in the dinginess and filth of a dismal Dubu." But Science had not been entirely defeated: "However this object was photographed, and this is the next best record to the object itself."[124]

Hurley's savages are represented by their artifacts, rather than in person: "Part of the committee of welcome, Goaribi, N.G."

F. E. Williams, then assistant government anthropologist and later the author of many papers and a number of substantial anthropological monographs on Papuan ethnology, was prompted to write a report called *The Collection of Curios and the Preservation of Native Culture,* which stressed that "not every one that saith Science, Science, is a scientist."[125] Williams foregrounded ethical issues in insisting that the scientific claims were not the only ones that were relevant; questions about the "influence, for good or evil, of the collector upon the native" had to be raised. He even suggested that the sacral objects of Purari Delta secret cults provided "an example of an object which (at least from one point of view) should never occupy a place in a museum" because of the serious disturbance in native religious life that their loss caused. Though "absurd creations of wicker-work," they were "possessed of another meaning in the dimness and obscurity of their own environment."[126] Williams thus employed the same figure of darkness and partial invisibility as Hurley, but to a different purpose: the absurdity of the figures was in the viewer's eye, the viewer being identified with the outsider, perhaps the reader, or even the writer in his ordinary persona. But the writer was also the expert, who had some knowledge of native religion as a functioning system and who could therefore discern what might and might not be extracted from it without inflicting damage.[127] Although Williams's use of the tropes of obscurity and dimness aired the attribution of radical savagery that had been central to Hurley's text, darkness thus also marked the boundary between the vision of the casual collector and that of the anthropologist. Though the terms had changed, the issue was the same as that in Johann Reinhold Forster's quarrel with the ignorant and avaricious seamen who competed with him in the curiosity market. Williams policed the boundary by emphasizing differences between various forms of unsystematic collecting that privileged the spectacular, the grotesque, and artifacts allegedly representative of "vanishing cultures" and more thorough and systematic collecting that appropriated a totality in the manner of Von Hügel and Gordon: "The ideal Papuan Collection would be one in which each of the principal cultural areas was thoroughly represented, in its material culture generally."[128]

Williams's suggestion that the claims of science should not override the interests of the natives remains commendable, and he drew attention to the power relations that often made the appropriation of specimens possible: "There are many things which the native is genuinely unwilling to part with; but there is nothing which, with a little show of bluff or authority you cannot get out of him."[129] It is not clear, however, that the underlying motivation was primarily ethical; or perhaps the point is that ethics were constituted in the context of colonial administration. The ceremonies that Williams was anxious to see preserved were delicate mechanisms, "easily thrown out of gear by bungling," susceptible to being encouraged or corroded respectively by the sympathetic interest or ignorant interference of white men. "It is much as if one were playing some game of makebelieve—tea parties or doctors or any other—with a child. Follow her lead carefully, and all goes smoothly; but break the sequence, do something out of keeping with her notion of the game, and there will be an outburst:— 'All right, you've spoilt the whole show: I won't play.'"[130]

In colonial Papua, there was hence an underlying fear that the native, though child to white adult, and female to male, could refuse to play the game if mishandled; and Lieutenant Governor Murray's statement about the Hurley controversy made it quite clear that a local economy of power, rather than questions of general principle, was the nub of the matter. "Whether taking the possessions of natives who were outside the influence and control of the Government can be called robbery in a legal sense may be left for lawyers to discuss. But the action was one that no Administrator could acquiesce in, because it places immense difficulties in the path of the Administration which is endeavouring to get the wild natives under control."[131]

The previous chapter began with consideration of a narrative—a narrative which located the origins of asymmetry between white and native people in an exchange relation. A thirst for Western commodities was imputed to the indigenous actors, which led them to subordinate themselves through imbalanced transactions, to alienate their land, and perhaps to offer their labor for exploitation. In this story tribal peoples are the authors of their own dominance by Europeans. I have put forward alternative accounts of these early exchange relations. In the case presented by Hurley, the tribal people were in fact absent from the transactions which ostensibly constituted their engagement with the civilized world; their willingness to receive what Hurley substituted for their goods was presumed on his part, and the introduction of an analogy with Father Christmas must be seen as distinctly idiosyncratic. The encounter that was not really an one can hardly be seen outside the space of colonial fiction, but it does mark both the signifying power of certain pioneers and their disproportionate capacity to discover places and create relationships.

I have emphasized two propositions: a specific one, that in certain phases of contact and colonial history, indigenous people are no less powerful and no less able to appropriate than the whites who imagine themselves as intruders; and a general one, that indigenous perceptions of, and reactions to, foreign people and goods must be taken seriously. Hence the other alternative account I offered envisages a process of local appropriation for local ends and situates colonial dominance in part in the unforeseen consequences of engagement in trade, and in part in processes such as annexation and appropriation which were not, in any sense, initiated by islanders. Neither the French annexation of the Marquesas nor the assault upon the traditional Tahitian aristocracy were in any sense prefigured by early interests in iron, muskets, and fabric. These relations of displacement and dominance were effected through the practical projects of the various agents of colonialism described in this chapter: explorers, missionaries, planters, ethnologists, administrators, pioneers. Their interests in material artifacts attested at once to the mutability of such things and to the particularity of their projects. Some of these people had far less impact than others; the projects of some classes were related more to the ways in which others might be imagined and represented, rather than practically controlled, but they must all ultimately be seen in the global context of European dominance. There is thus an overall level at which Murray's statement applies to everything from Forster's gentle legislation to Hurley's misogynist dehumanization: they were all "endeavouring to get the wild natives under control." This is also why the conceit in the symmetry of my chapter titles must now be repudiated: indigenous appropriation may be compared with European appropriation to establish that both sides have creatively changed the purposes of abducted treasures, represented the other, and imagined a narrative of contact objectified in artifacts of alterity and artifacts of history. Those propositions remain valid, but analytical fictions are created to subvert and be subverted in turn; one of the ends of an exposition of parallel processes can be the exposure of their fundamental difference.

5

The Discovery of the Gift: Exchange and Identity in the Contemporary Pacific

> Wamirans constantly reminded me that they define their world, themselves, and their relationships in terms of food. To bring their beliefs into a framework that I could more easily grasp, they often explained, "We are taro people, but where you come from, people are money people." Time and again I was told, "In your place people are different. They work for money. That is their life. That is who they are."
>
> Miriam Kahn, *Always Hungry, Never Greedy*, 1986

Histories of the sort I've discussed here add up to the global process of imperialism, and imperialism is considered one of the most important causes of the "globalization" of culture, a topic that has received increasing academic attention.[1] Perhaps in popular perceptions more than scholarly discourse there is a certain crude modernism and Eurocentrism in some views of this process which take it for granted that internationalization entails homogenization, specifically, the assimilation of other cultures to Euro-American models. It is assumed that the popularity of manufactured consumer items in Asia attests to the immense appeal of Euro-American values and goods, even though East Asian production and technical innovation have eclipsed Europe and the United States as far as many consumer items are concerned. Such notions, like the idea that Eastern Europe has finally been won over to what was all along a better form of sociality and economy, perpetuate the same kind of misreading of others' perceptions and intentions that characterized colonial views of peripheral barter. In each case, appearances may be misleading, and representations of introduced artifacts and models of social organization need to be interpreted in the context of the place into which they are introduced, and not taken as essences that have merely been moved physically from places of origin. Nevertheless, imperial dominance and intensive contact have had effects, and so the privileging of local appropriation over the values of the world system would be equally inadequate and equally conducive to moments of political blindness. It is important to recognize that material products, as well as belief systems such as Christianity, or resources such as literacy, are always acted upon and reformulated by indigenous populations, but these acts of derivation and displacement take place as political circumstances change, and the real ramifications of the entanglement of local polities in wider relations need to be appreciated, rather than denied by some search for an authentically different culture.

It would seem important, then, to avoid establishing any theoretical principle about the relative significance of external dominance or global relations as against local autonomy and appropriation; transposition is instead a process that has variable content according to the political dynamics of colonial encounters and international relations. In some contexts, indigenous peoples may well denigrate their own culture and, regarding everything that is imported as better, draw upon the discourses of the dominant culture in attempting to modernize themselves (though it cannot be imagined that this ever takes place without semantic shifts, without some alteration to the content of borrowed languages). Elsewhere, the power of indigenous appropriation may be marked by manifestly subversive and ironic reproductions of European behaviors and activities. *Trobriand Cricket,*[2] a film that in many ways anticipated the anthropological interests in cultural hybridization and transposition of the late 1980s, is always delightful because the game's anticolonial mischief and parody is unmistakable. But I think James Clifford is wrong to regard the umpire's possession of an Adidas plastic bag (from which he dispenses betel nut) as an element of this parody.[3] This interpretation reiterates the assumption that material culture is a kind of index of acculturation, here inverted and valorized as subversive appropriation; but not all European artifacts are taken by Pacific Islanders as badges of Western culture, of the larger array that the game subverts. In any case, there is a more general sense in which the subsumption of displaced objects and imitated activities to the example of a game or parody can produce politically consequential misinterpretations.

In the area of exchange, the "distortion" of the meanings of objects such as guns through recontextualization might stand as evidence for mimicry, and I have piled up cases of indigenous and European appropriations, imagining a limitless succession of cultural reconstructions of the identities of things. I have stressed all along that material culture types do not have stable identities within particular cultures, and their renaming and recontextualization may be motivated in a variety of ways: ironically, the assumption that displacement amounts to parody presupposes the essentialist tenet that I have tried to displace—that an original identity is salient to recontextualization. The question is of some importance for the broader understanding of the nature of colonial contact and its ramifications.

For both Europeans and Pacific Islanders, the artifacts of the other were sometimes used for nothing particularly important (the plastic bag could well have been used in the unreflective and mundane way that indigenous containers would be used daily); more consequential uses included various ways of mediating, objectifying, and incorporating the history of contact—however that was understood. Imports exemplified a wider range of transactions and encounters, and the ways in which the objects were construed refracted larger moral evaluations of foreigners and one's intercourse with them. In many cases what was done with the other's artifacts could appear to be a complete travesty of proper meanings—the missionary's conversion of a figure into an idol, the Samoan construction of the "papalagi ship"—but terms such as "travesty" and "parody" are misleading insofar as they impute a subversive desire to render something funny and ludicrous.[4] Such subversion certainly is a feature of colonial representations produced by both dominant and subordinate groups, but the appearance of parody in the copying of institutions, practices, and objects from one's own tradition may distort the intentions of those doing the copying.[5] Hence the cargo-cult house in the shape of a colonial bungalow can only be a parody for us;[6] for the Fijian the official British imitation of chiefly customs could only be absurd; but perhaps in both these cases copying is appropriation, a project engaged in to specify alterity and to incorporate the powers of the other. The political seriousness of the intercultural transaction is diminished if acquisition and reproduction are understood primarily as burlesque imitation.

In earlier sections of this book, some of the ramifications of contact between Europeans and islanders have been discussed; the question arises of how the longer history of economic interpenetration has generated new conceptions of objects and exchange in colonized societies. Thus far I have considered early barter and trade, particularly in the first half of the nineteenth century, but what of the more recent past and present? Most rural Pacific Islands communities have experienced several waves of economic change over the last century, associated with formal colonial rule, plantation development, multinational fishing and forestry, and international aid channeled through both "decolonizing" metropolitan regimes and postcolonial independent states. The emphasis in the interpretation of early barter was upon the local incorporation of apparently intrusive goods and presences, but can such a model be sustained after long histories of engagement with wage work and commercial farming? Or have distinctive local conceptions been effaced through homogenization in a global village?

The questions about exchange with which I commenced have been placed in the background by the focus on changes of meaning in objects themselves. This analytical progression from exchange to consumption was motivated in part by dissatisfaction with anthropological models which privileged forms of exchange and neglected the cultural constitution of objects and interests in objects. It has been shown that the meanings of things are frequently saturated by larger narratives—as in the Marquesans' historicized guns or missionaries' artifacts of conversion—and moreover that these singular representations often determine the shape of exchange. The Marquesans, for instance, sometimes construed muskets actually received through barter as gifts from powerful and distant European monarchs; the fact that rejected idols were presented to missionaries for display as trophies, rather than acquired through purchase, was similarly central to evangelical propaganda. In these cases, understandings of the biographies of objects demanded a particular transaction form. Irrespective of the fashion in which things actually circulated, an association between a particular artifact and (say) giving rather than barter was expected and understood. This is not to suggest that movements of objects and varieties of transactions are inescapably diverse. It is obvious that modern capitalism entails certain relations founded in wage work, and that objects and services generally take the form of alienable commodities. But things which are in principle alienable can be moved into circuits of gift giving which, even in industrial societies, are hardly restricted to the private sphere of the family. Gifts among executives or between them and their secretaries may, for instance, be quite crucial to the structuring of relations and hierarchies within the localized elite cultures of corporations and bureaucracies. Similarly, Polynesian societies were in most cases dominated economically by hierarchical relations of dependence upon chiefs which made the values attached to gifts quite asymmetric: what passed upward counted as offerings, while what was redistributed downward manifested the generosity of the king or queen and the vitalizing wealth of the sacred polity.[7] Those relations could be said to amount to a chiefly mode of production, but the array of transactions within any particular Polynesian society cannot be assimilated to that model—just as the Melanesian gift economy postulated by Strathern does not incorporate all Melanesian prestations. Within these exchange regimes, certain relations were specific to transactions in particular kinds of things, such as food, while special artifacts such as heirlooms were governed by quite peculiar principles which did not apply to exchange relations in general.

The proposition that transaction forms are to some extent specific to fields of objects, goods, services, relations, and so on must thus be qualified to acknowledge the importance of the larger systemic context—wage relations, chieftainship, or gift conversions.[8] At another level, however, I wish to extend the claims of the argument by transposing some propositions about material culture to the domain of exchange. Cross-cultural copying, borrowing, and incorporation have been shown to be crucial in the field of the artifactual; here it is argued that despite the fact that anthropologists have generally interpreted clan economies in terms of the systems of local relations and meanings, analogous relations of reaction and appropriation operate at the level of exchange forms themselves. It is not just that local trade and gift giving can be shown in various ways to have changed, as a result of colonialism and capitalism, but that modes of representing transactions are now constituted historically and often oppositionally, especially with respect to reified ethnic categories of "natives" and "others."

Transformations of Fijian Ceremonies

Solevu, the large-scale presentations of "valuables of the land" described in Chapter 2, still take place frequently in rural Fiji, although how they fit into the larger system has changed. It is worth examining the distinctively modern salience of these events—which, being formal, ritualized, communal affairs, have a distinctively "traditional" appearance.[9]

The old *solevu* were grounded in the diversification of specialized craft production: that is, certain villages or groups manufactured things such as pottery, mats, salt, wooden ornaments, and barkcloth. With certain exceptions,[10] many of these articles could have been produced anywhere, or at least in more places than they were produced, but the pattern of specialization and consequent mutual dependence fitted well with the tremendous importance of alliance in Fijian society: the reproduction of persons was (and in rural groups still is) seen to depend upon paths, maternal links, and exchange. Hence *solevu* were (and are) virtually always presentations between affines and generally take the form of gifts to a group from whom a wife is being received, or to the maternal kin of a child or deceased person. The fact that the same valuables were not produced everywhere was thus not the result of an uneven distribution of natural resources but was socially contrived so as to sustain an environment in which major presentations brought *different* valuables into an area. Ceremonies could of course have taken place without differentiated production and extralocal imports, but the central feature of the Fijian ceremonies—in contrast, as was noted, with those of other groups such as the Marquesans—was the distinctness and asymmetry of two sides. What was presented to the mother's or wife's people was not simply a quantity of goods but valuables "of the land," which expressed through their singularity the corresponding singularity of the debt, the relationship. Taking a wife, as the mythical man Tabua discovered, could not be compensated for with food or labor; the debt was registered at a distinct level, in (fictively magical) valuables which had to be brought from elsewhere. What was central to these transactions, then, was the expression of qualitative difference.

It is not surprising that this system of specialized production could make use of things which were not produced within it. At some point—probably in the early twentieth century—Fijians began to make extensive use of European oil lamps, and by the mid-twentieth century, if not earlier, kerosene had become an important exchange valuable in marriage ceremonies and other presentations.[11] In 1988 it was always presented in a particular form, in twenty-liter drums, and stores of these were separate from domestic supplies of kerosene for lighting.[12] At large ceremonies such as marriages, and at the smaller presentations which take place prior to these in order to bring the property of one side together, long lines of men and women bring forward drums and mats respectively: it is not always enunciated that these are men's and women's valuables, but such an identification is quite manifest in the practice itself. Women make mats, and presumably men, in the past, would have brought forward other things such as the wooden bowls which were their craft products. Kerosene is purchased by men, and men are the primary controllers of domestic cash, but the money is obtained from farming—work which is in fact roughly shared. Hence there is a degree of elision of labor which arises from this change in the content of what is ceremonially given. Previously, what men and women contributed was in fact almost exclusively produced through male and female work (although men probably cut the pandanus which was subsequently made into mats, as they do today, and women might have contributed in incidental ways to men's valuables). To some extent, the novel fact of a disguised female contribution to "male" valuables would be thought not to matter by Fijians, because at the crucial moment when the principal presentation is made, it is very clear that this is a collective act, and the senior man who formally makes the speech of presentation, expressing respect for the receiving party and ritually apologizing for the paucity and poor quality of what is offered—his words belied by visible abundance—is understood to speak for the side, the *mataqali*. However, during the earlier phase of the ceremony male and female contributions are matched against each other, and at this point it would have to be said that the articulation of ceremonial exchange with commercial farming means that women contribute disproportionately, in a manner which did not take place before the acquisition of valuables was mediated by cash. There have been similar but more extreme developments in the New Guinea highlands, where big-men have appropriated the work of women in coffee plantations for prestigious purchases such as trucks.[13] In the Fijian case, this inequality is primarily an issue from an external, analytical perspective, and is not regarded as being important by either women or men. Women are quite aware that they work harder than men but regard this as the basis for reciprocity in matters of importance to them (such as church contributions). My interest here is primarily in the importance which is attached to *solevu* by Fijians; it is not just the content of relations that has changed but also their form and the mode in which cultural value is made explicit.

I was told on a number of occasions that the way *solevu* worked in the Sigatoka valley was that mats were presented by upstream groups to those downstream,[14] while drums moved upriver against mats. It was asserted that it was impossible for drums to be given by people higher up to those lower down, which puzzled me because I had witnessed a number of presentations at which this actually had taken place. There was a simple basis for the statement: the villages upriver had less access to shops, town, and such goods as kerosene, and it was thus said to be appropriate that drums move from people closer to the coast up into the interior (until the early seventies there was no road past the village of Keiyasi, which is only about half way up the valley). Discussion with older people suggested that this actually did take place up until the late 1950s or early 1960s; they acknowledged that subsequently, and especially recently, drums would often move in the other direction (the road now goes much further up the valley, and since people from the upper villages often go down to the market town of Sigatoka for the day to sell cash crops and go shopping, they have effectively the same access to kerosene as those much lower down). These circumstances are important not merely as illustrations of localized change or the use of an imported product in ceremonial exchange—such substitutions and incorporations are widely attested to— but also because recent developments suggest a shift in the underlying logic of exchange.

Previously, there was a great emphasis on presentation of the valuables produced by one's own group, or of other extralocal manufactured articles (such as wooden bowls from another allied group), that is, of goods which were external from the perspective of the receiving people. The whole array of ceremonies across the region clearly constituted a complex movement of specialized products, in which what was locally distinctive—and in a sense incommensurate—had the particular cultural value of expressing affinal debt.[15] Insofar as it is the case that drums are now presented by each group to all their exchange partners, the system has been reoriented toward difference based on quantity rather than kind. This stems from the importance of the ceremonies in the rhetoric of Fijian identity.

Fijian marriage in the upland interior is constituted through a series of presentations, which I will review briefly here.[16] Fijians make a distinction between proper customary marriage and elopement,[17] which is equated with the practice of white foreigners (vavalagi). The essence of this distinction is that in proper marriage (vamau), the choice of spouse and the timing of a series of elaborate feasts are made communally, while elopement is a spontaneous, individual affair. This dichotomy is telling ideologically but not practically significant, since "elopement" is often tacitly agreed to and should always be eventually followed by a compressed version of the presentations which constitute a formal marriage. Conversely, the choice of partner is not arranged without consultation, and marriage could not proceed without at least the acquiescence of the couple. It is significant, though, that Fijians actually represent the singularity of the customary ceremony in terms of a dichotomy between collective and individual interest.

A proposal may be initiated by an informal gift of cash or fabric from the man to the woman,[18] but from the wider perspective is marked by an offering of whale teeth between the clans; these are to be sent back in the unusual circumstance (given the likelihood of prior discussion) of the suit being rejected. Once agreement has been reached, the tabua often "rest" for a while, since the male side may need time to acquire or raise a sufficient number of cattle, as well as a few pigs, to provide for two very substantial ceremonies. The next stage is the vavanua, when the husband's people travel to the prospective wife's village, present valuables and cash, and are feasted; this is followed after an interval of a few months by the dresu ivola, which takes place when the couple sign a legally necessary declaration of their intention to marry. This has gradually been transformed from a small feast associated with this technical requirement into a full-scale ceremony, where almost as much property as is offered at the actual marriage will be presented from the husband's side to the wife's. Two or three months after this, the main ceremony will take place. For some time before a large vamau, the routine of life in the husband's village will be transformed by intensive preparations. A number of temporary structures will be erected for eating and sleeping; there will be several trips up nearby mountains to kava plantations, both to provide for the considerable amount of drinking which will take place around the ceremonies and to make up packages of this important cash crop for sale in town to cover the cost of other supplies. Women may stay up all night to finish their mats, and men will be actively collecting firewood; as the day for the arrival of the wife's people approaches, the village will begin to fill up with other relatives and visitors, and a sequence of small prestations will begin, through which the husband's side bring their *iyau* and *tabua* together.

The marriage itself will feature several ceremonies; on their arrival the wife's group will make an *isevusevu*, an offering of kava roots presented by any visitors on their arrival in a village or polity; this is reciprocated by a formal presentation of a bowl of the prepared drink, and these occasions are marked by an enormous amount of less formal drinking,[19] around the clock in smaller groups. There are usually two substantial presentations of property from the male side, one of which is the climax of the whole occasion. This takes place outside in the well-tended grassy areas that English observers in Fiji sometimes called "the village green," where a substantial group will be sitting respectfully as mats, drums, and other valuables such as pots and European fabric are stacked up. Occasionally a live pig or cow may be tethered nearby. The most important element of these gifts is a substantial number of *tabua*—perhaps forty to sixty. Although the flow of goods is thus generally from the husband's to the wife's side, the latter bring a substantial quantity of household goods—cloth, pillows, mosquito nets, saucepans, two or three articles of European furniture, and perhaps also a radio and Primus lamp.

It must be apparent that one of the most striking features of these occasions is the quantity of property offered, and the general sense of excess. Indeed, the abundance of mats, drums, and *tabua* to be presented are constantly remarked upon in the lead-up to the ceremonies, and this is also the reference point for later recollection. On the crucial point of what the presentations of valuables are supposed to effect, men volunteer a remarkably unambiguous statement: the goods are "the price of the bride."[20] More generally, explication of the overall meaning of the ceremonies relates to an idea of purchase:[21] once the presentations have taken place, it is said tersely that "for them" (or "for us," depending on the affiliation of the speaker), "it is finished"—it is as if a definitive transaction has taken place, and there is no subsequent association between the woman and her natal group.

What is notable here is the discrepancy between a notion of such a precise and bounded transaction and the wider ramifications which marriage tangibly has. Even with regard to the woman herself, it is true that she cannot work much with her natal kin, but she will do so occasionally and will certainly sustain strong links—manifest in mutual visiting—with her brothers and other relatives. In the larger field of relations, the general indebtedness of a group to the people from whom their wives and mothers come is manifold and profound, especially as it appears for the next generation in the relation between son or daughter (vasu)[22] and mother's brother (koko). There is a strong sense, especially for men, that the koko should periodically be visited, and it is impossible simply to call in briefly at the mother's village; if this is a distant place, and if visits are infrequent, a man should stay for at least a couple of weeks, drinking a lot of kava and staying up all night talking, as well as assisting with whatever routine work is going on. Although vasu do make contributions when their mother's brother's people are mounting a substantial solevu, or when they are raising funds to build a new church, indebtedness is not quantitative and material—to be offset or restituted through work—but is instead registered in sociality and engagement.

Women do not explain marriage presentations in the same way as men; they do not adduce the purchase/sale or price idioms. They suggest more straightforwardly that there is a great accumulation of valuables "because, in Fiji, a woman is a sacred thing."[23] At one level, this is to imply a one-to-one relationship between the worth of the mats, drums, and tabua and the worth of the woman; and this would be consistent with the male account. But in another sense the women's view is perhaps truer to the processual logic of these exchange relations: as I argued earlier, the primary and original significance of the tabua is as a marker of exchange, of the movement of singular valuables against women. The practical endurance of mutual but asymmetrical enchainment makes it plain that the values of goods and persons are not written off against each other. Debt is a persisting condition which must be periodically addressed and recursively acknowledged through presentations, rather than a consequence of one gift which can be repaid. Presentations evince relations which evolve and ramify; they do not exist in a relation of equivalence to other presentations. From one angle, particular marriage solevu are only elements of much longer histories of affinity, and since these groups exchange spouses there is much consolidation and mutual confounding of wife-giving and wife-taking relations. However, the Tabua myth signals the paradigmatic and founding character of marriage as far as a much wider set of relations is concerned: the display of a relationship between valuables and women creates value in both. Hence a woman is "a sacred thing," and *iyau* can represent value and express debt in a wider range of transactions.

My point is that the male statements about price and purchase could convey a false view of marriage presentations. Although I have disagreed with Strathern's totalization of gift relations into a "Melanesian gift economy," I take much of her argument to apply to the practical ramifications of exchange and affinity in this part of Fiji; here persons and relations produce gifts which are inalienable in principle. But where does this analysis leave the claim that the pile of mats and drums is "the price of the bride"? Any interpretation which systematically excludes propositions that have been expressed forcefully by a group of actors (here the men if not the women) must be in its own way false, or at least incomplete. Pacific Islanders frequently offer analogies between forms of internal exchange and cash transactions or European economic relations, and the rhetoric which these claims and comparisons serve must be attended to; it is not satisfactory to dismiss such statements as marginal accretions arising from the partial contamination of a kinship economy by commercial dealings.[24]

Just as material objects are often assimilated to local categories, the notion of price can be seen to have undergone some mutation through recontextualization. Its particular sense provides the basis for a wider view of the motivation of the male account. Something said frequently during *solevu* is that the work of a marriage (or that required by any other ceremony) is "difficult" *(dredre)*. In observations and asides in the midst of many tasks such as cutting wood, butchering cattle, making mats, and bringing valuables together, this fact of difficulty is alluded to. These remarks relate both to the work of the whole occasion and to the property offered, the woman's "price." The cattle and drums are said to be difficult because of the monetary value they represent; informants will point out, as carcasses lie out in an open space prior to presentation, that these are worth between $200 and $400 or even $500 each, and that each new full drum of kerosene costs about $12.[25] The worth and difficulty of these are said to be superseded, though, by *tabua*. Whale teeth are frequently said to be "heavy" in a sense which precisely mirrors the connotations of "weighty" in English;[26] their difficulty is similarly reflected in prices of $60 to $100 for large teeth, which are the only teeth acceptable in important presentations.

All the talk about "difficulty" reveals a morality of price. In a market situation, a price may be too high or too low, but the ease or difficulty of assembling the price of a thing is irrelevant to moral calculation: whether a purchaser can buy outright or needs to sacrifice and take out loans has no bearing on the justice of an amount. But in Noikoro the fact of difficulty is central. Although there are certain quantitative notions about what should be contributed—two drums per man, four mats per woman—in practice there is much variation, and people often have no clear idea of the numerical quantities of what actually has been given. The commitment is to present an abundant and difficult quantity of valuables, not any specific number. This is also why a system which formerly turned upon qualitative difference has changed to accommodate the substitution of like for like: drums for drums, mats for mats. Insofar as the ceremony has come to be appreciated primarily as a display of commitment to the way of the land, quantity rather than distinction becomes the measure of dedication.

The references which are often made to the cash value of exchange goods enunciate the fact that cattle, kerosene, and whale teeth are not fixed within the kinship economy of ceremonies and relationships. This sense of a lack of containment stems from a broader understanding of kinds of social life. These rural Fijians postulate a dilemma between two paths: the way of the land and the way of money, which are seen to stand in tension, if not to be incompatible.[27] The former is expressed in respectful behavior, relatedness, daily rituals such as those of kava drinking, and above all in major ceremonies, while the path of money is understood as an individualistic pursuit of business and personal gain, which can only be effectively pursued if kinship obligations and sociality are neglected. It should be stressed that this is a cultural polarity which fails to reflect a great deal of practical interpenetration between the domains of cash crops and ceremonial activities; it is arguable, in fact, that the latter energizes the former through creating demand for cash and produce.[28] Ironically, the model of dual sectors (traditional and modern, subsistence and capitalist) postulated in much theorization of modernization, development, and imperialism fails to reflect the actualities of the rural Fijian economy but does correspond at some level with the perceptions among rural people and Fijians generally. As in many other parts of the world, there is a strong identification of the countryside with tradition and the past; in some cases these ideas denigrate rural peoples seen as backward, but in Fiji the reserve of custom and authenticity is affirmed in opposition to the values and behavior of others. Fiji-Indians, white foreigners, and many urban Fijians are stereotypically thought to pursue work, commerce, and careers and to lack kinship and customs of respect. Efficacy in one domain corrodes social value in the other.[29] This proportionate relationship was directly attested to one afternoon during a relatively small ceremony. A man next to me remarked upon the fine appearance of the pile of pots, drums, and mats, adding in the next breath: "In Fiji it is difficult. We are poor." This further expresses what might be seen as a general operation in Fijian estimations of persons and relations—value in one domain energizes value in another—but in this case the relationship entails inversion. Fijians constantly make ethnocentric claims about the social value of their own order: they have real kinship and real mutual caring; old people are looked after; and unlike white foreigners, they are genuine Christians (true enough). Neotraditional culture is thus distinguished from its indigenous antecedents by a profoundly oppositional orientation. Elsewhere in the Pacific, the main contrast is with ways attributed to whites, but in Fiji indigenous and customary values are also upheld against Fiji-Indian culture. Insofar as it contributes to ethnic distrust, this ideology thus has a negative side, but here I am more concerned with the way in which the instability of things which could be either commodities or exchange valuables and the compelling image of alternate paths permit Fijians to translate a sense that they are "poor" and handicapped in commerce into a sense of moral superiority. This is why "price" becomes the appropriate reduction of a complex series of gifts.

I suggest that this polarization is central to Fijian culture in its distinctively neotraditional form—as it is elsewhere in the Pacific, with predictable variations[30]—but it should be noted that the morality of these juxtaposed terms is not always construed in the same way. There are many rural Fijians who are less committed to customary ceremonies than those whose views have been quoted, who often live in small homesteads away from villages and concentrate upon their own commercial projects. They work hard and say that men who stay in the villages spend too much time drinking kava and never accomplish anything. Although Fijians' sociality is generally characterized in the terms that I have set out, the primarily affirmative view of these ways reflects the point of view of the sort of people an anthropologist is likely to take up with—a group committed to customary ways and distrustful of those who have stepped away from them.[31] These moral and political ideas can perhaps be specified through examining a particular thing—not an artifact, but an animal.

I have noted that cattle are an important component of *solevu*. They are called *bulumakau* (bull and cow) by Fijians, and from the perspective of many Fijians, *bulumakau* differ from cattle. Cattle, as we understand them, are basically commodity animals; they are not individual creatures and are convertible above all into kilogram-weights of various grades of meat which have market values. The meaning of *bulumakau*, by contrast, was established around the turn of the century on the basis of the significance of pigs. In rural Fiji, domestic pigs are never killed for an ordinary meal and usually mark the presence of a visitor or the occasion of a feast.[32] In 1908 a colonial officer noted that cattle "are beginning in Native estimation to take the place of pigs. At gatherings when feasts are made, nowadays much more beef than pork is in evidence."[33]

Presumably, pork was formerly used in all ceremonies, but the modern use of *bulumakau* expresses the differentiation of events on the basis of the kinds of animals which are offered and consumed: *bulumakau* are reserved for the most important occasions—essentially marriage and death—where they are both presented as carcasses with valuables and slaughtered for feasting (the feast not strictly being a component of the presentation). People in western Fiji who are committed to the way of the land strongly hold the view that *bulumakau* are raised for ceremonies; a man when asked why he farmed them at all might say, "because of the old lady, because of Joanna, because of Johnny," meaning that the animals would be needed for feasts when his mother died, and for gifts associated with his daughter's and more particularly his son's marriages. However, many people do farm cattle commercially, and one of the principal ways in which rural Fijians pursue the "path of money" is through grazing; even those Fijians who claim that their herds are for ceremonial purposes sell individual beasts periodically. The *bulumakau* thus has an unstable character: as its origins in a gift from a European trader to a Fijian chief in the 1830s might suggest, it is potentially a commodity or a gift, an animal which is valuable because of its association with ceremonies and gifts in the way of the land, and also an animal which is valuable in that it may have a price of $400. This duality, though, is precisely what makes ceremonial presentations of "difficult" things like whale teeth and cattle such a poignant context for the expression of modern rural Fijian identity. *Tabua*, too, are commodities, often pawned to Chinese or Indian shopkeepers or purchased from them when a ceremony is approaching. The value of internal exchange is paradoxically expressed through the market value of things which are not sold: the men who drew my attention to the value of cattle, drums, and whale teeth were using monetary value as a measure and metaphor for their dedication to custom, to the ways of the land.

The convertibility of things and the possibility that they could be sold rather than consumed through grand customary marriage presentations thus permit the explicit expression of the singularity and worth of the Fijian way. The dedication of energy is marked by the possibility of its absence, or its socially unproductive redirection into business. From the perspective of the history of anthropology, there is a certain irony: while late nineteenth- and early twentieth-century schools often postulated that customs were reproduced simply because certain savage peoples were bound to adhere to their traditions, in this case it is precisely a certain sense of choice that makes it possible for Fijian custom to be privileged in moral terms.

The Disclosure of Reciprocity

People who are entangled at once in a kinship economy and in petty commodity production draw a market metaphor, the notion of price, into the context of life-cycle ceremonies. Perhaps this is obvious: what else should one expect to occur? My argument, however, is intended to suggest a broader critique by drawing attention to features of the meanings of modern rituals and kinship relations in the constitution of local identity in island societies. While very few anthropologists actually suppress the facts of contact history and engagement in plantation or migrant labor, the dominant approach to interpretation and explanation in Melanesian anthropology has been to render them completely marginal. My aim is not to suggest that the topic of contact history should displace cultural inquiry but rather to demonstrate that the meanings of exchange relations and ceremonies are historically constituted. That is, indigenous comparisons between local and foreign white practices are not contingent on marginal observations for the benefit of a visiting stranger; they instead express a set of contrasting values through which older cultural relations and activities have been refracted, made explicit, and revalued. This distinctly modern culture is neotraditional in the sense that "tradition"—an authentic core of indigenous precedents which are necessarily distinguished from foreign or "modern" ways of life—stands as an explicit reference point for practice and for moral and political adjudications.

Wider images of reciprocity and sociality, as well as particular ceremonies, are drawn into such objectifications of local identity. The notion of the "Fijian way of life" embraces attitudes toward relationships, daily behavior, and many aspects of etiquette, as well as recognized customary occasions such as *solevu*. For instance, there is a common feeling that whenever someone walks past a house he or she should be invited in for food and tea; if one walks through a village, such invitations are likely to be issued from many dwellings. This expresses politeness rather than an expectation that such invitations will be taken up, but people do in fact eat or take tea in one anothers' houses frequently and casually. Whether this was done earlier or not, the point is that the practice has acquired novel value. It is cited with pride in explanations to strangers (such as anthropologists) of what the Fijian way consists in: "Among you *vavalagi* this is not possible. If you see someone coming you shut your door."[34] It should be emphasized that although this picture of the Fijian way is an idealization often enunciated for outsiders, it is not merely a facade of no internal relevance. The account masks predictable tensions about land and many other things, but the image of communities suffused with kinship and reciprocity is one that Fijians attempt to sustain among themselves and that has practical as well as rhetorical effect.

This moral construction of indigenous manners has a number of other features. One relating particularly to internal exchange is a prohibition upon cash transactions within villages. In neotraditional Fiji, villages (as opposed to towns) are rule-governed in a number of conspicuous ways. Forms of respect which might be relaxed elsewhere are supposed to be observed; raucous games are said (by older people) to be prohibited; nothing should be carried or worn high on the body; and hats should not be worn. These *tabu* apply in a more intense form in the vicinity of the chiefly house in which certain important ceremonies take place; women will not walk past such a house carrying loads. While small shops are found in some Fijian villages, they are generally in peripheral areas or are actually outside village boundary fences.[35] Buying and selling (of meat, for instance) between villages can and does take place in other spaces, such as at football fields, which are external to villages. While we have seen that cash is often incorporated into ceremonial exchange, there are parallels elsewhere in the Pacific to this suppression, or notional suppression, of buying and selling within the community. As Jocelyn Linnekin has written, rural "Hawaiians say that monetary transactions have no place within the village. As one informant explained, 'Keanae is a small place. The minute you sell, you going to get into trouble. You *give*, don't sell. When you give, something tastes good; but when you sell, it not going to taste so good.'"[36]

Here the approbation of what is notionally distinctive to native culture is conspicuous, but it is important to reiterate that a re-ification, even if relatively homogeneous, may be subject to con-flicting assessments. Work in the "invention of tradition" genre almost always assumes that people assert that their traditions are good, but there has been as much scope for self-critique in indigenous re-flections on cultural difference as has always characterized our play on us and them.[37] The stereotyping of foreigners as commercial individ-uals unconstrained by the burden of kinship is thus engaged in by some Fijians who want to modernize themselves and get rid of the shackles of custom and the chiefly hierarchy, by young urban women who are sick of arranged marriages—though of course "arrangement" only became recognizable through the presence of another practice that could be taken as its opposite. Dissident Fijians refer to the same emblems of customary life as those who affirm the path of the land, rejecting rather than celebrating them. As in relativist anthropology, what is foreign serves as a counterexample and an alternative to one's own culture.

The particular character of Fijian ambivalence with respect to the way of the land reflects the circumstances of an independent nation dominated by a "traditional" indigenous elite and the Methodist church, as indigenized and hegemonic as the state. Disaffected com-moners would inevitably challenge "customary" values as well as par-ticular economic and social asymmetries, but comparable forms of antitraditionalism are found among some urban islanders who stigma-tize as "archaic" the folklore versions of their own culture purveyed in nationalist rhetoric.

The people described by Linnekin are at a much greater remove from antecedent "traditional" (as opposed to neotraditional) society than most Papua New Guinea or Fijian groups. It is thus not surprising that their affirmations of local life and identity depend on highly generalized and stereotyped images (such as mutual respect and reciprocity) rather than the particular ceremonial cycles privileged by the Fijians, or the gifts of taro which the Wamira people of eastern Papua, described by Miriam Kahn, [38] represent as being central to their way of life. An older anthropological terminology would have recognized degrees of "acculturation" here. In some cases local kinship structures are dramatically attenuated; people may have been Christian in some sense for one hundred or one hundred and fifty years. Elsewhere, there are greater degrees of continuity in ritual life; older men and women may have been born prior to colonial pacification or religious conversion. While different histories have of course had profound ramifications, it is this commonsense notion of "more" or "less" change that we must be suspicious of. Anything like quantitative measurement of the effects of contact overlooks a basic consequence of any kind of engagement, whether limited and peripheral or profound and destructive: all Oceanic societies have come into relations with external groups which have been available for symbolic elaboration in oppositional terms. Moreover, this potential for symbolic elaboration has, by now, mostly been rhetorically exploited, most significantly in the domain of exchange. As many forms of exchange continue to have complex ramifications in the context of the production and reproduction of kinship relations, there has been a tendency for indigenous people to emphasize the fact of reciprocity in their own transactions, that is, to emphasize the ways in which these presentations differ most from the "money life" of white foreigners. While the contrasting objectification and articulation of the meaning of indigenous sociality has taken many forms, the assertion that local reciprocity is emblematic of a kinship order is prominent in many areas. This local rendering of larger economic contrasts brings the analysis of this book around full circle: while I argued earlier that the older anthropological construct of the gift depended more upon an inversion of the category of the commodity than upon anything which really existed in indigenous Oceanic societies, Pacific Islanders have now created customs of reciprocity and an idea of the gift. For you or I to decide that the gift/commodity distinction is theoretically untenable would seem a case of shutting the stable door after the concept has bolted. Of course, this is not really a matter of the derivation or transmission of ideas but one of the emergence of a neotraditional culture through oppositional practices: engagement with markets and wage relations has created difference in a domain which is represented as separate from, and anterior to, the world of money. Particularly when islanders have experienced these relations at a geographical distance from their own homes, through engaging in indentured labor and migration, they have experienced another kind of exchange and economy and been able to recognize their own from an external vantage point. By making custom (or *kastom*) explicit, and through a sociality based on rules and reciprocity, islanders seem to have become more traditional than they could ever have been before. Ironically, the models which anthropology imagined for pristine societies have been approximated through acculturation.

Discoveries

The prisms of anthropological theory produce several ways of seeing objects. Most theories of prestations, whether Maussian, Marxist, or neither, tend, insofar as they are dedicated to the analysis of transactions, to leave the nature of things exchanged as an absent space, a matter of no particular consequence for the preconditions or outcomes of exchange. This is to say not that particular commentators absurdly suppose that objects are uniform, but that all that counts theoretically is the social relationship; hence a gift of a ritual ax, or of food or sex, can only figure analytically as a gift. At the same time, it is apparent that the logic of the relations which these movements engender cannot be subsumed into a unitary model. Fijian ceremonies may consist of sequences of "gifts," but offerings of valuables recursively acknowledge debt and allay malaise, offerings of food acknowledge presentations and have no bearing on debt, and debt is engendered by relations rather than transactions. The nature of what is presented is indissociable from the ramifications of the transaction.

When we do take objects seriously, we seem to jump to an assumption that they are badges of some personal or collective identity. While Daniel Miller acknowledged that "the object may lend itself equally to the expression of difference . . . and to the expression of unity," his argument, discussed earlier, made the subject-object process central; hence the objectification of identity is theoretically privileged. Many of Miller's specific claims are relevant to the Pacific, but no discussion of the region can neglect colonialism, which makes the objectification of difference and history more conspicuous than, or at least as conspicuous as, ethnic or subcultural affirmation. The history of colonial contact has provided a master context for the various narratives and fragments of narratives presented here, and for anthropology this perhaps offers an alternate framework to the juxtaposition of us and them, which in turn makes other ways of seeing social and geographical difference possible. Against prevailing anthropological visions of stable cultures, I have insisted that island societies have been profoundly affected by relationships with dominant European powers and their local extensions and expressions; this contact has been interpreted broadly, in the sense that the ramifications of contact predated, and now persist beyond, the period of formal colonial rule. But colonialism was not a monolithic metropolitan enterprise that had some kind of uniform "impact" in colonized places; on both sides, interests in entanglement were uneven and differentiated, between chiefs and commoners, between indigenous men and indigenous women, and between the explorers and natural philosophers who appropriated the space of male reason in opposition to the licentious feminized curiosity of common sailors. Almost by definition, colonial entanglement and struggle turn upon the difference between indigenous peoples and foreigners, natives and intruders, but recognition that this axis is fundamental should not obscure or marginalize the crucial fragmentation of knowledge and interests on both sides, the struggles which always take place within both the metropolitan project of colonialism and the indigenous project of appropriating or reacting to colonial intrusion.

The sense of urgency about this basis for analysis has not, however, enabled me to write an account of Pacific exchange within the colonial and "postcolonial" periods, which is in some sense self-contained; the facts of colonial history do not themselves provide a sufficient context for interpretation. My concern is with entanglement rather than colonial "penetration"—I find myself unable to deploy the feminizing images of indigenous places which have proved so seductive for many writers on imperialism and the world system. While the profound asymmetries of colonialism cannot be overlooked, any theory which recapitulates the pioneers' ideology of vacant or passive spaces for European conquest and achievement must falsely diminish the prior dynamics of local systems, their relative autonomy, and their capacity for resistance. That is why a chapter on permutations of debt and forms of exchange in Pacific societies was a necessity: it could not be supposed that the processes of early barter and subsequent transformation arose merely from the conjuncture of cultural contact.

Anthropology has tended to operate at two levels—the ethnographic and the theoretical. Although the former reveals a great deal about local nuances and the particular expressions of cultural meaning in exchange relations, theoretical discussion has almost always privileged the general type, such as the gift, or general theorizing of production, consumption, and circulation in economic anthropology. Here I have sought to collapse some of these separations and place difference between the societies of a region in the foreground. This has submerged the issue central to much anthropological writing—the contrast between "their" customs and "ours"—and drawn the analysis of economic forms such as debts and prestations into a comparative historical analysis. I have devoted more space to the stories of colonialism than to exposition of the forms of prestations in indigenous systems, but in a certain analytical sense, these domains of discussion should be seen to have the same weight. If inadequate and overgeneralized notions of "gift economies" are displaced by more locally particular models of prestations, alienability, and debts, and if this discussion is integrated with the interpretation of the cultural differentiation of artifacts, some sense can be made of the process of colonial contact in different areas.

Objects have been central in these transcultural histories; they have often marked alterity and particular strategies for dealing with it—through appropriation and incorporation or distancing and recontextualizing. Some things mark the (partial) acquisition of the capacities or attributes of the other; others express indeterminacy and a bridge between apparently incompatible systems; others now stand for totalities formerly unrepresented, which are discovered, as explicit forms, through the process of contact.

In the Pacific, the word "discovery" is tangled up with the great voyages of exploration; Wallis, Bougainville, and Cook "discovered" islands that had been inhabited for hundreds or thousands of years by their indigenous owners. The exposure of something that is, in some sense, already known is appropriately present in some older senses of the verb: through confession, a criminal might for instance "discover" or disclose his guilt; "discover" could simply mean to expose, reveal, or uncover anything. In these terms, the process of contact in the Pacific has produced a great deal of "discovery": just as George Keate could write in 1788 that the pilfering engaged in by the Belauans suggested "a satire on society," an exposure of the failure of civilization to sustain the spontaneous order which appeared to exist in such places as the "Pelew Islands," Pacific Islanders have used selective constructs of other societies as foils for explicit models of their own sociality, which are linked with analogous projects of affirmation or criticism of the customary regime. While contact with groups recognized as others of course has precontact and prehistoric counterparts, the marked character of difference and the consequent degree of discovery through the colonial encounter are clearly unprecedented. The histories of cultures in the Pacific Islands in the nineteenth and twentieth centuries have been marked, above all, by this process of rendering local practice explicit through politicized juxtaposition to whatever is taken to be European custom, whatever stands as "foreign."[39]

This is the point that (stereotypically speaking) both the local ethnographer of a culture "out of time" and the theorist of the global system must both miss: contemporary culture and sociality are constituted historically, locally, and willfully. I have mapped the ways in which indigenous exchange systems responded to external trade, the ways in which European collecting encoded various hierarchizing and legislative projects, and the ways in which modern exchange now operates as a vehicle for the mediation of perceptions of the larger world of money and the local world of kinship. The notion of entanglement aims to capture the dialectic of international inequalities and local appropriations; it energizes a perspective situated beyond the argument between proponents of the view that the world system is essentially determinate of local social systems and those asserting the relative autonomy of individual groups and cultures.[40]

I have emphasized the continuing dynamism of local societies, but for many other writers cultural difference and plurality have long been on the point of extinction: Malinowski lamented the fact in the opening pages of *Argonauts of the Western Pacific*, his great work on Melanesian exchange, and it is still possible, sixty years later, for ethnographic film producers to display a "Disappearing World." The technology which has enabled us to measure this vanishing heterogeneity, this process through which the world system has become encompassing, consists in the visual inspection of material culture.

Thatch is replaced by tin, wood and bark by plastic, local fabric by factory output—everywhere authenticity yields the ground of identity to sameness and junk. If there is one commonsense theory that this book has been directed against, it is this curious idea that artifacts are subjects rather than objects, things which produce or express cultural change while standing as fixed and stable entities themselves. Although I have tried to exorcize certain ways of imagining colonialism through gender imagery, there is another kind of sexual metaphor that I cannot resist. Bearing in mind confusions about true and false rings, I have insisted upon the promiscuity of objects and imagined playful, powerful, politicized affairs constituted through moments of desire, incorporation, intransigence, and risk; giddy moments in which shared histories or their absence become crucial; and moments in which prior meanings and affiliations can be violently distorted. Although the outcomes of liaisons with artifacts cannot be predicted, there is a sense in which both positive ramifications and political damage can always run beyond initial expectations; it is perhaps this instability, historicity, and lack of historical containment that epitomizes the entanglement we all have with objects.

NOTES

INDEX

Notes

Introduction

1. Fra. Paolino de San Bartolomeo, A *Voyage to the East Indies* . . *Collected from Observations Made during a Residence of Thirteen Years, between 1776 and 1789, in Districts Little Frequented by Europeans* (London: John Davis, 1800), p. 156.

2. J. R. Forster, note to ibid. Forster supplied the notes in the course of preparing a translation of Paolino's work into German. The English translation (by William Johnston) was from this text rather than the original and includes the annotations.

3. In an important recent book the us/them opposition is self-consciously offered as an analytic fiction, a contrivance justified by theoretical ends (Marilyn Strathern, *The Gender of the Gift: Problems with Women and Problems with Society in Melanesia*, Berkeley: University of California Press, 1988, pp. 16–17, 38). Without denying the specificity of Strathern's intentions and the value of her theoretical innovations at another level, I find this merely a subterfuge: it does not matter whether one entertains a naive idea that there is some underlying truth to we/they, European/Melanesian oppositions or regards these as devices that can generate literary and theoretical effects. The point is rather that such constructions are taken to be apt at any level. I share James Clifford's sense that "all dichotomizing concepts should probably be held in suspicion . . . If all essentializing modes of thought must also be held in suspense, then we should attempt to think of cultures not as organically unified or traditionally continuous but rather as negotiated, present processes" (*The Predicament of Culture*, Cambridge, Mass.: Harvard University Press, p. 273).

4. The claim here that the focus on recontextualization and the mutability of things is "new" is not to be taken as a claim of originality on my part; the debt to other writers such as Arjun Appadurai is made clear in Chapter 1, and it will be evident that it is the expression and theoretical direction of these ideas which is novel, rather than the observation of transformation in itself.

5. Adrienne Kaeppler, *Cook Voyage Artifacts in Leningrad, Berne, and Florence Museums* (Honolulu: Bishop Museum, 1978), p. vii. It should be noted that a more recent article of Kaeppler's ("Museums of the World: Stages for the Study of Ethnohistory," in Susan M. Pearce, ed., *Museum Studies in Material Culture*, London: Leicester University Press, 1989, esp. p. 83) deals in part with the process of recontextualization that is taken as a central model here.

6. W. C. Sturtevant, *Guide to Field Collecting of Ethnographic Specimens* (Washington: Smithsonian Institution Press, 1977), p. 2. Further: "beyond a certain level" items of material culture "do not reflect subjective bias on the

part of the researcher. They are also unique in their unchanging nature thus allowing re-examination at will" (Barrie Reynolds, "The Relevance of Material Culture to Anthropology," *Journal of the Anthropological Society of Oxford* 14, 1983, 217).

7. The borrowing of exotic motifs, images, and styles in European art and design is not a topic I pursue here, but there is an extensive literature; see, for example, John Sweetman, *The Oriental Obsession* (Cambridge: Cambridge University Press, 1988).

1. Objects, Exchange, Anthropology

1. For a discussion of the philosophical background to anthropology's tendency to distance others, see Johannes Fabian, *Time and the Other: How Anthropology Makes Its Object* (New York: Columbia University Press, 1983).

2. W. H. Auden, "Musée des Beaux Arts," in *Collected Shorter Poems* (London: Faber and Faber, 1966), p. 123.

3. I am conscious that "we" is a highly problematic pronoun, especially if it is assumed that my intention is to contrast some unlocated "Western culture" with tribals or others. The point of the juxtaposition is of course to establish similarities which undo such oppositions. Along with Marianna Torgovnick, I "use the 'we' strategically, to prevent myself and my reader from backing away, too easily, from the systems of us/them thinking that structure all discourse about the civilized and the primitive"; what is crucial is that the "we" produces "a sense of discomfort or misfit. The 'we' is necessary to expose a shared illusion: the illusion of a representative primitive 'them' as opposed to a monolithic, unified, powerful, 'us.' It is necessary to reveal the 'us' as fragmented along lines of gender, national origin, class, political sympathies, race, and dozens of other categories and preferences that will determine individual readers' resistance to being part of the cultural 'we'" (*Gone Primitive: Savage Intellects, Modern Lives*, Chicago: University of Chicago Press, 1990, p. 4). Hence my "we," though sometimes juxtaposed to non-Westerners, makes no claims about the culture of rural Scotland, for instance; it refers instead to educated, primarily middle-class urban people who have self-conscious interests in "culture." Such interests (my interests) are certainly constituted from a class position, but it should not be thought that the pleasure of museums or other peoples' artifacts is specifically bourgeois or elite in opposition to some hypothetical mass culture: in Sydney, for instance, more people go every weekend to the Powerhouse, the technology and design museum, than attend major football matches.

4. These constructions are expressed in a rather extreme form in a book which makes close parallels between the psychic development of the individual and

social evolution: E. Sagan, *At the Dawn of Tyranny* (London: Faber and Faber, 1985); their presence in what may otherwise be radical cultural critiques is attested to by the preoccupation of Gilles Deleuze and Félix Guattari with "nomad thought" among other primitivist tropes (Deleuze and Guattari, *Mille plateaux*, Paris: Minuit, 1980).

5. Karl Marx, *Capital* (Moscow: Progress Publishers, n.d. [orig. 1867]), I, 37.

6. The debate about barter and the origins of money was of course prominent in Western economic theory (cf. Caroline Humphrey and Stephen Hugh-Jones, "Introduction," in *Barter, Exchange and Value*, Cambridge: Cambridge University Press, in press), but this debate does not concern us here.

7. James G. Frazer, *Questions on the Customs Beliefs, and Languages of Savages* (Cambridge: Cambridge University Press, 1907), p. 29.

8. For much earlier evocations of barter as a primitive absence, standing for the lack of money, see Boemus's *Fardle of Fashions* (Latin original, 1520), quoted in Margaret T. Hodgen, *Early Anthropology in the Sixteenth and Seventeenth Centuries* (Philadelphia: University of Pennsylvania Press, 1964), p. 197.

9. P. J. H. Grierson, *The Silent Trade* (London: Macmillan, 1903).

10. I have not italicized "kula," because here and in most other instances I am talking about the anthropological construct rather than the indigenous practices out of which the "system" has been made. I do not dispute that exchange practices in the Massim region constitute a system, but I would not want to equate that with anthropology's "Kula ring."

11. Notably the *hiri*—a pots-for-sago system operating along the Papuan coast. See F. R. Barton, "Annual Trading Expedition to the Papuan Gulf," in C. G. Seligman, *The Melanesians of British New Guinea* (Cambridge: Cambridge University Press, 1910), and Murray Groves, "Hiri," in *The Encyclopaedia of Papua New Guinea* (Melbourne: Melbourne University Press). Footage of Mailu and the *lagatoi* canoes appears in the later version of Frank Hurley's film, *Pearls and Savages* (1923). Although it is generally true that Seligman's sections on trade emphasized utilitarian transactions, he was also aware of more ceremonial activity and quoted from colonial reports to the effect that certain expeditions from the southern Massim "were principally concerned with the exchange of the circulating articles of native wealth . . . trade was only a secondary consideration" (Seligman, quoting M. Gilmour from the *Annual Report of British New Guinea* for 1904–1905, in *The Melanesians of British New Guinea*, p. 529).

12. B. Malinowski, "Kula: The Circulating Exchange of Valuables in the Archipelagoes of Eastern New Guinea," *Man* 20 (1920), 98. The main publication was, of course, *Argonauts of the Western Pacific* (London: Routledge, 1922).

13. Martha Macintyre and Michael W. Young, "The Persistence of Traditional Trade and Ceremonial Exchange in the Massim," in R. J. May and Hank Nelson, eds., *Melanesia: Beyond Diversity* (Canberra: Research School of

Pacific Studies, Australian National University, 1982); Nancy D. Munn, *The Fame of Gawa: A Symbolic Study of Value Transformation in a Massim (Papua New Guinea) Society* (Cambridge: Cambridge University Press, 1986); Roger M. Keesing, "New Lessons from Old Shells," in Jukka Siikala, ed., *Culture and History in the Pacific* (Helsinki: Finnish Anthropological Society, in press).

14. Malinowski did, at various stages, establish more complex classifications of transactions (for instance in *Argonauts*, 177ff.), but the point of concern here is the rhetorical centrality of the kula gift, which is in any case the point that his work tends to be reduced to in broader anthropological understanding and even in his own distillations (as, for example, in the discussion of exchange and reciprocity in *Crime and Custom in Savage Society*, London: Routledge, 1926).

15. Martha Macintyre, "Changing Paths: An Historical Ethnography of the Traders of Tubetube" (Ph.D. diss., Australian National University, 1983).

16. C. A. Gregory, *Gifts and Commodities* (London: Academic Press, 1982), p. 42.

17. C. A. Gregory, "Kula Gift Exchange and Capitalist Commodity Exchange: A Comparison," in *The Kula: New Perspectives on Massim Exchange* (Cambridge: Cambridge University Press, 1983), p. 109.

18. Ibid., p. 104.

19. In rural India, for instance, gifts within caste relations generally take the opposite form—the receiver is of higher rank. See Jonathan P. Parry, *Caste and Kinship in Kangra* (London: Routledge and Kegan Paul, 1979), p. 5 and *passim*, and Gloria Goodwin Raheja, *The Poison in the Gift: Ritual, Prestation, and the Dominant Caste in a North Indian Village* (Chicago: University of Chicago Press, 1988).

20. My method privileges illustration over terminological specification, but for the definition-minded reader it may be useful if I make it clear that I use the term "transaction" highly inclusively to cover any commodity or noncommodity exchange; "gift" is mainly used to refer to the Maussian construct and certain prestations contrasted with commodity transactions in the minds of actors or observers; because sections of the following argument are precisely concerned to suggest that "gifts" in certain societies do not take the Maussian form, it has been neither stylistically practical nor theoretically desirable to use the word "gift" in any single restricted sense. The term "prestation" is not equated with gift but includes a wider range of presentations and exchanges, such as the offerings in hierarchical societies like the Oceanic chiefdoms (see Chapter 2).

21. Marcel Mauss, *The Gift: Forms and Functions of Exchange in Archaic Societies* (London: Routledge, 1966), p. 31, cited in *Gifts and Commodities*, p. 18. The recontextualization of Mauss in Marxist terms is somewhat clearer in a later article: "The key to understanding gift giving is apprehension of the

fact that things in tribal economies are produced by non-alienated labour. This creates a special bond between a producer and his/her product, a bond that is broken in capitalist society based on alienated wage-labour. Mauss's analysis focussed upon the 'indissoluble bond' between things and persons in gift economies and argued that 'to give something is to give part of oneself' [*The Gift*, p. 10]. Gifts therefore become embodied with the 'spirit' of the giver and this 'force' in the thing given compels the recipient to make a return" ("Gifts," in J. Eatwell, M. Milgate, and P. Newman, eds., *The New Palgrave: A Dictionary of Economics*, London: Macmillan, 1987, p. 525).

However, unless there is some further theoretical reformulation, this is rather misleading. Mauss's approach had almost no interest in labor or consequent associations between people and their products.

22. For a valuable and extended discussion, see Maureen Mackenzie, *Androgynous Objects: String Bags and Gender in the Central Highlands of New Guinea* (London: Harwood Academic Publishers, in press), which emphasizes that notions of multiple authorship mean that the sacred male work of decorating and elaborating upon (western New Guinea highlands) string bags initially produced by women does not erase the productive contribution of the latter.

23. Jonathan P. Parry, "*The Gift*, the Indian Gift, and the 'Indian Gift,'" *Man* 21 (1986), 453–473.

24. The approach put forward more recently by C. A. Gregory and J. C. Altman is much closer to that advanced here. They suggest that three categories of relations should be investigated: relations between transactors, relations between transactors and objects, and relations between the objects. The first admits specific questions such as the history of the relationship, the second questions such as rights of disposal on the part of givers and receivers, and the third remains unsatisfactorily restricted to such questions as equivalence and quantity (*Observing the Economy*, London: Routledge, 1989, p. 204). However, it is methodologically unproductive to suggest that "the aim should be to construct a synoptic table of the categories of transactors involved, the types of objects, and the forms of exchange" (ibid., pp. 204–205). I cannot see that this could lead to anything other than a rigid typology which would suppress the contested and mutable character of value; what is crucial is the process and progression of transactions, through which the meanings of objects and relations can be changed.

25. It is hardly insignificant that this marking encircles the body of the woman and usually not that of the man: the wife is of course defined to a much greater extent by the married state than the husband.

26. Tony Tanner, *Adultery in the Novel: Contract and Transgression* (Baltimore: Johns Hopkins University Press, 1979), p. 340.

27. Ibid., p. 341.

28. *"Kitomwa* are those valuables that are the property of an individual. They are perhaps best defined as being entirely unencumbered by debt" (Macintyre, "Changing Paths," chap. 3). The importance of this rather confusing category is discussed further in Chapter 2 below.

29. This extract from an unpublished interview was generously provided by Martha Macintyre. A shorter quotation appears in chapter 3 of "Changing Paths."

30. This argument was developed at length in an earlier paper; Nicholas Thomas, "Forms of Personification and Prestations," *Mankind* 15 (1985), 223–230.

31. A. Weiner, "Inalienable Wealth," *American Ethnologist* 12 (1985), 210.

32. Ibid., p. 223. The argument, particularly with respect to cloth, has been generalized to other parts of Oceania in several articles, including "Plus précieux que l'or: relations et échanges entre hommes et femmes dans les sociétés d'Océanie," *Annales* 37 (1982), 222–245, and "Why Cloth? Wealth, Gender, and Power in Oceania," in Annette Weiner and Jane Schneider, eds., *Cloth and Human Experience* (Washington: Smithsonian Institution Press, 1989).

33. Weiner, "Inalienable Wealth," p. 224.

34. My survey of arguments here suggests that, outside the technical field of material culture studies, objects have been generally neglected in cultural and economic anthropology. For a more extended critique along these lines, see Daniel Miller, *Material Culture and Mass Consumption* (Oxford: Basil Blackwell, 1987). It should perhaps be noted that the substantivist school in economic anthropology was more open than others to questions of this kind but rarely discussed the meanings of things in any sustained or focused way (see for example Anne M. Chapman, "Port of Trade Enclaves in Aztec and Maya Civilizations," in Karl Polanyi, Conrad M. Arensberg, and Harry W. Pearson, eds., *Trade and Market in the Early Empires*, Chicago: Gateway, 1957, pp. 126–127). This may be a consequence of their emphasis on regionally extensive trade systems rather than localized economies.

35. Cf. *OED* under "alien," "alienate," etc. Weiner ("Inalienable Wealth," p. 225 n. 1) notes that *immeuble* is translated as "indestructible" by I. Cunnison, but she does not add that this is obviously a partial and inadequate rendering. For other criticisms of the translation, see J. Parry, *"The Gift," Man* 21 (1986), 453–473.

36. Weiner, "Inalienable Wealth," p. 211.

37. Miller, *Material Culture and Mass Consumption*, p. 214.

38. Ibid., esp. pp. 190–191.

39. Ibid., p. 169.

40. J. Keller, "Woven World: Neotraditional Symbols of Unity in Vanuatu," *Mankind* 18 (1988), 3.

41. Cf. MacKenzie, *Androgynous Objects.*

42. A. Appadurai, "Introduction: Commodities and the Politics of Value," in

Arjun Appadurai, ed., *The Social Life of Things: Commodities in Cultural Perspective* (Cambridge: Cambridge University Press, 1986), p. 13, italics removed.

43. Ibid.

44. Ibid., p. 15.

45. The perspective of the colonial periphery makes it impossible to accept Appadurai's characterization of barter as "the exchange of objects for one another *without* reference to money and *with* maximum feasible reduction of social, cultural, political, or personal transaction costs" (ibid., p. 9). This is theoretically economical but probably remote from much of what has been represented, or rather misrepresented, as barter. I will argue in Chapter 3 that the cultural burden of these transactions is heavy; the notion that they are in some sense asocial or straightforward is, in any case, rather unsatisfactory: a relationship of hostility or foreignness seems to be equated with a lack of sociality. To the contrary, it is clear that barter often takes place precisely in order to define and state ethnic difference and distance (see, for example, Caroline Humphrey, "Fair Dealing, Just Rewards: Barter in a Buddhist Culture of Northeast Nepal," in Caroline Humphrey and Stephen Hugh-Jones, eds., *Barter, Exchange, and Value*, Cambridge: Cambridge University Press, in press).

46. For instance, Nicholas Modjeska's recent article poses the questions, in relation to Sepik barter, "How will these women value their respective products? Does the exchange ratio represent an equilibrium of embodied labours or social utilities?" ("Exchange Value and Melanesian Trade Reconsidered," *Mankind* 15, 1985, 153). His conclusion, however, constructively suggests that political context overdetermines narrower economic factors (such as supply and demand): it is proposed that presuppositions about power influenced supply and particular transactors' expectations about their hegemonic or subordinate status in the market (pp. 160–161).

47. Robert J. Foster, "Value without Equivalence: Exchange and Replacement in a Melanesian Society," *Man* 25 (1990), 403. This article was especially helpful for my own understanding of these vexed issues.

48. Marilyn Strathern, *The Gender of the Gift: Problems with Women and Problems with Society in Melanesia* (Berkeley: University of California Press, 1988), pp. 176–182 and *passim*. Strathern explores the ways in which things exchanged, the attributes of persons, and their relations are drawn into relations of comparison, juxtaposition, and mutual valorization. These arguments are expressed in various ways at different points of her complex and rewarding book, and I see my reductions of the argument, and their exemplification in the analysis of Fijian ceremonies (Chapters 2 and 5), as having been influenced by her account rather than as faithful to the intentions of the whole book or any particular section.

49. Munn, *The Fame of Gawa*, chap. 1, presents the conceptual framework abstractly.
50. The textbook demonstration of this is Paul Bohannon, "The Impact of Money on an African Subsistence Economy," in George Dalton, ed., *Tribal and Peasant Economies* (New York: Natural History Press, 1967), pp. 123–128. See also Paul Bohannon and Laura Bohannon, *Tiv Economy* (Evanston: Northwestern University Press, 1968).
51. Gayatri Chakravorty Spivak, "Translator's Preface," in Jacques Derrida, *Of Grammatology* (Baltimore: Johns Hopkins University Press, 1974), p. xv.
52. Ibid., p. xviii.

2. The Permutations of Debt

1. James Clifford, *The Predicament of Culture* (Cambridge, Mass.: Harvard University Press, 1988), p. 32.
2. W. E. Armstrong, "Rossel Island Money," *Economic Journal* 34 (1924), 423–429; see also his book *Rossel Island* (Cambridge: Cambridge University Press, 1928).
3. The assault upon such usage goes back to Malinowski himself: "I cannot follow Professor Seligman in his use of the word *currency* [in *Melanesians of British New Guinea*, 1910] . . . *Currency* as a rule means a medium of exchange and standard of value, and none of the Massim valuables fulfill these functions" (*Argonauts of the Western Pacific*, London: Routledge, 1922, p. 499 n.). Of course, the point that kula valuables are in fact exchange media and standards of value in certain respects has been central to recent critique.
4. John Liep, "Ranked Exchange in Yela (Rossel Island)," in Jerry Leach and Edmund Leach, eds., *The Kula: New Perspectives on Massim Exchange* (Cambridge: Cambridge University Press, 1983), pp. 504, 509.
5. J. H. L. Waterhouse, *Roviana and English Dictionary* (Sydney: Epworth Press, 1928); A. M. Hocart, "Trade and Money," MS, Hocart Papers, Turnbull Library, Wellington, New Zealand, p. 1; cf. Martha Macintyre, "Changing Paths: An Historical Ethnography of the Traders of Tubetube" (Ph.D. diss., Australian National University), p. 125: "Bwanabwana people often refer to shell valuables as 'Papuan money,' offering sustained and logical comparisons with 'European money' . . . They recognize that there are important differences between money and shell valuables, but they insisted that the similarities were relevant to my understanding of exchange in the region." See also Rena Lederman, What Gifts Engender (Cambridge: Cambridge University Press, 1986) pp. 231–232, for comparisons among the Mendi of the Papua New Guinea highlands.
6. It is obvious, though, that supply and scarcity are sometimes important. Eu-

ropean goods (such as iron axes) which are initially highly valued often depreciate as contact proceeds and their availability increases; there were no doubt counterparts to this in precontact development, as warfare, migrations, and other factors altered the patterns of regional trading. The consumption-oriented perspective upon value employed here incorporates the utilitarian and meaningful considerations which have generally been opposed in economic anthropology.

7. J. F. Collier and M. Z. Rosaldo, "Politics and Gender in Simple Societies," in Sherry B. Ortner and Harriet Whitehead, eds., *Sexual Meanings: The Cultural Construction of Gender and Sexuality* (Cambridge: Cambridge University Press, 1981), esp. pp. 278–279; the argument was developed in the Melanesian context by Marilyn Strathern in "Kinship and Economy: Constitutive Orders of a Provisional Kind," *American Ethnologist* 12 (1985), 191–209. Nicholas Modjeska's article "Production and Inequality: Perspectives from Central New Guinea" (in Andrew Strathern, ed., *Inequality in the New Guinea Highlands*, Cambridge: Cambridge University Press, 1982, esp. pp. 55–57) was also important but dealt with distinctions in production systems which are not precisely coterminous with the oppositions that have become more central in recent debate (see particularly M. Strathern and M. Godelier, eds., *Big Men and Great Men: Personifications of Power in Melanesia*, Cambridge: Cambridge University Press, 1991). The range of possible variation is made particularly clear in Margaret Jolly's study of forms of substitution in north Vanuatu societies ("Soaring Hawks and Grounded Persons," in Strathern and Godelier, *Big Men and Great Men*). Apart from these and the other works mentioned here, I have been helped by Alfred Gell, "Inter-tribal Commodity Barter and Reproductive Gift Exchange in Old Melanesia," in Caroline Humphrey and Stephen Hugh-Jones, eds., *Barter, Exchange, and Value* (Cambridge: Cambridge University Press, in press).

8. Michael Nihill, "'Worlds at War with Themselves': Notions of the Antisociety in Anganen Ceremonial Exchange," *Oceania* 58 (1988), 258.

9. Michael Wood, "Brideservice Societies and the Kamula," *Canberra Anthropology* 8 (1) (1987), 8; for more extended analysis see his book *The Substance of Sociality: Domination and Exchange among the Kamula* (London: Harwood Academic Publishers, in press). For the eastern highlands compare Maurice Godelier, *The Making of Great Men* (Cambridge: Cambridge University Press, 1986), p. 171.

10. Strathern, "Kinship and Economy," p. 204.

11. The close parallels which formerly existed in warfare and headhunting are apparent from Martha Macintyre, "Warfare and the Changing Context of 'Kune' on Tubetube," *Journal of Pacific History* 18 (1983), 11–34, but wider similarities in gender relations and the uses of valuables can also be discerned (Macintyre, "Changing Paths," and personal communication).

12. There were at least three main types: *mbakia, poata,* and *mbariki* (in descending order of value). The first were distinguished by an orange or amber band and were very finely polished; *poata* were the same as *mbakia* but white; and *mbariki* were said to be much more roughly produced (T. Russell, "The Culture of Marovo," *Journal of the Polynesian Society* 57, 1948, 320–321; see Gus Piko, "Choiseul Currency," *Journal of the Solomon Islands Museum Association* 4, 1976, 97–110, for other regional varieties). An indigenous account recorded by George Carter in the mid-1970s does not discuss the uses of various forms but does class together a much wider array of exchange-media: "1. bakiha [*mbakia* in Hocart's spelling]—white clam-shell (hio); 2. bakiha—red one side (hio); 3. kalo—whale's teeth; 4. rade—porpoise's teeth; 5. kibukibu—beads of cowry shell used for necklace; bareke [*mbariki*]—larger than bakiha but rough finish (clam shell—veruveru); 7. hokata—armlet made from (hio); 8. rotana—decorated armlet made from pandanus leaves; 9. taraka medaka—woven flat string of pandanus leaves; 10. bururape—necklace of cowry shell and fruit of trees; 11. dala—hio and turtle shell; 12. buroku—a long and round woven rope of pandanus leaves; 13. huneke—coconut leaves (basket); 14. barekoto—second class buha (cloth); 15. kalala—banyan tree (bark for cloth)" (G. Vudere, "Saikile," Carter MSS, Pacific Manuscripts Bureau, microfilm, p. 4). It is significant that the pandanus and cloth products are listed, since these were probably articles exchanged by women overlooked in the earlier accounts.

13. Hocart, "Trade and Money," p. 1.

14. For extensive discussion, see J. Hogendorn and M. Johnson, *The Shell Money of the Slave Trade* (Cambridge: Cambridge University Press, 1986).

15. Hocart, "The Cult of the Dead in Eddystone of the Solomons," *Journal of the Royal Anthropological Institute* 52 (1922), 78, 266, 277, 279; "Warfare in Eddystone of the Solomons," *Journal of the Royal Anthropological Institute* 61 (1931), 308, 316–317.

16. "Trade and Money," p. 5. Cash equivalents for various grades of shells are also given in other relatively early sources (e.g., B. Somerville, "Ethnographical Notes in New Georgia," *Journal of the Anthropological Institute* 26, 1896, 405).

17. Ibid., pp. 10–11.

18. Hocart, "Warfare in Eddystone," p. 306.

19. Ibid., pp. 305–306; cf. H. B. Guppy, *The Solomon Islands and Their Natives* (London: Swann Sonnenschein, Lowrey and Co., 1887), pp. 32–33; J. F. Goldie, "The People of New Georgia," *Proceedings of the Royal Society of Queensland* 12 (1909), 27.

20. Here I follow I. Kopytoff's discussion of slavery in "The Cultural Biography of Things: Commoditization as Process," in Arjun Appadurai, ed., *The Social Life of Things* (Cambridge: Cambridge University Press, 1986), p. 65.

21. Vudere, "Saikile," p. 6. This was written by a Christian islander who would not have seen such customs in the same terms as those who actually practiced them. An earlier account was given by the naturalist Charles Woodford: ". . . with reference to the treatment of women that when a girl arrives at the age of puberty she is known as a Bimbolo having been previously a vineke. When she is Bimbolo she is temporarily a prostitute during a periodical feast or festival and is free to all the men of the town she may choose. After this should she be married she becomes a Bakalinge. There is another class of women chiefly slaves from *Sambana* who are called Mangota and who are prostituted all their lives" (MS Diary, 15 March 1887, in Woodford Papers, microfilm, Department of Pacific and Southeast Asian History, Australian National University, Canberra).

22. Hocart, "Warfare in Eddystone," p. 318.

23. Ibid., p. 270.

24. Macintyre, "Changing Paths," p. 119. The glosses in square brackets of Tubetube words are derived from Macintyre's glossary. For more extended discussion of *kitoms* or *kitomwa*, as they are in various cognates, see Munn, *Fame of Gawa*, pp. 151–155, and a number of the chapters in Leach and Leach, *The Kula*.

25. This argument is drawn from Nicholas Thomas, *Marquesan Societies* (Oxford: Oxford University Press, 1990), pp. 31–33.

26. Wood, *The Substance of Sociality.*

27. Marilyn Strathern, *The Gender of the Gift: Problems with Women and Problems with Society in Melanesia* (Berkeley: University of California Press, 1988), p. 161.

28. Lisette Josephides, *The Production of Inequality: Gender and Exchange amongst the Kewa* (London: Tavistock, 1985); see also articles cited in Strathern, *The Gender of the Gift.*

29. Strathern's prefatory discussion (*The Gender of the Gift*, p. 10) makes the "fictional" character of the gift/commodity contrast quite clear, and insofar as her analysis is understood in these terms, my critique is misdirected to the extent that it merely affirms that alienation is a feature of Melanesian exchange. That is, I appear to offer an empirical corrective to what is not an empirical argument. While I am aware that the discussion here does not do justice to the status of Strathern's concepts, it is not clear to me that enunciated premises effectively permeate or encircle the entire structure of a text. Hence, despite Strathern's methodological stipulations, much of the actual analysis of *The Gender of the Gift* does appear to make substantive claims, or—given the constituted discourses through which it can be understood—can only be read as if it does so. It will be apparent, though, that some of my reservations about the theoretical formulas of *The Gender of the Gift* relate to the logic internal to the fictions rather than the cruder issue of substantive adequacy.

30. Ibid., p. 161.
31. Similarly, it is not important if mats are made from purchased rolls of dried and softened pandanus, which are available in the frequently visited urban markets.
32. This is true of western Fiji but not the rest of the group, where a Tongan-type division of labor applies: women do not garden.
33. Strathern, *The Gender of the Gift*, p. 156.
34. This brief discussion derives from more extensive analysis, especially *Marquesan Societies*, pp. 82–85.
35. Macintyre ("Changing Paths," p. 120 n. 12) refers to a case in which a shell was named after a man, but the stories associated with it derided his foolishness in disposing of it for several bags of rice. It is clear in this instance that what is known about the valuable relates to a transactor's accomplishment, and not to the social relationship produced between transactors. This exemplifies the broader argument of the introductory chapter that gifts and other transactions may sustain various meanings (rather than merely relate to a movement of commodities) but that these do not necessarily take the form of a debt or a bond between giver and receiver.
36. Margaret Jolly, "People and Their Products in South Pentecost," in *Vanuatu: Politics, Economics, and Ritual in Island Melanesia* (Sydney: Academic Press, 1981) pp. 286–287, quoted in *The Gender of the Gift*, p. 155.
37. Strathern, *The Gender of the Gift*, p. 155.
38. Ibid., p. 162.
39. Ibid., pp. 328–339.
40. I am not suggesting, of course, that Strathern fails to acknowledge diversity within the region, which is alluded to at many points; my point is rather that difference within Melanesia is submerged analytically.
41. Strathern, *The Gender of the Gift*, p. 134.
42. The discussion here and elsewhere is based upon archival studies and fieldwork in 1988 in the Noikoro area of the western interior of the main island of Viti Levu. Although exchange ceremonies of roughly the type described took place throughout Fiji, and although the general claim (that the Fijian system turned upon complex processes of value conversion) holds for the whole island group, much else of what is said applies only to the upland interior; kinship terminology and ritual, among other things, were distinctive in a number of ways. The main difference between this area and the coastal polities which are much better documented is one that has perhaps been overstressed to the exclusion of other kinds of social variation: the upland polities were relatively unconsolidated politically, and there were no regionally extensive networks of tributary relations which encompassed subordinate places. However, all Fijian societies were (and in a modified way still are) hierarchically structured by chieftainship.

Over the last hundred years the area has been transformed in various ways by Christianity and colonial rule; settlements in hill forts were amalgamated in more accessible valleys, for instance. Most interior villages are now occupied by 100–300 people, who practice various forms of horticulture, collecting, fishing, and hunting; of several cash crops, kava is perhaps the most important; the demand for this nonalcoholic narcotic beverage among urban Fijians and Fiji-Indians is high. For additional information on Fiji, see T. J. Macnaught, *The Fijian Colonial Experience* (Canberra: Research School of Pacific Studies, Australian National University, 1982), and, for a good ethnographic account of an area close to Noikoro, C. S. Belshaw, *Under the Ivi Tree: Society and Economic Growth in Rural Fiji* (London: Routledge, 1964). There are extensive references to the anthropological literature in N. Thomas, *Planets around the Sun: Dynamics and Contradictions of the Fijian Matanitu* (Sydney: Oceania Monographs, 1986), and Marshall Sahlins, *Islands of History* (Chicago: University of Chicago Press, 1985).

43. *Report on the Decrease of the Native Population* (Suva, Fiji: Government Printer, 1896), p. 60; Basil Thomson, *The Fijians: A Study in the Decay of Custom* (London: Macmillan, 1908), p. 281. Note, however, that in addition to *solevu*, there were said to be other occasions upon which some sort of unceremonial barter *(veisau)* took place (mentioned, for instance, by Charles Wilkes in *Narrative of the United States Exploring Expedition*, Philadelphia: Lea and Blanchard, 1845, III, 301). This seems also to have been referred to by the word *voli*, which came to mean "cash buying and selling" in the second half of the nineteenth century (David Cargill, "A Grammar of the Feejeean Language," MS, Mitchell Library, Sydney, 1839).

44. G. C. Henderson, ed., *The Journal of Thomas Williams* (Sydney: Angus and Robertson, 1931), I, 163–164.

45. A. A. A. Von Hügel, *The Fiji Journals of Baron Von Hügel*, ed. Jane Roth and Steven Hooper (Suva: Fiji Museum, in press), 7 July 1875. (The original manuscript is at the Cambridge University Museum of Archaeology and Anthropology, Cambridge.)

46. Colo East Provincial Council Minutes, 1899, National Archives of Fiji, Suva (hereafter cited as NAF).

47. But such assistance was no doubt reciprocal and is likely to have been provided in the context of established relations of alliance.

48. Jean de Marzan was in Fiji from 1893 until 1927 and in the eastern upland interior of Viti Levu much of that time after 1898; he obviously had a reasonable knowledge of some Fijian dialects and seems to have made dedicated ethnographic inquiries.

49. De Marzan noted that these grievous consequences arose only from old debts, not from modern commercial ones: "The Fijian . . . is negligent in freeing himself of his debts in stores—debts which he says cause no sickness"; see

"Customs and Beliefs in Upland Viti Levu," tr. and ed. N. Thomas, *Domodomo: Fiji Museum Journal* 5 (4) (1987), 58.

50. Colo East Provincial Council, 10–11 December 1901, NAF. A more senior official thought that the people ought to be allowed to "make some small solevu."

51. *Siriawa na mate kemutou maliwa; kua ni leqwa;* these expressions always conclude with *mana!* after which everyone says *e jina,* "let it, the prestation, be true and efficacious." These terms are in the Noikoro dialect of the western interior of Viti Levu, but the kava ceremony now has a fairly standard form throughout the group. The use of *mana* and *dina* (in the Bauan dialect, now standard Fijian) are reported in early accounts.

52. Mauss, *The Gift: Forms and Functions of Exchange in Archaic Societies* (London: Routledge, 1966), p. 22; Mauss's citations to Malinowski's *Argonauts* (1922) omitted.

53. Ibid., p. 29.

54. Jerry Leach, "Introduction," in Leach and Leach, *The Kula,* p. 3.

55. *Yau* is the verb, *i-* the nominalizing prefix. See A. M. Hocart's glossary (*The Northern States of Fiji,* London: Royal Anthropological Institute, 1954, p. 294); A. Capell, *New Fijian Dictionary* (Suva: Government Printer, 1941), p. 289; and also D. Toganivalu, "Ai yaya kei yau," *Transactions of the Fijian Society for 1917,* 1.

56. The nature of contemporary exchange is discussed further in Chapter 5.

57. Sahlins, "Raw Women, Cooked Men, and Other 'Great Things' of the Fiji Islands," in Paula Brown and D. Tuzin, eds., *The Ethnography of Cannibalism* (Washington: Society for Psychological Anthropology, 1983), p. 72.

58. "How Fijians First Became Cannibals," MS Stanmore Papers, University Museum of Archaeology and Anthropology, Cambridge; in the hand of E. Heffernan, perhaps collected in 1877 from Namosi (as it is in a fascicle so dated), but said to have taken place at Vatukarasa on the coast in the Nadroga area. It should be pointed out that, given the weight that both I and Sahlins (see note 60) place upon it, the text of this myth is not especially satisfactory: there is no Fijian version, and the translation is clearly rather free.

59. See Chapter 5 for further discussion.

60. Sahlins has provided an extended analysis of the narrative with particular respect to cannibalism and the constitution of chieftainship through marriage and the substitution of raw women for cooked men (enemies' bodies, and here the teeth, interpreted, somewhat implausibly, as a transformation of Tabua's body) ("Raw Women, Cooked Men"; cf. *Islands of History,* chap. 3). However, the fact that in this cultural structure women of the land are appropriated by an invasive foreigner chief leads him to see Fijian marriage in general as hypergamous, which is to overlook intra-Fijian variation and assimilate ordinary to elite marriage; cf. C. Toren, "Review Article—*Islands of History*," *Critique of Anthropology* 8 (3) (1988), 115. The "stranger king" model must be

applied with some caution, since in some instances transactions between a foreign chief and taukei involving the substitution of imported wealth for wives are not connected with the foundation of chiefly lineages (as in the Vunaqumu tradition cited below); in the myth discussed here, it is not directly suggested that the man is, or becomes, a chief, although there are obviously parallels with other chiefly genealogical narratives.

61. This has been pursued by Fergus Clunie, *Yalo i Viti: A Fiji Museum Catalogue* (Suva: Fiji Museum, 1986), pp. 160–161, whose stress on the *tabua* as a "symbolic woman" is broadly consistent with the analysis here. My point, though, is that it is the facts of alliance, exchange, and exchangeability which are signified, rather than the woman herself.

62. I accept Sahlins's suggestion that the reference in the English text to a miracle could easily have translated *cakamana*, to work *mana* ("Raw Women, Cooked Men," p. 73 n. 2).

63. This is underlined by the wide currency of a folk etymology—*tabua* were formerly made of other materials such as wood, and *ta-bua* may be said to mean cut-wood (of a certain species). It is apparently true that matter other than ivory was formerly used (cf. Toganivalu, "Ai yaya," pp. 8–9), but Capell in *The New Fijian Dictionary* (p. 16) sternly points out that the etymology is apocryphal, which is precisely the point: the sign is arbitrary. Contemporary usage explains the unavoidable character of certain obligations because soliciting gifts of *tabua* have been made, and a *tabua* is "a venerated thing"—the Fijian construction is also passive-cum-adjectival *(e kia na kwa dokai)*, neatly expressing the sense in which all the weight is bestowed upon, rather than exactly intrinsic to, the teeth.

64. Brewster, "Genealogies and Histories of the Matanitu or Tribal Governments of Central Viti Levu (Great Fiji)," MS, University Museum of Archaeology and Anthropology, Cambridge, p. 85. Note that in this case the "stranger-chief," in contrast to Sahlins's stranger-king, does not become ruler and seems in no sense to have been incorporated into the genealogy.

65. In this particular case it is notable that there is a kind of equivalent of the incest prohibition at the level of the production of valuables. Most forms of *iyau* other than *tabua* were made by women, although this is not an absolute rule. What is significant is the fact that now (at least) unmarried women do not produce *iyau*; that is, they produce it only as wives in their husband's places but never in their natal villages. If this really was general, the consequence would have been that the exchange of valuables for a woman was itself contingent upon former exchange; in this political economy production can follow only from circulation and from a radical dissociation of the woman from her natal group, since she moves to create the "valuables of the land," which are then substituted for further women (from her own group, since the system is essentially based on restricted exchange).

66. Sir Arthur Gordon (*Fiji: Records of Private and of Public Life, 1875–1880,*

Edinburgh: privately published, 1897–1912, II, 104) mentions passing through a village where many men were engaged in making pillows. He does not say that these were specifically for exchange, but given the durability of such things, it is not likely that many men at any one time would have been making their own.

67. De Marzan, "Customs and Beliefs," p. 50.

68. For parallels with respect to shell valuables, see Robert J. Foster, "Value without Equivalence: Exchange and Replacement in a Melanesian Society," *Man* 25 (1990), 408.

69. Clunie, *Yalo i Viti*, pp. 159–165; Thomas Williams, *Fiji and the Fijians* (London: Alexander Heylin, 1858), I, 159; Wilkes, *Narrative*, p. 354.

70. There is not much oral information forthcoming now on artifacts of these types, but a few Fijians I asked thought that, unlike such things as headrests, they would have been "family property."

71. But some were sold or given to Europeans.

72. Niel Gunson, "Great Women and Friendship Contract Rites in Pre-Christian Tahiti," *Journal of the Polynesian Society* 73 (1964), 54–57.

73. Berthold Seemann, *Viti: An Account of a Government Mission to the Vitian or Fijian Islands* (Cambridge: Macmillan, 1862), p. 187.

74. *Popoi*, prepared breadfruit paste.

75. P. Chaulet, "Notices géographiques, ethnographiques et religieuses sur les îles Marquises," MS, Archives, Congregation of the Sacred Hearts of Jesus and Mary, Rome, p. 92; slightly abbreviated in translation.

76. For discussion of types of feasts and ceremony, see Thomas, *Marquesan Societies*, pp. 89–97.

77. It must be emphasized, though, that from the point of view of the early accounts, the mutability and fluidity of political relations and hierarchy is conspicuous; formal propositions of the kind made here seem to bear little relation to the competitive processes which incorporated strategic marriages, feasting, and warfare.

78. Alfred Gell, *Metamorphosis of the Cassowaries: Umeda Society, Language, and Ritual* (London: Athlone, 1975), pp. 17–18; for a substantial expansion of the arguments there to deal with the articulation of external and internal exchange in New Guinea societies generally, see Gell, "Inter-tribal Commodity Barter and Reproductive Gift Exchange." There is scope also for applying a version of the argument to eastern Polynesia, since a lack of dense exchange networks does correlate with an emphasis upon internal exchange in-kind, but this would have to be proposed in a qualified way, since some trade took place within island groups.

79. This is to some extent analogous to the distinction between bridewealth and brideservice regimes but relates specifically to the form of ceremonial exchange and may not directly correspond to other processes.

80. See for example Macintyre, "Warfare and the Changing Context of *Kune* on Tubetube," pp. 29–30.

81. Miriam Kahn, *Always Hungry, Never Greedy: Food and the Expression of Gender in a Melanesian Society* (Cambridge: Cambridge University Press, 1986), esp. chap. 8. Kahn distinguishes between integrative feasts signifying group solidarity and a more political and competitive form. My comparison with the Marquesas obviously relates mainly to the latter (which she compares with the Goodenough case at pp. 147–148), although the distinction could no doubt be sustained for all three societies. Competitive feasting in my analysis of Marquesan society has a fundamental place in political processes.

82. Michael W. Young, *Fighting with Food* (Cambridge: Cambridge University Press, 1971); *Magicians of Manumanua* (Berkeley: University of California Press, 1983); "Abutu in Kalauna: A Retrospect," *Mankind* 15 (1985), 184–197.

83. Young, "Ceremonial Visiting on Goodenough Island," in Leach and Leach, *The Kula*, pp. 395–396.

84. Brian J. Egloff, "The Kula before Malinowski: A Changing Configuration," *Mankind* 11 (1978), 433–434.

85. See particularly Clunie, *Yalo i Viti*, but the forceful claims made for the importance of Tongan influence are not all documented with adequate precision.

86. S. J. P. Hooper, "A Study of Valuables in the Chiefdom of Lau, Fiji" (Ph.D. diss., University of Cambridge, 1982); cf. I. Hughes, "Good Money after Bad: Inflation and Devaluation in the Colonial Process," *Mankind* 11 (1978), 308–318; Andrew Strathern, *The Rope of Moka* (Cambridge: Cambridge University Press, 1971), on the circulation of pearl shell in the New Guinea highlands after the introduction of larger quantities by white prospectors.

3. *The Indigenous Appropriation of European Things*

1. Cf. Caroline Humphrey and Stephen Hugh-Jones, "Introduction," in Humphrey and Hugh-Jones, eds., *Barter, Exchange, and Value* (Cambridge: Cambridge University Press, in press).

2. Julia Blackburn, *The White Men: The First Response of Aboriginal Peoples to the White Men* (London: Orbis, 1979), p. 50.

3. Ian Creery, *The Inuit (Eskimo) of Canada* (London: Minority Rights Group, 1983 [Report No. 60]), p. 4.

4. J. Renton (writing in the 1860s), cited in Judith A. Bennett, *Wealth of the Solomons* (Honolulu: University of Hawaii Press, 1987), p. 23.

5. S. Tuhanuku, "Trade Unions and Politics," in Peter Larmour and S. Tarua, eds., *Solomon Islands Politics* (Suva: Institute of Pacific Studies, 1983), p. 117.

6. Actually, missionary vessels *(vaka lotu)* or even ships containing missionaries

only visited Niue several decades after initial contact, but it is typical of oral traditions in these societies, in which Christianity has become extremely important, that mission contact is attributed the historic role and represented as the civilizing force: "they brought the light."

7. [J. Lupo], "The Story of Niue," *Journal of the Polynesian Society* 32 (1923), 240.

8. In Tanna, the objects received were also wrapped up; this may well have related to fear of pollution or contamination.

9. John Elphinstone Erskine, *Journal of a Cruise among the Islands of the Western Pacific* (London: John Murray, 1853), p. 27.

10. Ibid., p. 30.

11. J. J. de Labillardière, *An Account of a Voyage in Search of La Pérouse . . . 1791–94* (London: Stockdale, 1800), II, 131. The Frenchmen seem to have understood correctly what the "queen" said: the first expression should be *ikai fakatau*, "not for purchase," and the second *'a 'au pe*, meaning "it's for you, please"—the way that gifts are pressed (thanks to Aletta Biersack and 'Okusi Mahina for this information).

12. Betsy Towers, *Moctezuma* log, 11 December 1848, MS, microfilm, Pacific Manuscript Bureau (hereafter cited as PMB) 302 (this was written by the captain's wife but unfortunately could not be said to convey any distinctive women's perspective). There are several similar references, but also a few which mention limited quantities of food ("a few Bananas") being brought off (see William Swain, *William Hamilton* log, 9 October 1836, PMB 672; Mathias Smith, *Richard Mitchell* log, 3 January, 21 October 1837, PMB 889; Edward P. Brown, *Noble* log, 20 May 1842, PMB 687). It is notable that the European experience in Vanuatu was generally also that weapons, but not food, was offered (see discussion in Chapter 4).

13. These could not have been offered in the absence of a European demand for things of native manufacture, which fed the metropolitan thirst for "artificial curiosities." But it could not be supposed that this dictated what was brought off in canoes by the Niue people (or any other islanders) since they had various other goods, such as mats, which could have met this interest but which they chose not to supply. There is, in any case, no sense from any of the accounts that visitors to Niue had much influence over what was made available to them. Most barter took place between ships and canoes, and few visitors actually landed.

14. Despite some violence in the course of contact, this was notable in the first British visit to Tahiti (see the account of Wallis's voyage in J. Hawkesworth, *An Account of the Voyages . . . for Making Discoveries in the Southern Hemisphere*, London: Strahan and Cadell, 1773, I, 438–439).

15. Cf. Bernard Smith, *European Vision and the South Pacific*, 2d ed. (Melbourne: Oxford University Press, 1985), p. 30.

16. Marshall Sahlins, *Historical Metaphors and Mythical Realities* (Ann Arbor:

University of Michigan Press, 1981), p. 40. See also Caroline Ralston, "Ordinary Women in Early Post-contact Hawaii," in *Family and Gender in the Pacific: Domestic Contradictions and the Colonial Impact* (Cambridge: Cambridge University Press, 1989). The Hawaiian explanation is probably also appropriate to Tahiti, where sexual liaisons were generally with commoner women.

17. Although I am not concerned to pursue the issue here, it should be noted that Sahlins's interpretation of the Hawaiian events has been challenged by other scholars (see, for example, J. Friedman, "Cook, Culture, and the World System," *Journal of Pacific History* 20, 1985, 191–201).

18. As was the case on certain other small and arid islands (Niue was of the raised coral structure, which meant that water supplies were limited), there seem to have been no pigs or dogs on the island at the time of early contact, and they may not have been introduced until the 1860s. Fowl were no doubt kept but perhaps for feathers rather than food; other than vegetables, fish would have been important in the diet.

19. William Gill, *Gems from the Coral Islands; or, Incidents of Contrast between Savage and Christian Life* (London: Yates and Alexander, ca. 1856), p. 339.

20. T. H. Hood, *Notes of a Cruise in HMS "Fawn" in the Western Pacific* (Edinburgh: Edmonston and Douglas, 1863), p. 20; A. W. Murray, *Missions in Western Polynesia* (London: John Snow, 1863); Julius L. Brenchley, *Jottings during the Cruise of H.M.S. "Curaçoa" among the South Sea Islands in 1865* (London: Longmans Green, 1873), p. 34.

21. See James Cook, *The Journals of Captain James Cook*, ed. J. C. Beaglehole (Cambridge: Cambridge University Press/Hakluyt Society, 1955–1967), II, 434–437.

22. For another interpretation of early contact with Niue, see Sue McLachlan, "Savage Island or Savage History? An Interpretation of Early European Contact with Niue," *Pacific Studies* 6 (1982), 26–51, which emphasizes the invasive character of Cook's action. It unfortunately lacks a comparative perspective: Cook, and other European explorers, approached contact in essentially the same way at a number of islands, but the characteristics of encounters and longer-term outcomes of course differed. Local cultural structures are obviously crucial for any understanding of specific developments.

23. Alan Howard, "Cannibal Chiefs and the Charter for Rebellion in Rotuman Myth," *Pacific Studies* 10 (1986), 1–27; N. Thomas, *Marquesan Societies* (Oxford: Oxford University Press, 1990); Sahlins on the Ku-Lono alternation in Hawaiian cosmology in *Historical Metaphors*, pp. 10–12.

24. Thomas, *Marquesan Societies*, pp. 119–120.

25. Brenchley, *Jottings*, pp. 28–29; cf. Basil Thomson, *Savage Island: An Account of a Sojourn in Niue and Tonga* (London: Murray, 1902), pp. 34–35, 96. George Turner noted that "they have no king. Of old they had kings, but

as they were the high-priests as well, and were supposed to cause the food to grow, the people got angry with them in times of scarcity, and killed them; and as one after another was killed, the end of it was that no-one wished to be king" (*Nineteen Years in Polynesia*, London: John Snow, 1861, p. 469). Katharine Luomola has discussed rituals of chief- or god-killing and related practices in "Symbolic Slaying in Niue: Post-European Changes in a Dramatic Ritual Context," in Niel Gunson, ed., *The Changing Pacific* (Melbourne: Oxford University Press, 1978). She mentions oral accounts blaming individual islanders who had traveled on a mission ship in 1830 for epidemics, and another account of a later Christian Niuean who was rejected and forced to flee from the island after a residence in Samoa; he was later permitted to settle but was nevertheless regarded as a source of pollution and infection (pp. 146–147). The association between these interactions and epidemics was no doubt important but does not by itself explain the consistent attitude of hostility from the time of Cook, which was only beginning to be qualified when Erskine visited. Missionary success led to a different situation in the 1860s. Luomola refers to the need for a "ritually neutralizing period for foreign objects to divest themselves of their foreign sanctity" and suggests that there were links between this "fear of ritual pollution" and "anxiety about non-conformity by strangers, particularly Tongan invaders" (ibid., p. 147). Although these aspects were significant, the historical grounds for the attitude toward foreignness need to be specified. There was an antipathy toward political domination and chiefly predation, rather than a vague fear of "non-conformity."

26. Edwin M. Loeb, *History and Traditions of Niue* (Honolulu: Bishop Museum, 1926), p. 166; Thomson, *Savage Island*, pp. 76–77.

27. Hood, *Notes of a Cruise*, p. 23.

28. Cook, *Journals*, II, 366.

29. In addition to introducing many European artifacts, early voyagers also effected a great deal of movement of indigenous material culture around the islands. A Tahitian with Cook at Easter Island in 1774 was enthusiastically collecting a distinctive kind of dark local barkcloth which he expected would be highly appreciated back in Tahiti, while the red feathers referred to here were acquired by the explorers in Tonga in part because it was known that they were esteemed highly in Tahiti. On the first voyage it had not been possible to obtain the "chief mourner's costumes" adorned with pearl shell, which particularly fascinated the Europeans (see next chapter), but the later visitors found that the desire for Tongan feathers was so intense that these could be used to purchase the ceremonial garments.

30. Cook, *Journals*, II, 369.

31. The reasons were probably similar to those in the Hawaiian case, discussed above.

32. Urey Lisiansky, *A Voyage around the World . . . 1803–6* (London: John Booth, 1814), p. 82.

33. A. J. von Krusenstern, *Voyage round the World in the Years 1803 . . . 1806*, trans. Richard Belgrave Hoppner (London: John Murray, 1813), I, 132.
34. Lisiansky, *Voyage*, pp. 67–68.
35. N. Korobitsyn, extracts from journal, in A. I. Andreev, ed., *Russian Discoveries in the Pacific Ocean and North America* (Moscow: Academy of Sciences, 1944), p. 170; F. Shemelin, *Journal of the First Voyage of the Russians around the World* (St. Petersburg: 1815–1818), I, 134 (these both in Russian; my thanks to Daniel Tumarkin and Raya Topchian for advice about and translation of these sources). In a few cases pigs were obtained for whale teeth, which already were, or were incorporated into, Marquesan valuables (N. Appleton, *Concord* log, 10 October 1801, PMB 200). But traders often failed to carry these: Isaac Iselin noted that although pigs were "pretty abundant," they could not get "a very great supply" because they carried no whale teeth (*Journal of a Trading Voyage*, New York: McIlroy and Emmett, n.d., pp. 39, 43).
36. David Porter, *Journal of a Cruise Made to the Pacific Ocean*, 2d ed. (New York: Wiley and Halsted, 1822), II, 98–104. For fuller discussion of these events, see Thomas, *Marquesan Societies*, pp. 133–139.
37. Porter, *Journal*, II, 36.
38. Thomas Dornin, journal kept on board the U.S. frigate *Brandywine*, entry under July 1829, Navy Department Records, National Archives, Washington.
39. Hiram Paulding, *Journal of a Cruise in the U.S. Schooner "Dolphin"* (New York: Carvill, 1831), pp. 59–60.
40. See, e.g., J. Shillibeer, *A Narrative of the Briton's Voyage to Pitcairn's Island* (Taunton: J. W. Marriot, 1817), pp. 64–65. It should be made clear that it was not merely the novelty of firearms which had these consequences but also their use in Porter's intervention: guns had been used earlier, and the word *puhi*, possibly derived from Tahitian, was recorded during the Russian visit of 1804 (Lisiansky, *Voyage*, p. 324).
41. C. Forbes, *Indus* log, undated entry of 1815 headed "Marquesas Islands," PMB 202.
42. Camille de Rocquefeuil, *Journal d'un voyage autour du monde . . . 1816–1819* (Paris: Ponthieu, Lesage and Gide, 1823), I, 299.
43. For more detailed discussions of this history, see Thomas, *Marquesan Societies*, pp. 145–161.
44. David Darling, "Report of a Visit to the Outstations Connected with the Windward Islands Mission," MS, South Seas Letters, Council for World Mission Collections, School of Oriental and African Studies, London; Thomas, *Marquesan Societies*, pp. 151–152. On Tahitian developments see Colin Newbury, *Tahiti Nui* (Honolulu: University of Hawaii Press, 1980), and Niel Gunson, "Pomare II of Tahiti and Polynesian Imperialism," *Journal of Pacific History* 4 (1969), 65–82.
45. It is not clear that these pigs could be used in the crucial ceremonies for deceased chiefs and priests; there seems to have been a requirement that these

were *tapu* animals raised specifically for such events. For a discussion of variation in similar prescriptions concerning acquired versus nurtured pigs, see Margaret Jolly, "Soaring Hawks and Grounded Persons," in *Great Men and Big Men: Personifications of Power in Melanesia* (Cambridge: Cambridge University Press, 1991).

46. I assume that analysis of indigenous demand in barter and cross-cultural trade must entail this kind of reference to the language of classification, or at least to what classifications and estimations are implicit in practice. Hence it seems wrong of Salisbury to assume that "matches, razor-blades, kerosene, lamp-wicks, knives, needles, and nails have no counterpart in native society"; this leads him to suggest that "larger European goods" are "novel capital investments" (*From Stone to Steel: Economic Consequences of Technological Change in New Guinea*, Melbourne: Melbourne University Press, 1962, pp. 195–196). What is missing here is any account of the ways in which these new things were actually conceptualized by the highlands people with whom Salisbury worked; it seems very possible, for instance, that knives and iron hatchets were assimilated to local categories, which is certainly what happened in most parts of the Pacific. It should be added, though, that *From Stone to Steel* offers a fascinating account of the process of exchange, especially between the ethnographer and the locals, the value of which is hardly diminished by the author's now dated formalistic economism (which in any case embodied some interesting qualifications).

47. See George Stubbs, *Kangaroo*, ca. 1772–1774, reproduced as color plate 1 in Smith, *European Vision*; Stubbs was not on the voyage; he painted from a stuffed specimen which had been brought back and presumably drew upon others' sketches.

48. See *OED* under "platypus."

49. On the other hand, in the Sa language of South Pentecost, Vanuatu, the same word is used for guns and bows and arrows (Margaret Jolly, personal communication).

50. S. Henry and J. Kent, "Missions," *South Asian Register* 4 (1828), 351–352; reprinted in part in the *Journal of Pacific History* 4 (1969), 82.

51. This term, used by some missionary observers, actually referred to quite a different kind of medical condition, but it also could refer more generally to what was morally corrupt: in the missionary perspective, in particular, it would seem appropriate that both French literature and excessive drinking could be connected with the word.

52. Quoted in Douglas L. Oliver, *Ancient Tahitian Society* (Canberra: Australian National University Press, 1974), I, 258.

53. G. Cheever, *Emerald* log, 5 August 1834 microfilm, Department of Pacific and Southeast Asian History, Australian National University. The missionary accounts of this prohibition are referred to by Niel Gunson, "On the Incidence

of Alcoholism and Intemperance in Early Pacific Missions," *Journal of Pacific History* 1 (1966), 58.

54. Gunson, "The Incidence of Alcoholism," p. 52, quoting Daniel Tyerman and George Bennett (writing in 1821) in James Montgomery, ed., *Journal of Voyages and Travels* (London: John Snow, 1831), I, 80.

55. The missionaries distilled spirits for their own consumption as well as for trade with passing vessels. On the voyage out to the Pacific one Mrs. Gregory "was frequently quarrelg [*sic*] with the Steward for more wine" although the allowance was a bottle a day "besides porter and brandy" (Gunson, "The Incidence of Alcoholism," p. 47).

56. Ron Brunton, *The Abandoned Narcotic* (Cambridge: Cambridge University Press, 1989).

57. J. Eagleston, "Ups and Downs through Life," MS, 1831–1836, on microfilm, typescript copy, Department of Pacific and Southeast Asian History, Australian National University, p. 286.

58. Cf. Marshall Sahlins's discussion of the sense in which the *lotu* represented the "true religion" for Fijians even before they could adopt it (*Islands of History*, Chicago: University of Chicago Press, 1985, pp. 37–38).

59. This is in A. Capell, *New Fijian Dictionary* (Suva: Government Printer, 1941), but it is not clear at what date the usage developed.

60. John Turnbull, *A Voyage round the World . . . 1800–1804*, 2d ed. (London: Alexander Maxwell, 1813), p. 208.

61. Sahlins, *Historical Metaphors*, pp. 28–29 and *passim*.

62. Charles Wilkes, *Narrative of the United States Exploring Expedition* (Philadelphia: Lea and Blanchard, 1845), II, 137.

63. See Eagleston, "Ups and Downs," pp. 275–281, 283, 285, 295ff., 336–337; Richard B. Lyth, "Tongan and Feejeean Reminiscences," MS, 1850–51, Mitchell Library, Sydney; R. G. Ward, "The Bêche de Mer Trade," in R. G. Ward, ed., *Man in the Pacific Islands* (Oxford: Clarendon Press, 1972), pp. 103–104.

64. N. Thomas, *Out of Time: History and Evolution in Anthropological Discourse* (Cambridge: Cambridge University Press, 1989), pp. 82–83.

65. D. Toganivalu, "Ai yau kei na yaya vakaviti," *Transactions of the Fijian Society for 1917*, p. 8.

66. Cheever, *Emerald* log, 25 July 1834. "One of them happened to be leaning over the gangway [when a whale appeared nearby] . . . he was frightened out of his wits . . . We told them that Whales teeth came from these fish & then they wanted us to go kill him. Phillips [a Rewa chief] muzzled his gun & would hardly believe us when told that a musket shot would not hurt him."

67. W. Lockerby, "Directions for the Feegee Islands" (written ca. 1811), ed. E. Dodge, *Journal of Pacific History* 7 (1972), 184.

68. Cheever, *Emerald* log, 23 June 1834; compare his account of a subsequent

visit in June 1835. One Englishman in particular, Mr. Emery, was regarded as reliable; the others were seen as a set of rogues.

69. Cheever, *Emerald* log, 5 August 1834.

70. H. Phillips, letter to Eagleston, 27 September 1830, with Eagleston manuscript "Ups and Downs."

71. Eagleston, "Ups and Downs," pp. 287–288.

72. It might be going too far to presume that this reflected the tendency in Fijian ceremonial exchange for prestations of manufactured articles of one sort or another to be followed by *magiti*, feasts—typically of pork and various tubers such as taro or yams. However, it is notable that food was almost always given (as distinct from offered as trade) in a cooked form.

73. E.g., Eagleston, "Ups and Downs," p. 275.

74. Ibid., pp. 250, 289.

75. Ibid., p. 282.

76. N. Thomas, *Planets around the Sun: Dynamics and Contradictions of the Fijian "Matanitu"* (Sydney: Oceania Monographs), pp. 9–11, and *passim*; Thomas Williams, *Fiji and the Fijians* (London: Heylin, 1858), chap. 2; on Cakaudrove specifically, see S. Sayes, "Cakaudrove: Ideology and Reality in a Fijian Confederation" (Ph.D. diss., Australian National University, 1983), chap. 1.

77. E.g., Horatio Hale, *United States Exploring Expedition: Ethnology and Philology* (Philadelphia: Lea and Blanchard, 1846), p. 50.

78. R. A. Derrick, *A History of Fiji* (Suva: Government Printer, 1950), pp. 44–45. For one of the earliest tellings of the Charles Savage story, see Eagleston, "Ups and Downs," p. 304. The general idea that confederations were essentially postcontact developments was prevalent in early missionary ethnographic and historical notes and appeared in print in Williams, *Fiji and the Fijians*, p. 18, and subsequently in many other works.

79. S. Sayes, "The Paths of the Land: Early Political Hierarchies in Cakaudrove, Fiji," *Journal of Pacific History* 19 (1984), 4–8 and *passim*; Thomas, *Planets*, p. 7.

80. E.g., Wilkes, *U.S. Exploring Expedition*, III, 123; residents of the Rewa village of Kasavu were said themselves to be the source of the account of the massacre there (David Cargill, *Memoir of Mrs. Margaret Cargill . . . Including Notices of the Progress of Christianity in Tonga and Feejee*, London: John Mason, 1841, pp. 281–282). P. E. Tatawaqa assembled some Fijian traditions of Savage early this century ("Charley Savage," *Transactions of the Fijian Society for 1912*).

81. Eagleston, "Ups and Downs," p. 287.

82. Cheever, *Emerald* log, 21 May 1834.

83. Wilkes, *U.S. Exploring Expedition*, III, 131–133; on the structural significance of this type of conflict, see Thomas, *Planets*, pp. 30–31.

84. These events are discussed in many sources, Wilkes, *U.S. Exploring Expedition*, III, 63–65, and J. Waterhouse, *The King and People of Fiji* (London: Wesleyan Conference Office, 1866), being among the more accessible, while D. Toganivalu's "History of Bau" (MS, National Archives of Fiji, Suva) provides an important internal account. For analysis, see Sayes, "Cakaudrove," chap. 7, and Thomas, *Planets*, pp. 56–57.

85. This is clearly so of Eagleston, who made a number of voyages and was probably more consequential than most of the others.

86. Ben Finney, *Big-Men and Business* (Canberra: Australian National University Press, 1973), p. 32; see also Andrew Strathern, *The Rope of Moka* (Cambridge: Cambridge University Press, 1971), and Daryl Feil, *Ways of Exchange* (St. Lucia: University of Queensland Press, 1984).

87. A. Strathern, *Rope of Moka*; Steven Hooper, "A Study of Valuables in the Chiefdom of Lau, Fiji" (Ph.D. diss., University of Cambridge, 1982), p. 87.

88. The only tortoiseshell articles in Fergus Clunie's Fiji museum catalogue are hairdressing needles (*Yalo i Viti: A Fiji Museum Catalogue*, Suva: Fiji Museum, 1986, items 78–79).

89. Sandalwood dust was used in the hair in ceremonial contexts; this may be a long term consequence of the trade and is now often replaced with Johnson's Baby Powder.

90. E.g., Eagleston, "Ups and Downs," pp. 341, 349; cf. Ward, "The Bêche de Mer Trade," pp. 111, 114.

91. Pork and tubers were often obtained from other islands such as Rotuma.

92. For an account of an especially large presentation and feast, see G. C. Henderson, ed., *The Journal of Thomas Williams* (Sydney: Angus and Robertson, 1931), II, 347ff.

93. The population decreased from about 20,000 in 1840 to roughly 5,000 in the 1880s.

94. Finney, *Big-Men and Business*, p. 123.

95. Ibid, pp. 128–137. The fact that the eastern highlands were lumped together with Goroka in his material for the purposes of this broader discussion meant that the differences which were later central to Modjeska's and Godelier's comparisons were suppressed.

96. It does not seem coincidental that the several economic anthropologists with similar concerns happened to work with a society with one of the most elaborate value-conversion systems—the various Tolai groups (see Richard Salisbury, *Vunamami: Economic Transformations in a Traditional Society*, Melbourne: Melbourne University Press, 1970; T. S. Epstein, *Capitalism, Primitive and Modern*, Manchester: Manchester University Press, 1968; A. L. Epstein, *Matupit: Land, Politics, and Change among the Tolai of New Britain*, Canberra: Australian National University Press, 1969).

4. The European Appropriation of Indigenous Things

1. The development of collecting and curiosity cabinets, and of ethnological collecting specifically, are much larger topics than can be pursued here, but see Oliver Impey and Arthur MacGregor, eds., *The Origins of Museums: The Cabinet of Curiosities in Sixteenth and Seventeenth Century Europe* (Oxford: Oxford University Press, 1985); chaps. 27–33 deal with American, Asian, and African material in early collections, though in a documentary rather than interpretative way. G. Stocking, ed., *Objects and Others: Essays on Museums and Material Culture* (Madison: University of Wisconsin Press, 1986), contains useful essays mainly on late nineteenth- and twentieth-century museums; there is also an extensive literature within museum and material culture studies on issues associated with the implications of various types of displays, cultural property, the politics of representation, and so on. See for instance Adrienne Kaeppler, "Museums of the World," Peter Gathercole, "The Fetishism of Artefacts," and E. Hooper-Greenhill, "The Museum in the Disciplinary Society," all in Susan M. Pearce, ed., *Museum Studies in Material Culture* (London: Leicester University Press, 1989); also valuable are Brian Durrans, "The Future of the Other: Changing Cultures on Display in Ethnographic Museums," in Robert Lumley, ed., *The Museum Time-Machine* (London: Routledge, 1985), and Sally Price's more provocative and wide-ranging *Primitive Art in Civilized Places* (Chicago: University of Chicago Press, 1989). For more theoretically stimulating discussion, see James Clifford, *The Predicament of Culture* (Cambridge, Mass.: Harvard University Press, 1988), chaps. 9 and 10, and Marianna Torgovnick, *Gone Primitive: Savage Intellects, Modern Lives* (Chicago: University of Chicago Press, 1990). Almost all of these studies deal with metropolitan institutions' and aficionados' interests, rather than the concerns of various collectors active in the colonized countries, which I attempt to address more directly here.

2. My emphasis upon the diversity and the internal tensions of colonial projects here parallels a broader wave of interest in anthropological and historical scholarship. See Ann L. Stoler, "Rethinking Colonial Categories: European Communities and the Boundaries of Rule," *Comparative Studies in Society and History* 31 (1989), 135–136; Jean Comaroff and John L. Comaroff, "Through the Looking Glass: Colonial Encounters of the First Kind," *Journal of Historical Sociology* 1 (1988), 6–32; and the papers in a special issue of *American Ethnologist* 16 (4) (1989) devoted to "Tensions of Empire" (ed. Frederick Cooper and Ann L. Stoler). My interest in juxtaposing explorers', missionaries', and administrators' interests and perceptions also owes a great deal to Margaret Jolly's forthcoming work on gender and the colonial history of Vanuatu ("Engendering Colonialism: Women and History in Vanuatu," manuscript).

3. Keate was not on the voyage himself but wrote the book on the basis of the papers of, and extended interviews with, participants. The story had features which could hardly have failed to attract considerable public attention (and Keate's publication was, in fact, commercially very successful)—Captain Wilson and the crew of the *Antelope* were wrecked on Belau, where they stayed for several months, enjoying good relations with the inhabitants, while building a new vessel, with which they sailed to Macao. Another aspect which aroused great public interest was the Belauan chiefly man Prince Leboo, who accompanied Wilson back to London and had a similar impact upon various aristocratic circles as the Tahitian Omai.

4. "Curios" is a later, nineteenth-century, term (cf. *OED*). On the natural/artificial distinction, see Margaret T. Hodgen, *Early Anthropology in the Sixteenth and Seventeenth Centuries* (Philadelphia: University of Pennsylvania Press, 1964), pp. 111–112, where the development of a distinct interest in "artificial rarities" is discussed (this is also touched upon by a number of contributors to Impey and MacGregor, *The Origins of Museums*). A distinction is quite clear from a kind of catalogue (which incidentally was among the books taken by Joseph Banks on Cook's first circumnavigation), C. Biron's *Curiositez de la nature et de l'art* (Paris: Jean Moreau, 1703), which itemized minerals, plants, animals, and works of art from various parts of the world. The artificial category included a "miroir du métail du Japon," "différents houragans, ou petits paniers faits d'écorces d'arbres par les Sauvages du Canada," manuscripts in the Malabar language, and diverse other things which were mostly described briefly and unsystematically.

5. This is apparent even from titles such as Anonymous, *A Voyage to the East Indies in 1747 and 1748 . . . Interspersed with Many Useful and Curious Observations and Anecdotes* (London: T. Becket and P. A. Dehondt, 1762); Mary Wortley Montagu, *Letters . . . Written during Her Travels in Europe, Asia, and Africa . . . Which Contain among Other Curious Relations, Accounts of the Policy and Manners of the Turks* (London: Homer, 1764). A list of such eighteenth-century titles could easily be considerably expanded. Toward the middle of the nineteenth century, the word "curious" ceases to refer to reports, descriptions, notices, and voyages, and is instead characteristic of customs, festivals, races, dress, and so on; that is, it ceases to be an attribute of the inquirer or the inquiry and is objectified and externalized.

6. Edmund Burke, *A Philosophical Enquiry into the Origin of Our Ideas of the Sublime and Beautiful*, ed. J. Boulton (Oxford: Basil Blackwell, 1958 [orig. 1757]), p. 31. Rüdiger Joppien and Bernard Smith discuss the relevance of this passage to Hodges's Cook voyage paintings in *The Art of Captain Cook's Voyages* (Melbourne: Oxford University Press, 1985), II, 31–32. I am not suggesting, of course, that these ideas were generally subscribed to in the late eighteenth century; in both philosophical disquisitions and certain travel works

(such as those of Monboddo and Mungo Park) there seems to be no problem or ambivalence about the idea of "scientific curiosity." The point is, however, that an opposition between the masculine work of reason and infantile or feminine curiosity (grounded in the passions) was highly salient in the discourses of these particular voyages.

7. James Cook, *The Journals of Captain James Cook*, ed. J. C. Beaglehole (Cambridge: Cambridge University Press/Hakluyt Society, 1955–1967), II, 254.

8. George Keate, *An Account of the Pelew Islands*, 3d ed. (London: G. Nicol, 1789), p. vii.

9. Ibid., pp. vii-viii.

10. Ibid., p. xiii.

11. I do not discuss the French voyages in any detail here, but the same general range of attitudes is exhibited; see for instance L. de Bougainville, *A Voyage round the World* (London: Nourse, 1772), I, 258–259, concerning Tahiti.

12. See e.g., George Forster on the inhabitants of Tanna and Malekula, discussed by Margaret Jolly, "'Illnatured Comparisons': Racism and Relativism in Perceptions of Ni-Vanuatu on Cook's Second Voyage," *History and Anthropology* 5 (1991), in press.

13. Bernard Smith, *European Vision and the South Pacific*, 2d ed. (Oxford: Melbourne University Press, 1985), p. 123, citing Sydney Parkinson, *A Journal of a Voyage to the South Seas in "HMS Endeavour"* (London: S. Parkinson, 1773), pp. 90, 129–130, and 96. Tattooing was frequently described as curious; see Cook on the Marquesas (*Journals*, II, 374). From the first voyage, Joseph Banks's journal is especially replete with expressions of curiosity and similarly ambivalent reactions. The costume of the "chief mourner" in Tahitian mortuary ceremonies—which aroused the interest of other members of the voyage—was "most Fantastical tho not unbecoming" (J. C. Beaglehole, ed., *The "Endeavour" Journal of Sir Joseph Banks*, Sydney: Public Library of New South Wales/Angus and Robertson, 1962, I, 288).

14. Cook, *Journals*, II, 272, 375.

15. Johann Reinhold Forster, *The "Resolution" Journal of Johann Reinhold Forster*, ed. Michael E. Hoare (London: Hakluyt Society, 1982), pp. 300, 360, 491.

16. George Forster, *A Voyage round the World, in His Brittanic Majesty's Sloop "Resolution"* (London: B. White, 1777), II, 213.

17. [John Marra], *Journal of the Resolution's Voyage in 1772–75* (London: Newbery, 1775), p. 163. Unfortunately there is no way of establishing whether these words, or any other sentence, derive from the original text of the author, the gunner's mate, or the work's educated editor, thought by J. C. Beaglehole to be David Henry, the editor of *Gentleman's Magazine* (see his "Introduction" to Cook, *Journals*, II, cliii–clv).

18. Smith, *European Vision*, p. 124. Parkinson's statements are all from the first voyage; those quoted of Cook, and of the Forsters, are all from the second.

19. Johann Reinhold Forster, *Journal*, p. 377.
20. George Forster, *Voyage*, II, 220, 233.
21. Johann Reinhold Forster, *Journal*, pp. 644, 300. The first observation related to Tonga, the second Queen Charlotte Sound, New Zealand. As Smith noted, the attitudes toward "any work which involved unnatural proportions in the human figure" were generally far more negative than those toward abstract design (*European Vision*, pp. 125–126). This view was shared by slightly later French visitors (among them J. J. de Labillardière, *Relation du voyage à la recherche de La Pérouse*, Paris: Jansen, an VIII [1800], II, 105, Table des Planches—in separately paginated appended material, referring to fig. 22 in plate 32.
22. Johann Reinhold Forster, *Observations Made during a Voyage round the World on Physical Geography, Natural History, and Ethic Philosophy* (London: G. Robinson, 1778), p. 418.
23. Ibid., pp. 421–422; cf. George Forster, *Voyage*, II, 292, 324.
24. The account offered by Johann Reinhold Forster and others essentially corresponded with the Melanesia/Polynesia division which was proposed by Dumont D'Urville in the 1830s; see Nicholas Thomas, "The Force of Ethnology," *Current Anthropology* 30 (1989), 29–30; on adjudications about women, see Margaret Jolly, "Engendering Colonialism: Women and History in Vanuatu" (manuscript).
25. See e.g., Cook, *Journals*, II, 541, concerning the apparent affiliations of New Caledonian languages. Similar discussions appear in the numerous publications associated with later voyages, such as that of the missionary ship *Duff* (James Wilson, *A Missionary Voyage in the Southern Pacific Ocean*, London: Chapman, 1799, especially the "preliminary discourse" which draws on Cook narratives among other publications for a systematic anthropological exposition).
26. See Rhys Jones, "Images of Natural Man," in J. Bonnemains, E. Forsyth and B. Smith, eds., *Baudin in Australian Waters* (Melbourne; Oxford University Press, 1988), and the graphic material in the book as a whole. Some references were made to the "wretchedness" of huts and domestic utensils, but this attitude seemed to apply mainly to the former; the women's baskets were certainly appreciated and taken as a manifestation of industry. It is relevant here that Maori, Australian, and Tierra del Fuegian artifacts could be placed together in one engraving (plate 26 in Parkinson's *Voyage round the World*), and it might be noted that John Frederick Miller, who made a series of drawings of artifacts for Joseph Banks, took the same overall approach to the whole range of material (see reproductions in Joppien and Smith, *The Art of Captain Cook's Voyages*, I).
27. Norman Bryson, "Chardin and the Text of Still Life," *Critical Inquiry* 15 (1989), 227, 231.
28. Those demarcations appeared, to some extent, in late nineteenth-century co-

lonial writings: see, for example, Henry M. Stanley, *Through Darkest Africa* (London: Sampson Low, 1890), I, 156, 175, 244, 370; II, 91, 93, 320, 367, 369. Here artifacts are mostly the types characteristic of a particular tribe or race; we are shown the "Milk Vessel of the Wahuma," for instance.

29. J. J. de Labillardière, *An Account of a Voyage in Search of La Pérouse* (London: Stockdale, 1800), II, 224–225.

30. New Caledonians were not categorized as "savages" in opposition to the "inhabitants" of the Friendly Islands in the captions to the plates in the English edition, but the illustrations themselves emphasized the warrior character of the Melanesians.

31. Labillardière, *Relation*, II, 107 (my translation of the caption; the English edition does not include illustrations). As was consistent with this emphasis, it was also conjectured—in the absence of any particular justification—that a mask which had been collected was used in battle ("that they may not be recognized by their enemies"—English ed., II, 249).

32. This might be traced in some later French voyage depictions of the Maori, which seem to emphasize the distortion and savage effect of certain weapons; see reports from Duperrey's 1824 visit in Isabel Ollivier, ed., *Extracts from New Zealand Journals Written on Ships under the Command of d'Entrecasteaux and Duperrey* (Wellington: Alexander Turnbull Library, 1986), pp. 199–201. Axes and other implements appear elegant, but links are made with customs such as the scarification and mutilation of the face during mourning.

33. These were in fact more conspicuous in a letter from the two Forsters (unpublished at the time) to an Italian scientist commenting upon artifacts that the latter had purchased. Here they wrote that "the belligerent people found in New Zealand are not very advanced in the arts. We brought back only some fishhooks crudely made" (translation in Adrienne Kaeppler, ed., *Cook Voyage Artifacts in Leningrad, Berne, and Florence Museums*, Honolulu: Bishop Museum, 1978, p. 72).

34. Johann Reinhold Forster, *Journal*, pp. 555–557; cf. p. 647, where at New Caledonia, in the absence of Cook, sailors refused to make a boat available to Forster to take him ashore. He angrily noted that this arose from their envy over the differences between their and his emoluments and identified his own projects with the public interest: "I get my money if I had not the opportunity to get one plant or bird described the whole Voyage. If I am disappointed the fault is not mine, but the public loses by it, who pays & whose chief views are thus defeated, by Men who are Servants to the public, & ought to promote, not hinder the common cause. But it cannot be reasonably expected from the people who have not sense enough to think reasonably & beyond the Sphere of their mean grovelling passions." It is notable, in the light of Burke's discussion, that the sailors' interests are here represented as "passions" in contrast,

presumably, to Forster's project of "reason" in the scientific pursuit of natural history.

35. Sparrman's material was presented to the Swedish Academy of Science and is now in the Statens Etnografiska Museum, Stockholm (J. Soderstrom, A. *Sparrman's Ethnographical Collection from Captain Cook's Second Expedition*, Stockholm: Ethnographical Museum, 1939); for the Forster material see [Peter Gathercole], *From the South Seas* (Oxford: Pitt Rivers Museum, 1971). The only catalogue of artificial curiosities specifically from the voyage to appear during the eighteenth century was Alexander Shaw's compilation of specimens of barkcloth (but see also the Leverian museum catalogue, discussed by Smith, *European Vision*, p. 127). Shaw had not himself been a participant on the voyage but made up a number of volumes which included printed introductory matter with actual specimens cut from much larger pieces: A *Catalogue of the Different Specimens of Cloth Collected in the Three Voyages of Captain Cook to the Southern Hemisphere, with a Particular Account of the Manner of Manufacturing the Same in the Various Islands of the South Seas* (London: compiled by and printed for the author, 1787 [there are several copies in the Mitchell and Dixson Libraries, Sydney]). While other facts such as navigational and astronomical observations were presented through official publications, this was merely a collection "of select specimens for a few friends" (Shaw, *Catalogue of the Different Specimens*, p. 2).

36. Johann Reinhold Forster, *Observations*, pp. 212–213.

37. Harriet Guest, "The Great Distinction: Figures of the Exotic in the Work of William Hodges," *Oxford Art Journal* 12 (2) (1989), 41–42.

38. E.g., Bronislaw Malinowski, *Argonauts of the Western Pacific* (London: Routledge, 1922), p. 511; Ben Finney, *Big-Men and Business* (Canberra: Australian National University Press, 1973), p. 12; Rena Lederman, *What Gifts Engender* (Cambridge: Cambridge University Press, 1986), pp. 3, 148, 181.

39. Nancy D. Munn, *The Fame of Gawa* (Cambridge: Cambridge University Press, 1986), p. 49.

40. Johann Reinhold Forster, *Journal*, p. 396. This type of "musical instrument, composed of reeds" is illustrated in James Cook, A *Voyage toward the South Pole, and around the World* (London: Strahan and Cadell, 1777), I, plate 21 (facing p. 220). The comparisons with the Greeks also enabled the astronomer William Wales, at least, to reflexively perceive Homer's account differently: "I must confess I have often been led to think the feats which Homer represents his heroes as performing with their spears, a little too marvellous . . . But since I have seen what these people [on Tanna] can do with their wooden spears, and them badly pointed, and not of a very hard nature, I have not the least exception to any one passage in the great poet on this account. But if I see fewer exceptions, I can find infinitely more beauties in him; as he has, I think, scarce an action, circumstance, or description of any kind whatever, relating

to the spear, which I have not seen and recognized among these people" (quoted in Cook, *Voyage toward the South Pole*, II, 83; cf. *Journals*, II, 862). There were certainly copies of Homer on the vessel, and this passage makes it clear the extent to which classical parallels did not merely provide a literary device for later composition, but actually informed vision and the manner in which people were "recognized" in the first instance. It is interesting that Wales should make such remarks in relation to the Tannese, rather than Tahitians or Tongans who were more frequently compared with the Greeks or Romans.

41. Johann Reinhold Forster, *Journal*, p. 398.
42. Keate, *Account of the Pelew Islands*, p. 289.
43. George Forster, *Voyage*, II, 312, 328: "We proceeded up the hill, and saw several extensive spots of ground which had been cleared of wood in order to be cultivated. The wretched tools of the natives, and the necessity of working very slowly with them . . . convinced us that this piece of ground, which comprehended near two acres, must have required a great deal of time and labour to clear."
44. For example, ibid., II, 299.
45. Keate, *Account of the Pelew Islands*, p. 312.
46. George Forster, *Voyage*, I, 177–180. William Hodges's painting, *View of Pickersgill Harbour, Dusky Bay* (in the National Maritime Museum; Joppien and Smith, *Art of Captain Cook's Voyages*, II, plate 18), provides a remarkable pictorial counterpart to this passage: the hillock upon which the observatory was set up is exposed to sunlight in a striking manner, in contrast to the heavy darkness of surrounding foliage; the sailor's slouching gait, which might be taken to suggest drunkenness, and the attachment of the ship to the land by a tree trunk suggest that the European presence is overwhelmed by, or subsumed into, the chaos of the luxuriant vegetation. While the inflection of the painting is thus quite at odds with Forster's celebration of the distinctness between the European presence and the virgin environment, the fact that the smoke and the cauldron are also visible suggests strongly that the text was influenced by the painting (which may well have been executed on the voyage), or perhaps vice versa.
47. The point of the argument here is not, however, that there were significant differences of perspective between Forster senior and junior, or between them and others on the voyage. Such differences did exist, but—as with the tension between impassioned curiosity and more scientific collecting—the ambivalence internal to particular voices is conspicuous. The fact that George Forster's reflective passage on Dusky Bay is roughly derived from a section of Johann Reinhold Forster's journal (pp. 265–266), exemplifies the sense in which particular texts contained both relativizing and distancing attitudes.
48. Johann Reinhold Forster, *Journal*, p. 396.
49. Keate, *Account of the Pelew Islands*, p. 337.

50. Ibid., p. 338.

51. It is not surprising, in this context, that Keate was also the author of a satirical novel in the style of Sterne (*Sketches from Nature in a Journey to Margate*, London: J. Dedsley, 1779).

52. Keate, *Account of the Pelew Islands*, p. 313.

53. Ibid., p. 314.

54. The discussion here is of course selective and illustrative, relating to Protestant rather than Catholic missionary work, although there were certain parallels. For an overview of Pacific evangelical missions up to 1860, see Niel Gunson, *Messengers of Grace: Evangelical Missionaries in the South Seas* (Melbourne: Oxford University Press, 1978), and James A. Boutilier, Daniel T. Hughes, and Sharon W. Tiffany, eds., *Mission, Church, and Sect in Oceania* (Lanham, Md.: University Press of America, 1978), for studies of various particular missions.

55. In many cases the alteration of dress and hair style were also constitutive of conversion.

56. Missionaries were often conscious that "converts" were Christians in a merely nominal sense, just as they could hardly avoid being aware of the nonreligious advantages (such as access to trade goods) which often induced chiefs and others to convert.

57. William Wyatt Gill, *Jottings from the Pacific* (London: Religious Tract Society, 1885), p. 15. Gill added that "the divinity is believed to have devoured the *essence*, so that only the refuse is in reality left! Like the dogma of transubstantiation nearer home, this doctrine requires a considerable amount of faith" (p. 16). The opportunity to denigrate Catholicism through comparison with non-Christian customs was rarely passed over.

58. John Williams, *A Narrative of Missionary Enterprises in the South-Sea Islands* (London: John Snow, 1838), p. 37.

59. See the quotation at the beginning of this section. Apart from this catalogue, and another from the late nineteenth century, there are few sources about the establishment and organization of this institution (for a brief account see Adrienne Kaeppler, *"Artificial Curiosities": An Exposition of Native Manufactures Collected on the Three Pacific Voyages of Captain James Cook, R.N.*, Honolulu: Bishop Museum, 1978, pp. 13–14). It included both natural history material ("horns of the ibex and antelope") and a wide array of artifacts from Asia, the Pacific, and Africa. It is not surprising that the "household idols" of Pomare were in a central case in the "Large Room"; "rejected idols" from other parts of the society group also seem to have been prominently displayed. The feature which distinguished these exhibitions from most personal collections and state museums was (apart from the emphasis on idols) the presence of artifacts associated with missionary activity and the process of conversion: "A shell, sounded to call the scholars to school, and the natives to their public worship,

in Oaho [sic] Sandwich Islands"; "A pair of shoes, worn by Mr. Ellis in moun-
tainous parts of the Island of Hawaii" (Anonymous, *Catalogue of the Missionary Museum, Austin Friars, Including Specimens in Natural History, Various Idols of Heathen Nations, Dresses, Manufactures, Domestic Utensils, Instruments of War, &c. &c. &c.*, London: W. Phillips, 1826, pp. 10, 17, 20). The museum was closed and the collection dispersed early this century.

60. This was a cheap and widely circulated four-page periodical which featured an engraving on the front, frequently depicting Hindu "idols" such as the Juggernaut or other Asian images and invariably appearing grotesque. On representations of the Juggernaut, see Ronald Inden, *Imagining India* (Oxford: Basil Blackwell, 1990).

61. *Missionary Sketches* no. 3 (October 1818), p. 1.

62. Ibid., p. 3.

63. Smith, *European Vision*, pp. 324–335.

64. *Ti'i*, cognate with Maori *tiki* and numerous related Polynesian terms, referring to an ancestor image.

65. *Missionary Sketches* no. 3 (October 1818), p. 2.

66. Thomas Williams, *Fiji and the Fijians* (London: Alexander Heylin, 1858), I, 215–216; Richard Moyle, ed., *The Samoan Journals of John Williams* (Canberra: Australian National University Press, 1984), pp. 83, 102, 264.

67. John Williams, *Missionary Enterprises*, p. 456. Certain popular syntheses carried particularly florid descriptions. An anonymous publication from about 1835 noted for instance that "often with the lozenge-shaped [clubs] they would cleave the skulls of their opponents" (*Missionary Notices: Tahiti and the Society Islands*, London: Religious Tract Society, ca. 1835, p. 83).

68. Richard B. Lyth, "List of Curiosities," in his "Tongan and Fijian Reminiscences," MS, Mitchell Library, Sydney, II, 5–9. I am extremely grateful to Laurel Heath, who helped me locate this document, for her advice on Lyth's papers in general.

69. A portrait of John Williams surrounded by idols and other artifacts (reproduced in Smith, *European Vision*, plate 203) also conveys this sense of accomplishment. Just as surrendered "idols" were trophies of victory, the possessor of such spoils appears as a successful hunter or soldier of Christ.

70. Thomas Baker, *Diary and Collected Papers* (Roneod: privately published; in Mitchell Library, Sydney), p. 89 (entry under 20 September 1864).

71. The use of a transaction to express the allegedly shallow attachment of indigenous people to their ritual objects, and their overwhelming desire to obtain trade goods, figured as a narrative device in the publications of later ethnological collectors; see, for instance, Frank Burnett, *Through Polynesia and Papua: Wanderings with a Camera in Southern Seas* (London: Francis Griffiths, 1911), pp. 120–121.

72. Thomas Williams, *Fiji and the Fijians*, I, 60.

73. Ibid., pp. 60–101.

74. For similar aesthetic appraisals, see Gill's description of the "admirable" carving and design of adz handles (*Jottings*, pp. 223–224).

75. "Some [spears] are armed with the thorns of the sting-ray, some are barbed, and some formed of a wood which bursts when moist, so that it can scarcely be extracted from a wound" (Thomas Williams, *Fiji and the Fijians*, I, 57).

76. Ibid., p. 77.

77. This trend, rather than the contextualization in warfare, is dominant in lists and drawings of clubs in Williams's unpublished papers. An annotated list of clubs refers exclusively to wood types and aesthetic properties, and no mention is made of horrific effect (Williams, "Rough Sketches of Places, Persons, and Things," MS, Mitchell Library, Sydney, 1844–ca. 1850). Unfortunately, the drawings which accompanied these notes have mostly been lost, but the few still in the volume clearly emphasize form and symmetry. I would not, however, argue that these images express a distinct missionary agenda to the extent that the earlier engravings express interests peculiar to Enlightenment voyagers and natural scientists; the engravings in Williams's book conformed with a genre found in many works of the second half of the nineteenth century (see, for instance, Stanley's *Through Darkest Africa*). It is rather the placing of images and texts, and the nature of comment, that is distinctive.

78. This material is analyzed in detail in N. Thomas, "Colonial Conversions: Difference, Hierarchy, and History in Early Twentieth Century Evangelical Propaganda," *Comparative Studies in Society and History*, in press.

79. *The Transformed Isle* (film, Australasian Methodist Missionary Society, ca. 1917), caption frame.

80. *Australian Methodist Missionary Review*, 4 September 1909.

81. E.g., John Williams, *Missionary Enterprises*, p. 5.

82. The next two sections of this chapter derive from N. Thomas, "Material Culture and Colonial Power: Ethnological Collecting and the Establishment of Colonial Rule in Fiji," *Man* 24 (1989), 41–56.

83. W. T. Pritchard, *Polynesian Reminiscences; or, Life in the South Pacific Islands* (London: Chapman and Hall, 1866), p. 253; Deryck Scarr, *I, the Very Bayonet: A Life of Sir John Bates Thurston* (Canberra: Australian National University Press, 1973), pp. 59–60; Scarr, *Fiji: A Short History* (Sydney: George Allen and Unwin Australia, 1984), pp. 35–41. The fullest discussions of settler and planter society can be found in John Young, "Evanescent Ascendancy: The Planter Community in Fiji," in J. W. Davidson and Deryck Scarr, eds., *Pacific Islands Portraits* (Canberra: Australian National University Press, 1973), and *Adventurous Spirits: Australian Migrant Society in Pre-Cession Fiji* (St. Lucia: University of Queensland Press, 1984). The cotton boom was caused by the lack of supply from the United States during the American Civil War.

84. Young, *Adventurous Spirits*, pp. 280–281, 309. Beginning in 1879, the demand for labor began to be met through the importation of indentured Indians, which was intensely controversial in the period up to its abolition and of decisive importance for subsequent Fijian history.

85. In fact it was the case that the first governor, Sir Arthur Gordon, felt that Fijian interests—as he perceived them—should be paramount. This perspective, together with certain protectionist doctrines which aimed to restrict Fijian participation in commerce and preserve village society, was subscribed to by most subsequent Fijian administrations. For the historical background see Scarr, *I, the Very Bayonet* and *Fiji*, although these works convey an elitist perspective in which J. B. Thurston (governor 1888–1897) is heroically central. Timothy J. Macnaught's *The Fijian Colonial Experience* (Canberra: Research School of Pacific Studies, Australian National University, 1982) provides a slightly less administration-oriented discussion of the period up to World War II.

86. Arthur Hamilton Gordon, letter to Wood, Nasaucoko, 14 July–14 August 1876, Stanmore Papers, British Library Add. MS. 49237.

87. A. A. A. Von Hügel, *The Fiji Journals of Baron Von Hügel*, ed. Jane Roth and Steven Hooper (Suva: Fiji Museum, in press), June 1875. This passage was actually a later summary of Von Hügel's early impressions of Fiji.

88. Fergus Clunie, *Yalo i Viti: A Fiji Museum Catalogue* (Suva: Fiji Museum, 1986), p. 190; cf. A. M. Hocart, *The Northern States of Fiji* (London: Royal Anthropological Institute, 1952), p. 53 n.2.

89. Charlotte Cameron, *Two Years in Southern Seas* (Boston: Small, Maynard, & Co., ca. 1920), pp. 128–129.

90. J. Edge-Partington and C. Heape, *An Album of the Weapons, Tools, Ornaments, Articles of Dress, &c. of the Natives of the Pacific* (Manchester: privately published, 1890–1898), p. 123.

91. Jane Roth and Steven Hooper, "Introduction" to Von Hügel, *Journals*. I am indebted to Mrs. Roth and Dr. Hooper, who generously made available the proofs of their forthcoming edition of the journals.

92. Von Hügel, *Journals*, 26 June 1875.

93. Ibid., 3 July 1875.

94. Ibid., 29 June 1875.

95. Ibid., 3 July 1875.

96. Ibid., 6 July 1875.

97. Ibid., 1 August 1875.

98. Ibid., 3–8 August 1875.

99. Constance F. Gordon Cumming, *At Home in Fiji* (Edinburgh: William Blackwood, 1881), I, 226–227. Maudslay was temporarily on Gordon's staff (see his *Life in the Pacific Fifty Years Ago*, London: Routledge, 1930); "Mr. Gordon" was Gordon's nephew. Some of the governor's collection went to the British Museum; other material collected by most of these people was later given to Von Hügel for the Cambridge collection, which also has Gordon

Cumming's sketchbooks of Fijian artifacts, landscapes, and so on, among other relevant archival materials. Information on Gordon Cumming and the general context of life at Nasova is scattered throughout Claudia Knapman's, *White Women in Fiji 1835–1930: The Ruin of Empire?* (Sydney: George Allen and Unwin Australia, 1986).

100. Lady Gordon quoted in Sir Arthur Hamilton Gordon (Lord Stanmore), *Fiji: Records of Private and of Public Life, 1875–1880* (Edinburgh: privately published, 1897–1912), I, 272, cf. 295.

101. Ibid., pp. 150–151.

102. Ibid., pp. 322–323. For other respect observances and presentations of whale teeth, see ibid., pp. 293, 325, 327.

103. Ibid., pp. 161–162.

104. Ibid., p. 291.

105. Ibid., p. 292. Lady Gordon was as enthusiastic as any of the others about Fijian artifacts and constantly remarked upon their interest and appeal in letters home (ibid., I, 269, 273–274, 291–299, 350, 404–411; II, 31–32, 65–66, 127, 149, 151, 159, 185–186, 229–230, 244, 517; III, 68–69, etc.). Her interest was partly ethnographic but more marked by the encompassment of Fijian products in European craft activities: for instance she had fine pieces of barkcloth made into things such as bonnets for herself and female friends and relatives at home (II, 41).

106. Hocart, letter to W. H. R. Rivers, MS, Haddon Papers, Cambridge University Library.

107. Gordon, *Fiji*, I, 210, 212. For further discussion see N. Thomas, "Sanitation and Seeing: The Creation of State Power in Early Colonial Fiji," *Comparative Studies in Society and History* 32 (1990), 149–170.

108. Anonymous, *Fiji: Remarks on the Address Delivered by Sir Arthur Gordon, by a Colonist* (Levuka, Fiji: privately published, 1879), p. 5.

109. E. Vickery, *Fiji at Sydney International Exhibition, 1879* (Sydney: Foster and Fairfax, 1879); W. K. Thomson, *Melbourne International Exposition, 1880–1881: Fijian Court, Catalogue of Exhibits, Together with a Short Description of the Soil, Climate, Products, and Resources of the Colony of Fiji* (Melbourne: Mason, Firth, and M'Cutcheon, 1880).

110. John Mackenzie, *Austral Africa: Losing It or Ruling It* (London: Sampson Low, 1887), p. 1. The significance of this departure point for Mackenzie's particular arguments for an expanded and modified imperial project in South Africa is beyond the scope of my discussion.

111. Miller emphasizes this in *Material Culture and Mass Consumption* (Oxford: Basil Blackwell, 1987); see discussion in Chapter 1.

112. See Paul Greenhalgh's *Ephemeral Vistas: The Expositions Universelles, Great Exhibitions, and World's Fairs, 1851–1939* (Manchester: Manchester University Press, 1988) for a valuable review; Timothy Mitchell has focused on the forms of representation and truth evoked by such exhibitions among

other forms of colonial discourse in *Colonising Egypt* (Cambridge: Cambridge University Press, 1988), particularly chap. 1.

113. I borrow Bernard Cohn's term; see also John Comaroff, "Images of Empire, Contests of Conscience: Models of Colonial Domination in South Africa," *American Ethnologist* 16 (1989), 661–685.

114. Cf. Thomas, "Sanitation and Seeing"; Asa Briggs, *The Age of Improvement* (London: Longmans, 1959), p. 441.

115. Anonymous, *Eine Reise durch die Deutschen Kolonien . . . V. Band, Südsee* (Berlin: Verlag Kolonialpolitischer Zeitschritften, 1911). Without even going into the content of images or captions, the sequence of subjects photographed in this album clearly imagines a developmental history: the viewer first sees landscapes, then (wild) plant life, then birds, then native physical types, native villages, and houses, then native canoes, fishing technologies, and handicrafts (the marks of an indigenous predisposition for industry), then the mission stations, native police, and "Rabaul, der Sitz des Gouverneurs" (the agents of pacification and order), consummated by various pictures of the European presence and commerce—wharfs, bungalows, warehouses, ships, road building, and plantations.

116. See Roger Thompson, *Australian Imperialism in the Pacific* (Melbourne: Melbourne University Press, 1980).

117. "Space itself was a text that had to be written before it could be interpreted"—Paul Carter, *The Road to Botany Bay* (London: Faber and Faber, 1987), p. 41.

118. Frank Hurley, *Pearls and Savages* (New York: Putnam, 1923), caption to plate facing p. 352. Julian Thomas's research and advice on Frank Hurley have been extremely helpful.

119. Ibid., p. 379. This passage, and the next, seem to be derived word for word from Hurley's article in the Sydney newspaper *The Sun*, 7 February 1923 (under the headlines "HEAD-HUNTERS' CITADEL / Gruesome Human Relics" and "VICTIMS' HEADS STUFFED / Hurley's Thrilling Exploration"). A series of Hurley's accounts were illustrated with photographs which also appeared in the book *Pearls and Savages*.

120. Hurley, *Pearls and Savages*, pp. 380–383.

121. Ibid., p. 383.

122. This point is insisted upon with considerable redundancy. Hurley noted, for instance, that among other things pillaged were "bits of wood, charms, seeds, and bush herbs—the purposes of which we know not" (ibid., p. 380). This lack of knowledge evidently had no bearing on the value of these specimens for science, however.

123. *The Sun*, 7, 8, 13 February, 21 March 1923.

124. *The Sun*, 21 March 1923.

125. F. E. Williams, *The Collection of Curios and the Preservation of Native Culture* (Port Moresby: Government Printer, 1923), p. 2. Williams began by

alluding to "the action of the Government regarding certain curios collected by a recent expedition" but did not actually name Hurley or enter into the details of that particular case.

126. Ibid., pp. 1, 9.

127. Hence the wicker figures, known as Kaiemunu were thus believed to "have oracular authority . . ." and were also "the symbol[s] of the unity of the group." Williams noted that "much could be said" on the topic, suggesting (admittedly with some justification) the great extent of his own knowledge of the area.

128. F. E. Williams, *The Collection of Curios*, p. 5.

129. Ibid., pp. 19–20.

130. Ibid., p. 18. The direct analogy here is of course between the girl and the ceremony, not the girl and the native, but I take my interpretation to be justified by the broader lines of Williams's colonial theory. Though occasionally cautious and relativistic, he clearly subscribed to the idea that indigenous populations could be and needed to be effectively managed, an idea which was implemented through indirect rule structures among more hierarchical native populations. The three general tasks essential to native policy were "Maintenance, Expurgation, and Expansion," meaning the preservation of cultures insofar as they are working wholes, subject to the judicious excision of social defects (expurgation), and cultural enrichment in the sense of introducing new items that "give the native a chance of fuller development than has hitherto been possible for him" ("Creed of a Government Anthropologist," in F. E. Williams, *"The Vailala Madness" and Other Essays*, ed. Erik Schwimmer, St. Lucia: University of Queensland Press, 1976 [the essay quoted originally published in 1939], p. 410 and *passim*). This management and improvement approach is quite consistent with the paternalistic image in the passage quoted.

131. *The Sun*, 7 February 1923.

5. The Discovery of the Gift

1. The issue was made fashionable in the 1960s and 1970s by Marshall McLuhan's work but has undergone a recent revival in debate around that most nebulous of terms in contemporary criticism, "postmodernism." See Mike Featherstone, ed., *Global Culture* (London: Sage, 1990), for some articles that seem to be part of the problem and others that offer useful clarification. Globalization has also received attention in the journal *Public Culture*.

2. *Trobriand Cricket: An Indigenous Response to Colonialism*, produced by Jerry Leach and Gary Kildea, 1975.

3. James Clifford, *The Predicament of Culture* (Cambridge, Mass.: Harvard University Press, 1988), p. 148.

4. Missionaries certainly attempted to make idols seem ridiculous, but not usually in an amusing or parodic fashion; as indicated above, many representations clearly aimed to make the figures threatening as well as absurd.

5. Jean Rouch's film *Les maîtres fous* (1954) shows West African participants in the Hauka cult possessed by various figures of colonial authority (the general, the doctor's wife, the governor, and so on). Although the ecstatic imitation of official gait and behavior could be interpreted as parody of the *Trobriand Cricket* sort, I think this would entail a radical misreading of the cult's orientation. I am grateful to Leslie Devereaux, who organized a screening and discussion of the film that coincided with my revision of this book.

6. I am indebted to Martha Macintyre for discussion of a "cargo cult" in the Massim region, New Guinea, from which I have abstracted this example.

7. See N. Thomas, *Marquesan Societies* (Oxford: Oxford University Press, 1990), pp. 31–33.

8. This is shorthand for systems of the kind found in Fiji, the western Solomons, and parts of New Guinea, which permitted complex conversions of value between people, relations, food, and mediating objects on the one side and valuables such as the New Georgia shell money on the other. The process of value conversion could tentatively provide the basis for a category of a certain kind of economy comparable to the chiefly system or the capitalist system. As with "feudal" economic relations, many general types at this level are discredited, but I refer to a "gift conversion" system here, not so much in order to initiate further typologizing, but simply to avoid talking about any "gift economy" as a whole. As argued in Chapter 1, gifts can be clearly and legitimately distinguished from commodities (and certain other transaction forms), but I cannot follow Strathern in setting up a unitary systemic category on the basis of this transaction form.

9. It is made clear below that the cultural constructions discussed are not shared, even by all the members of these interior western Fijian societies; and although the interpenetration of commercial farming and "customary" village life in the Noikoro area certainly has counterparts in much of the rest of Fiji, I would not wish to claim that the cultural ramifications described here have any corresponding generality. To avoid stylistic convolution I have sometimes referred not to "Noikoro people" or "some Noikoro perceptions" but to "Fijians" and "the Fijian perception"; but it should be understood that these observations have only a local basis.

10. Pots, for example, of course depend on proximate clay sources.

11. I have not been able to establish with any precision when drums of kerosene were first used in Fijian *solevu*, and no doubt their introduction took place at different times. Accounts of ceremonies in Vanua Levu and the small islands of eastern Fiji before World War I and in the 1930s make no reference to their use (A. M. Hocart, *Lau Island, Fiji*, Honolulu: Bishop Museum, 1929,

pp. 78–81; Laura Thompson, *Southern Lau: An Ethnography*, Honolulu: Bishop Museum, 1940, pp. 65, 73–74, 208; Buell Quain, *Fijian Village*, Chicago: University of Chicago Press, 1948, pp. 335–338); these passages all refer to marriage, ceremonial presentations, and so on, without mentioning offerings of goods other than mats, whale teeth, food, etc. Thompson in fact implies that at the time of her fieldwork coconut oil was still generally used for lighting. By the 1950s, however, kerosene was certainly used in western Viti Levu (C. S. Belshaw, *Under the Ivi Tree: Society and Economic Growth in Rural Fiji*, London: Routledge, 1964, pp. 128–130, plate 14); the impression I obtained from informants was that this had been the case much earlier as well.

12. The latter was kept in plastic bottles which were refilled in town and which could never be presented ceremonially. Although kerosene from drums might certainly be siphoned off occasionally for domestic purposes, drums were not generally treated as a supply which could be drawn upon for ordinary use as well as presentation; rather, they were firmly regarded as a kind of *iyau*, that is, as movable property for ceremonial offering.

13. See Lorraine Sexton, *Mothers of Money, Daughters of Coffee: The Wok Meri Movement* (Ann Arbor: UMI Research Press, 1986); the importance of trucks in highlands male competition is apparent in the informative film *Joe Leahy's Neighbours* (Bob Connolly and Robin Anderson, Ronin Films, Canberra, 1989).

14. The basic geographic dimensions in the valley are "high" and "low" (*i yata* and *i ra*). These terms also express social rank and its enactment in the spatial arrangement of houses, but they do not signify status in the larger context of the valley: a village upstream will not be of higher rank; rank is between clans (*mataqali* and *beto*) and persons rather than places.

15. I would not claim that this is true of the whole of Fiji, and in some areas much more balance is apparent in presentations between affinal sides (e.g., Hocart, *Lau Islands*, pp. 155–156); it must also be recognized that much of coastal and central Fiji was incorporated into tributary relationships which were quite different from the relative equivalence of status between the small polities of the Viti Levu interior. However, the articulation of specialized craft production and ceremonial exchange seems to have been very widespread (for Vanua Levu, for example, see Quain, *Fijian Village*, pp. 173–175).

16. For a more detailed account see N. Thomas, "Contrasts: Marriage and Identity in Western Fiji," unpublished article. I was surprised by how similar the Noikoro ceremonies which I witnessed were to those observed for a relatively close area thirty years earlier (Belshaw, *Under the Ivi Tree*, pp. 127–141). For further recent ethnographic material on Fijian marriage, see also Belaneish Teckle, "The Position of Women in Fiji," (Ph.D. diss., University of Sydney, 1986).

17. *Veitubataki*; see Teckle, "The Position of Women," for discussion of the relative incidence of formal and informal marriage and related questions.

18. In various contexts manufactured cloth off the roll is substituted for barkcloth; this clearly goes back to the time of conversion to Christianity, where *sulu* were introduced as the Christian counterparts to indigenous clothes. Long strips are often laid out across the ground for the bride to walk across; this use of cloth as a path to the land (a particular *vanua* or traditional polity) reflects the broader uses of barkcloth as a marker of transitions and transformations (cf. Marshall Sahlins, *Islands of History*, Chicago, University of Chicago Press, 1985, pp. 85–87).

19. But kava drinking is never completely unritualized in these areas and rarely even in town.

20. *Na isau ni yalewa*. *Isau* is grammatically a nominalization of *sau*, which can mean "to reply or repay" but is now the conventional term for the price of any ordinary or remarkable item purchased in a store. It is clear to anyone acquainted with local usage that this type of statement about presentations (which I heard on a number of occasions in general discussion as well as explanation volunteered specifically for my benefit) does not relate to some idea that the presentation is a response or reciprocation (as might be surmised etymologically) but makes a metaphor from the cash transactions which these cash-cropping communities are frequently engaged in. A related word, *idole*, is also used to refer to a presentation made subsequent to elopement or informal marriage, where proper presentations had not been made when the relationship was initiated. It was emphasized to me that this meant "repayment" or "replacement" in a strong sense, paradoxically being a stress on identity and equivalence of value in a term which is not actually used in market contexts.

21. The verb used is *voli*, which in early vocabularies is given as "barter" (e.g., David Cargill, "A Grammar of the Feejeean Language," MS, Mitchell Library Sydney), but which is now just the everyday word for purchase/sale. Its earlier meaning probably related to the exchange of goods which was supposed to take place quite distinctly from their transmission through *solevu*. From the perspective of the analysis of exchange offered here, it would obviously be desirable to have a fuller knowledge of these transactions, but they are extremely poorly documented in the ethnohistoric sources.

22. The *vasu* relationship is well known in the ethnography of the Fiji–west Polynesian region (see, for example, the work of A. M. Hocart), and it should be made clear that in the uplands of western Viti Levu it takes quite a different form from that described in published accounts. Although the *vasu* has a special status, there is not now any right to appropriate property from the mother's brother; and in fact the relationship is generally represented as one of special obligation and respect. Second, the term refers to both sister's sons *and* daughters, which is not generally the case elsewhere.

23. *E kia na kwa dokai; dokai* may be translated simply as "respected," but connotations verging on the sacred are no doubt linked with its extensive use in
the Fijian translation of the Bible and other Christian discourse such as ser-
mons; I heard it attached to *Kalou* (God) in usage analogous to "the Holy
Spirit," for instance. As I discussed in Chapter 2, this same phrase was used
in relation to whale teeth.

24. With reference to eastern Indonesia material, Susan McKinnon has discussed
another case in which particular cycles of affinal exchanges are characterized
in terms of "buying and selling" ("The Slave in the Gift and the Market in
Kinship," paper presented at the annual meeting of the American Anthropological Association, Washington, November 1989—I am grateful to her for a
copy of the paper and her comments on unpublished work of my own). Her
interpretation contrasts with mine in emphasizing that the idioms appropriated
from the market enable Tanimbarese to distinguish between certain types of
exchange, and this is perhaps a missing dimension of the argument here.

25. I refer to Fiji dollars, which in 1988 were worth about US$1.30.

26. This was once expressed during a truck ride to a ceremony. A woman picking
up my bag said, "Nick, this is heavy, what have you got in here, the *tabua* of
the woman?" The joke turned, of course, on the fact that (although teeth are
heavy), the heaviness of *tabua* is not primarily of a literal kind.

27. *Na itovo vavanua or vakaviti;* and *na calevu* (or *sala*) *ni lavo*. On the dichot-
omous structure of Fijian culture, see N. Thomas, "Substantivization and An-
thropological Discourse," in James W. Carrier, ed., *History and Tradition in
Melanesian Anthropology* (Berkeley: University of California Press, in press).
For slightly different interpretations, see Christina Toren, "Drinking Cash:
The Purification of Money through Ceremonial Exchange in Fiji," in Mau-
rice Bloch and Jonathan Parry, eds., *Money and the Morality of Exchange*
(Cambridge: Cambridge University Press, 1989).

28. This question has been discussed at great length by geographers and economic
anthropologists concerned with development questions in Fiji; the view dominant formerly—that ceremonies were primarily wasteful impediments to
growth—has now been substantially displaced. For a review of these issues,
see H. Rutz, "Ceremonial Exchange and Economic Development in Village
Fiji," *Economic Development and Cultural Change* 26 (1978), 777–805.

29. It should be emphasized that the dichotomy here is contextual in its political
and moral application. In discussions with foreigners (such as an anthropologist or tourist) great emphasis is placed upon the web of sharing and mutual
support which Fijian society is said to constitute, and which is alleged (with
some justification) to be lacking among *vavalagi* (white foreigners such as
Americans, Europeans, and Australians). Similarly, Fijian values are asserted
in opposition to what are claimed to be the individualistic and non-Christian
practices of Fiji-Indians; but it should be noted that these stereotypical views

emerge from particular rhetorical conversations and do not reflect the good relations often sustained with individual Fiji-Indians. Assertions of the value of the "way of the land" are also important in some intra-Fijian disputes, and it is complained that some of those more oriented toward commerce or an urban lifestyle have "picked up the habits of foreigners."

30. For Samoa, see Timothy J. O'Meara, "The Search for Money Meets the Cult of Cash," in V. Lockwood, T. Harding, and B. Wallace, eds., *Contemporary Pacific Society* (Honolulu: University of Hawaii Press, in press), and Jocelyn Linnekin, "Fine Mats and Money: Contending Exchange Paradigms in Colonial Samoa," *Anthropological Quarterly* (in press).

31. To a substantial extent, these divisions in Fijian communities relate to different religious affiliations: the people who might be called traditionalists are generally Methodists and Catholics, while Seventh-Day Adventists and those who have joined new groups such as the Assemblies of God are often ambivalent or critical toward customary activities and suggest that Methodists practice religion in a rather partial, one-day-a-week manner. While the dichotomy between the way of the land and the way of money is important in the perspectives of these modernist dissenters, the moral constructions discussed here are obviously not acquiesced in.

32. Domestically raised pigs (*gi*) are to be contrasted with those killed through hunting (*vore* or *puaka*, which is simply the general term for pig); the latter are consumed routinely and are usually cut up and boiled or curried. *Gi* will always be prepared in an earth oven, which in general is associated with ceremonial or feast food.

33. A. B. Joske, in Colo East Provincial Council Minutes, 1908, National Archives of Fiji, Suva, p. 66.

34. There are many accounts of this type of advertisement of Fijian culture: "A Japanese scholar recently asked me why Fijians living in villages he visited asked him, 'Do you like the Fijian way of life?' Having answered, 'Yes,' he was told that the Fijian way was good. Nothing is paid for. There is plenty to eat freely from the garden and the surrounding environment. People assist one another without monetary payment. If people want something, it is given at once. It is not paid for. This, the Fijian went on, is the Fijian way of life, the chiefly way, the way according to kinship. It is not, he said, the same with Europeans. Things are paid for. Many live alone and each family by itself" (Asesela Ravuvu, "Fiji: Contradictory Ideologies and Development," in Antony Hooper, ed., *Class and Culture in the South Pacific*, Suva: Institute for Pacific Studies, 1987, p. 239). This is here filtered by a Fijian anthropologist who has written a kind of cultural handbook (*Vaka i taukei: The Fijian Way of Life*, Suva: Institute for Pacific Studies, 1983) as well as an extended study of customary ceremonies (*The Fijian Ethos*, Suva: Institute for Pacific Studies, 1987).

35. Where shops are within villages, people are apt to dismiss this fact as being of any significance for the overall contrast between town *(tauni)* and village *(rara* or *koro)*; in one place everything operates on a money basis, in the other food can simply be grown and given. It is true, in fact, that village "stores" are often very small and aim to supply minor needs for tea, matches, tinned beef, and so on; virtually all substantial purchases are made in town.

36. Jocelyn Linnekin, *Children of the Land* (New Brunswick: Rutgers University Press, 1985), p. 137.

37. Eric Hobsbawm and Terence Ranger, eds., *The Invention of Tradition* (Cambridge: Cambridge University Press, 1983). My interest in "invention" is less consistent with this literature than Roy Wagner's discussion, *The Invention of Culture,* 2d ed. (Chicago: University of Chicago Press, 1981). Although Wagner makes only cursory reference to the historical context of cultural objectification (but see pp. 31–34), he does take invention as a necessary and continuing process, rather than a contrived and inauthentic one peculiar to particular phases of nation building. My position on these questions owes a great deal to Margaret Jolly's critique in "Custom and the Way of the Land: The Politics of Tradition in Vanuatu and Fiji," paper presented at the annual meeting of the Association for Social Anthropology in Oceania, Kauai, Hawaii, March 1990. The literature on this cluster of issues in the Pacific is now extensive; for a critical discussion and further references, see Roger Keesing, "Creating the Past: Custom and Identity in the Contemporary Pacific," *Contemporary Pacific* 1 (1989), 19–42.

38. Miriam Kahn, *Always Hungry, Never Greedy: Food and the Expression of Gender in a Melanesian Society* (Cambridge: Cambridge University Press, 1986).

39. This does not mean just European: the ways of Japanese soldiers in the western Pacific, and of Japanese colonists in Micronesia, have also, for instance, provided matter for islanders' reflections upon others and themselves.

40. The "world system" perspective has been associated especially with Immanuel Wallerstein's work (e.g., *The Modern World System,* New York: Academic Press, 1974), and in anthropology with such scholars as Eric Wolf *(Europe and the People without History,* Berkeley: University of California Press, 1982). Stephen Hugh-Jones has criticized Wolf from the perspective of Amazonian views of contact history in "The Gun and the Bow: Myths of White Men and Indians," *L'Homme* 106/107 (1988), 138–155. In the Pacific case Jonathan Friedman has enunciated the world-system perspective in "Cook, Culture, and the World System," *Journal of Pacific History* 20 (1985), 191–201. This approach has been forcefully criticized by Sahlins in terms that reiterate, rather than transcend, the opposition between local and global causality which produces the problem in the first place—see "Deserted Islands of History," *Critique of Anthropology* 8 (3) (1988), 41–51.

Index

Alienability, 24, 38, 39, 44, 48–51, 55–57, 66. *See also* Inalienability

Anthropology: and alterity, 3, 13–14, 206; and history, 36

Appadurai, Arjun, 27–30, 73, 217n45

Arago, Jacques, 84

Armstrong, W. E., 37–38

Australian Museum, 178

Baker, Thomas, 157

Banks, Joseph, 142–143, 238n13

Barter: stereotypes of, 10–11, 84–85, 183–184, 217n45; in indigenous systems, 46–48, 82; in colonial history, 84–100

Baskets, in Vanuatu, 26

Belau, 126, 148–151

Blackburn, Julia, 85

Bourdieu, Pierre, 2

Bridewealth/brideservice societies, 39–44, 52, 75–76, 122–123

Bryson, Norman, 137

Burke, Edmund, 127

Cakobau, 117, 122

Cambridge Museum of Archaeology and Ethnology, 169

Cannibalism, images of, 138–139, 152, 164–167, 177

Ceremonial exchange, Fijian, 54–55, 59–65, 191–200, 204

Cheever, George, 116

Christianity, indigenous conversion to, 152–155, 169, 186, 202

Clifford, James, 186

Clunie, Fergus, 165

Colonial administration: in Fiji, 167–177; in Papua, 181–183

Colonial encounters: gendered construction of, 2–3, 181, 183, 205; misrepresentation of, 35, 83–84, 87–88, 123–124, 185–186, 205, 207, 255n40; effects on exchange systems, 80–81, 189

Commodities, in Pacific, 39, 45–51, 91, 103

Commodity, theories of, 27–28

Cook, James, 90, 91, 92, 94, 106, 108, 125, 126, 128, 130; first voyage, 105, 129–130; second voyage, 130–137; third voyage, 130

Cultural constructions, 17–18, 27–30, 72–74, 87, 88, 90–91, 97, 101, 123–124, 176; sex, 17, 49, 91–92, 94–95; body parts, 17–18; rings, 18–21; motor scooters, 25; trucks, 29; money, 38, 196–197, 202, 218n5; shell valuables, 46–48, 51, 65–66, 118, 220n12; "slaves," 48; ritual powers, 50–51; whale teeth, 67–71, 75, 110–113, 197, 200; wooden pillows, 72–73; chiefs' ornaments, 74–75; iron axes, 87, 95–97, 105, 146, 232n46; weapons, 89–91, 105, 158–162, 168, 177, 241n40, 245n77; food, 90–91; pigs, 95, 96, 97, 199, 231n45; guns, 99–102, 104, 105, 115, 121; alcohol, 106–108; ships, 109; *nbouet* ("cannibal" knife), 138; musical instruments, 145; Belaun tureen, 149–150; "idols," 153–156, 162, 243n59; "cannibal" forks, 156, 165–167, 170; grass skirts, 168–169; stuffed heads, 125, 179–180; kerosene, 190–191; cattle, 199–200

Cumming, Constance F. Gordon, 170–171

Curiosity, 26, 126–128, 130, 137, 140, 152, 237nn5,6

Debt, 14, 36, 53, 62–65, 67–68, 91, 195

D'Entrecasteaux, Bruny, 90, 138–139

Derrick, R. A., 115

Discovery, notion of, 177–178, 206–207

Eagleston, J. H., 113, 114, 117

Edge-Partington, James, 167

Erskine, John Elphinstone, 89, 91